POETIC

Tristan Corbière

Wry-Blue Loves

By Peter Dale

POETRY

Edge to Edge: new and selected poems
One Another
Under the Breath

TRANSLATIONS

Dante: The Divine Comedy
Poems of Jules Laforgue
Poems of François Villon

PROSE

An Introduction to Rhyme

INTERVIEWS

Michael Hamburger in conversation with Peter Dale
Richard Wilbur in conversation with Peter Dale
Peter Dale in conversation with Cynthia Haven

Tristan Corbière

Wry-Blue Loves

Les Amours jaunes

and other poems

TRANSLATED AND INTRODUCED BY

PETER DALE

ANVIL PRESS POETRY

Published in 2005
by Anvil Press Poetry Ltd
Neptune House 70 Royal Hill London SE10 8RF
www.anvilpresspoetry.com

This book is published with financial assistance
from Arts Council England

Designed and set in Monotype Dante by Anvil
Printed and bound in England
by Cromwell Press, Trowbridge, Wiltshire

ISBN 0 85646 377 9

A catalogue record for this book
is available from the British Library

ACKNOWLEDGEMENTS

Parts of this translation have appeared in the following publications:

Acumen; *Agenda*; *Antigonish Review* (Canada); *Core*; *The Cumberland Review* (U.S.A.); *Delta*; *Exile* (Canada); *La Tribune Internationale des Langues Vivantes* (France); *Outposts*; *The Swansea Review*.

The author is grateful to Roland John of the Hippopotamus Press for permission to reprint translations revised from *Cross-Channel* and *Narrow Straits* which the press first published.

Table

Contents

Sérénade des sérénades

Raccrocs

Serenade of Serenades

Flukes

Armor

Gens de mer

Armorica

Seafarers

Outline of the Life of Corbière

ÉDOUARD-JOACHIM CORBIÈRE – later self-christened Tristan – was born to Marie-Angélique-Aspasie (née Puyo) and Antoine-Édouard Corbière on 18 July 1845 in the house of the maternal grandparents at Coat-Congar, Ploujean, near Morlaix. His childhood was spent on an estate called Le Launay,* rented by the family, a hundred yards or so from Coat-Congar. A sister, Lucie, was born in 1850; a brother, Edmond, in 1855.

In 1859, Tristan was sent to board in Pâques at the Lycée Impérial de Saint-Brieuc. An indifferent scholar, he won prizes, however, in Latin, and did well in French. Though unhappy at the school, a fish out of water, he discovered there talents as a caricaturist and as a budding poet. In autumn 1860, he was moved for reasons of his health to the Lycée Nantes where he could be a day pupil, staying with his doctor uncle Jules Chenantais who watched over his condition.

An acute bout of illness in 1861 left him virtually an invalid. His mother took him during the vacation on a convalescent trip to Provence. He later made similar trips to Cannes and Luchon.

Though more at ease in his new college, he suffered increasingly poor health and he was unable to take his baccalaureate in logic and rhetoric. At the end of this year he returned to the new family home in Morlaix where he stayed as an invalid, reading mainly the Romantics and his father's books. The Romantics are satirized and parodied throughout his work, but his father is echoed in complimentary fashion. Corbière, though thwarted by ill-health, had always wanted to emulate the maritime and literary exploits of his father who had been a good sea-captain and was a successful novelist.

On the advice of his uncle he went, in 1863, to stay in the summer residence of the Corbières at Roscoff because the climate was

---

* Later, a place of importance to Corbière as the house of an aunt Mme Le Bris (née Puyo) who he felt understood him best.

reputedly beneficial for those suffering rheumatism and pulmonary complaints. (No one has yet ascertained the exact nature of Corbière's illnesses.)* He lived alone in the large house and ate at Le Gad's *pension* in the rue de Port, where a group of Parisian painters used to meet during the summer, none of them well known today. With one of these painters, Jean-Louis Hamon, he travelled, in 1869, to Italy, visiting Naples, Florence, Castellamare, Sorrento and Capri. In the Hotel Pagano in Capri, he met Jean Benner, a painter from Alsace, who made some sketches of Corbière that are thought to be the best of him now surviving. Corbière, no mean draughtsman himself, also sketched a self-caricature in the hotel register. The fruits of this trip may be seen in the Italian poems of the section *Flukes* here.

In mid-April he returned to Morlaix. However, he outraged the locals by appearing on the balcony in a bishop's vestments which he had brought from Rome and consequently he was duly despatched to Roscoff.

In 1871, a Count Rodolphe de Battine arrived at Le Gad's, accompanied by a 'countess' who was actually an actress of Italian extraction called Armida-Josefina Cuchiani, professionally known as Herminie. The Count had been wounded at Le Mans and his account of the conditions there contributed to the poem 'The Pastoral of Conlie', the climax of the *Armorica* section in *Wry-Blue Loves*. Corbière established friendly relations with the couple and took them for trips in his cutter, and, later, in a larger yacht he had christened 'The Tristan'. The poems 'Steam-Boat' and 'To my Cutter "The Slaver"' seem to relate to these trips. In the course of one of these they attended the annual Breton celebration of the pardon of St Anne on 27th August. This triggered one of Corbière's greatest poems, 'The Wandering Minstrel and the Pardon of St Anne'. Soon he was head over heels in love with the actress whom he renamed, for some obscure reason, Marcelle. In October, Rodolphe and his so-called countess returned to Paris where, next spring, Corbière followed them in pursuit of Marcelle.

---

* Val Warner, in *The Centenary Corbière*, Carcanet, 1975, gives his condition as deformity brought on by arthritis, complicated by tuberculosis which finally killed him.

A friend provided a room for him, close to Marcelle's apartment, in the Cité Gaillard in Montmartre. Yet he moved a few weeks later to 10 rue Frochot in the 9th *arrondissement*.

He lived on a monthly allowance of 300 francs sent by his mother. In June he returned to Brittany with the Count and Marcelle who both stayed till the end of August. During this year he was working hard at his caricatures, mostly at the expense of the Communards. He also worked on the poems which became the *Serenade of Serenades* section of his book. In August 1873, he published this at his own expense, his only book of poems, *Les Amours jaunes* (Wry-Blue Loves). Several pieces from it appeared in *La Vie Parisienne*. The book, unfortunately, was an absolute flop, receiving only one review. This did not totally discourage him. During 1874 he continued to compose, corrected and improved in his own copy many of the poems of *Wry-Blue Loves*. He published prose pieces in *La Vie Parisienne*: 'The Casino of Dead Men' and 'The American Woman'. He also spent some time at Count Rodolphe's newly inherited château, Arguebelles, near Le Mans.

In the summer of 1874, he stayed for the last time in Roscoff with Rodolphe and Marcelle. Yet, despite his wavering health, he returned to Paris in the November. Several weeks later, he was found, in formal evening wear, unconscious on the floor of his apartment. He was taken by friends, including Rodolphe, to the Dubois Hospital where he stayed eighteen days until 6th January 1875. From here, he sent his mother a message: 'I'm in the Dubois [Wood Hospital] where they make coffins.' She arrived on 27th December. It is also recorded that Marcelle was a devoted attendant at his bedside.

His mother brought him back to Morlaix, to the family house on the Quai de Léon. At his request the room was filled with heather. Also at his request, on the last day of February 1875, his friend Le Gad was fetched to tell him all the news and gossip of Roscoff. But Corbière would not pay attention and said: 'Tomorrow I won't be here.'

He died the next day at ten o'clock in the evening, without requesting the last rites – a fact that upset his father greatly after his own late reversion to Catholicism before his death a few grieving months later.

This bare outline does not convey the underlying loneliness, the suicidal tendencies, the cross-dressing and other eccentricities among his dreadful practical jokes which filled the interstices between these salient dates. The true life of Corbière has not yet been written – largely because of the destruction of most of the biographical material. Only one letter of his adult life survives the tidyings-up of members of the family. It may be that the only true life is now to be found in his poems – the right place to look for the life of a poet.

The Influence of Corbière

THE INFLUENCE OF CORBIÈRE is difficult to define in any obviously concrete way in the work of his successors, in French or English. It is a matter of admission that he influenced Pound and Eliot but concrete exemplification of this tends to be transmitted through the medium of Laforgue whom he directly influenced. Laforgue spent much of his critical energy in fending off and obscuring any suggestion of direct influence from Corbière. He claimed that at the time he was writing *Les Complaintes** he had not known Corbière's work. This is put in question by his friend Kahn who says he introduced Corbière's work to him in 1880, five years before publication of Laforgue's first book. The depth of Laforgue's criticism of Corbière reveals much more than a passing acquaintance. The influence may be felt as an imitation of approach and attitudes rather than as direct verbal derivation, a similarity in approach to diction of conversational-ironic rather than literary vocabulary and a freer approach in formal matters. The influences have often been underplayed by Laforgue scholars and commentators – including myself hitherto. But Val Warner, a meticulous scholar of these influences, whose book is cited earlier, remarks:

> It is arguable that Corbière's most significant influence has not been direct, but via Laforgue. Yet controversy surrounds the exact measure of Laforgue's debt to Corbière ...

As translated by William Jay Smith in *Selected Writings of Jules Laforgue*, Grove Press, 1956, Laforgue put the position in a letter of August 1885 to Léo Trézenik as follows:

> Corbière has dash and I have humour; Corbière dazzles while I purr; I live by an absolute philosophy and not by eccentricity; I sit still while he frisks about; I know nothing of *amour jaune* –

---

* A verse translation of *Les Complaintes* may be found in the bilingual *Poems of Jules Laforgue*, Anvil Press, 2001.

my love is not yellow; it is white and the deep mauve of mourning. Corbière, moreover, doesn't bother about rhyme or stanza... and never with rhythms. I have wanted to create symphonic music and melody while Corbière goes on scraping that old fiddle of his.

He further remarks that they share, if anything, a Breton cast of soul – though Laforgue was never a Breton. The most obvious parallels between the two poets are the pervading use of irony, the use of disjunctive devices and a shared appreciation of Villon. Yet at the same time there are clear differences. Corbière is less experimental – impatient and cavalier, yes, in questions of traditional rhyme, caesura, the alternation of masculine and feminine rhymes, but no real revolutionary in these matters. On the other hand Laforgue, as he suggests, was precise, then experimental and inventive in these areas. Corbière was also conservative in form – in a Browningesque fashion – and never quite arrived at *vers libre* where Laforgue came into his own. The technical link between them is probably two-fold: both had a somewhat free and easy attitude to rules for the caesura and enjambment and both had scant regard for the older more rhetorical approach to diction, liking the mixture of literary, colloquial, technical and archaic diction to increase their disjunctive preferences.

There are one or two closer parallels. Laforgue may have been influenced by 'To a Young Lady' where Corbière initiates the theme of the girl at the piano so often repeated by Laforgue. The use of the troubadour persona by Corbière may have helped Laforgue to the pierrot persona. In this respect the draft poem Corbière left in his copy of *Les Amours jaunes*, 'Clown Hanged' (see *Other Poems*, p. 438), anticipates Laforgue's use and is close to his ironic self-mocking attitude to love. Yet Laforgue could not have seen it. There are some similarities in approach in writing of their fathers. Both parody Baudelaire. Both quote or near-quote Villon. Yet a critic as acute as Edgell Rickword remarks, in *Essays and Opinions 1921–31*, Carcanet, 1974:

> It is possible that certain tendencies in later French poetry may be traced to an origin in *Les Amours jaunes* ... Laforgue's sorrowful jesting from time to time is reminiscent.

A major difference is their use of imagery. Laforgue's use of sun, moon, sea, eye, rose-window imagery steadily moves towards the systematic and symbolic whereas Corbière's imagery is much more of a nonce affair. It would be difficult to develop any Symbolist theory of literature from Corbière.

It is not wise to over-emphasize their similarities; there is perhaps truth in the wry humour of Jarrell's comment: 'And yet Laforgue is as different from Corbière as even Laforgue wanted us to believe' (*Kipling, Auden & Co.*, Carcanet, 1981).

Corbière's influence on Pound and Eliot is inseparable from Laforgue's – confined to diction, irony, the urban and down-to-earth, chiefly; though Laforgue is mentioned most often. Donald Davie puts the case most simply:

> It is hardly too much to say that what Pound admired in these Frenchmen was what he admired also in Crabbe – the naming of quotidian or ignoble objects with an accuracy that depended on purging from the mind any sense of the associations that had accrued to them.
>
> [from *Pound*, Fontana Modern Masters]

In his own critical writing, his *Literary Essays*, however, Pound treats both poets as more or less equals:

> Corbière is hard-bitten, perhaps the most poignant poet since Villon, in very much Villon's manner. Laforgue was a better artist than any of these men save Corbière.

Eliot has a few more direct echoes of Corbière in his French poems and the opening of 'East Coker', but his interest shifted to the more sympathetic Baudelaire away from both Laforgue and Corbière who were staunchly anti-Christian.

Another English-speaking poet who felt the power of Corbière was Randall Jarrell who made some interesting versions of parts of *Rondels for After*, and a version of 'Poet by Default'. Equally interesting freer versions of 'The Wandering Minstrel and the Pardon of St Anne' and 'Blindman's Cries' have been made by Martin Bell (*Complete Poems*, ed. Peter Porter, Bloodaxe, 1988). Curiously, Bell seems to have re-applied the conversational-ironic approach to one of its originators and to have driven his versions further in that direction, to the exclusion of other aspects. C. H. Sisson published a version of 'The Pastoral of Conlie', entitled 'Conlie Ditch', in *Agenda* 15.4. But the list of occasional translations is endless.

One of the more recent poets to come under Corbière's abrasive spell is the poet John Berryman with his demotic voices and personae, his distancings through sending up literary devices and diction. The influence is freely admitted, for a change, in the dedication to his book *Love & Fame*.

Corbière should be read for himself, not his influence; he has a fierce compassion and empathy for the suffering of the individual that he can barely disguise and control with his distancing ironies. Above all, he is his own man, able to resist the blandishments of literary theory, social expectations, and the mollifications of religion.

A Note on the Translation

THIS TRANSLATION attempts to find equivalents to the form of Corbière's poems. Since he is a writer who delights in puns and word-play this is a difficult task: no non-native speaker can know the full range of suggestiveness and association of a foreign vocabulary and idiom; much of this kind of thing is not readily found in dictionaries and thesauruses, particularly for past writers using colloquial styles. Furthermore, if it were to be found, there would still be the problem of matching up the destination language. In consequence not all of the puns have an equivalent and some suggested by Corbière are not in exactly the same places in these English versions. Undoubtedly much has been missed. A fair impression of Corbière's method and essence may nevertheless have been indicated.

In the matter of form, similar problems of equivalence occur. Corbière is a traditional poet, using the traditional rules of metric and rhyme with a rough and ready accuracy modified by near-licence when occasion demanded. He most strikes a French reader as weird in his use of caesura (which he multiplies when necessary) and enjambment which he uses freely like an English writer of blank verse. Neither of these things can be made to look startlingly innovative in English; nor would they have appeared all that startling to an English reader of the period. To indicate something of his approach somewhat variable weights and lengths of line have been introduced and some rather odd cacophonous substitutions of metrical measures.

The poet was as eccentric in his use of punctuation as in most other things. Despite current English practice, his apparently over-elaborate usage has been presented as closely as possible. In earlier drafts his pointing had been updated but revision suggested that his own methods signalled his ploys and ambivalences better and, indeed, made his tone, quiddity, and intention clearer. His use of enormous rows of omission or hiatus points, though intrusive, has been retained also. His use of italic is frequently to signal some wordplay or allusion. It has been followed here in the same places even though, in some exigencies, the play on words has been moved to some other part of the line. Lastly, his use of the dash has been retained in representation of the French manner of indicating speech since it often seems that the device introduces some element of disjunction at one and the same time. A further consideration was that the degree to which it is actual voice, imagined voice, or words put in the mouth of someone is open to interpretation.

There are native French speakers who are none too sure of Corbière's precise meanings and intentions at various points. Quite a few things still baffle me in his poems. Where reference works and expert opinion have shared my doubts I have trusted to intuition, instinct and luck – a thing Corbière had little enough of. In several parts, I have had to put up with my own ignorance since the task of representing the poet in English would have vanished over a far horizon of decent hesitation or of my death before I could be confident in my knowledge. One comfort in this is that Corbière was a poet who managed to misquote even himself. The last excuse must be that this version, as was the original, is the work of a poet rather than of a scholar and must stand or fall on the quality of the poetry – as does its original.

In justification, one can only reiterate what Randall Jarrell wrote in a letter to Robert Lowell:

> I'm not a French expert, alas!... Just a Corbière enthusiast: I'm gradually getting a largish Corbière vocabulary, which isn't much used for any other French poets – I say this to their shame.

> [*Randall Jarrell's Letters*, ed. Mary Jarrell, Faber, p. 184]

This versification could not have been done without the meticulous researches of scholars like Pierre-Olivier Walzer, in his edition of *Œuvres complètes*, and Val Warner, in her edition of *The Centenary Corbière*. Such debts could never be repaid even if the full extent of them could be remembered over the long years and many versions. It is fair to say that the slips are the truly original contribution of mine. Finally I should like to thank Kit Yee Wong for checking for my errors in the French text.

A Short Bibliography

Charles Cros / Tristan Corbière: *Œuvres Complètes*
Corbière section edited by Pierre-Olivier Walzer, assisted by Francis
F. Burch for the letters: Gallimard (1970)

Tristan Corbière: *Les Amours jaunes*
Edited by Michel Dansel; introduction by Pierre Osenat: Librairie
Larousse (1970)

The Centenary Corbière: Poems and Prose
Edited and translated with an introduction by Val Warner: Carcanet
New Press (1974). Reprinted in the Fyfield Books series, 2003.
Bilingual

French Poetry 1820–1950
Selected, translated and introduced by William Rees: Penguin
Classics (1990)

The Poem Itself
Edited by Stanley Burnshaw: Schocken Books (1967)

The Truth of Poetry
Michael Hamburger: Anvil (1996)

These Jaundiced Loves
A translation of *Les Amours jaunes* by Christopher Pilling: Peterloo
Poets (1995)

Les Amours jaunes

À l'auteur du Négrier.

T. C.

Wry-Blue Loves

To the author of *The Slaver*

T. C.

À Marcelle

LE POÈTE ET LA CIGALE

Un poète ayant rimé,
                    IMPRIMÉ
Vit sa muse dépourvue
De marraine, et presque nue:
Pas le plus petit morceau
De vers… ou de vermisseau.
Il alla crier famine
Chez une blonde voisine,
La priant de lui prêter
Son petit nom pour rimer.
(C'était une rime en elle)
– Oh! je vous pairai, Marcelle,
Avant l'août, foi d'animal!
Intérêt et principal. –
La voisine est très prêteuse,
C'est son plus joli défaut:
– Quoi: c'est tout ce qu'il vous faut?
Votre Muse est bien heureuse…
Nuit et jour, à tout venant,
Rimez mon nom… Qu'il vous plaise!
Et moi j'en serai fort aise.

Voyons: chantez maintenant.

To Marcelle

THE POET AND THE CICADA

A poet having rhymed a bit
            PUBLISHED IT
And saw his Muse deprived, bereft
Of sponsor, almost naked: left
Not a square meal, nor a tetrahedral,
Of a sestet ... or a sesquipedal.
He went and cried out: starving, poor!
To a blonde girl who lived next door
And begged that she should lend her name,
Her christian name for his rhyme and fame.
(It was a rhyme that suited well.)
– Oh, I will pay you back, Marcelle,
By August – on my word as chancer!
Principal and interest I'll answer. –
My neighbour is most generous.
It was her nicest fault, indeed:
– What: so that is all you need?
Your Muse is most felicitous ...
For one and all, by night and day,
Rhyme on my name ... if that's your pleasure,
And me, I'm easy, by all measure.

Come on: now you sing away.

Ça

Ça?

What?...

SHAKESPEARE.

Des essais? – Allons donc, je n'ai pas essayé!
Étude? – Fainéant je n'ai jamais pillé.
Volume? – Trop broché pour être relié…
De la copie? – Hélas non, ce n'est pas payé!

Un poëme? – Merci, mais j'ai lavé ma lyre.
Un livre? –… Un livre, encor, est une chose à lire!…
Des papiers? – Non, non, Dieu merci, c'est cousu!
Album? – Ce n'est pas blanc, et c'est trop décousu.

Bouts-rimés? – Par quel bout?… Et ce n'est pas joli!
Un ouvrage? – Ce n'est poli ni repoli.
Chansons? – Je voudrais bien, ô ma petite Muse!…
Passe-temps? – Vous croyez, alors, que ça m'amuse?

– Vers?… vous avez flué des vers… – Non, c'est heurté.
– Ah, vous avez couru l'Originalité?…
– Non… c'est une drôlesse assez drôle, – *de rue* –
Qui court encor, sitôt qu'elle se sent courue.

– Du *chic* pur? – Eh qui me donnera des ficelles!
– Du haut vol? Du haut-mal? – Pas de râle, ni d'ailes!
– Chose à mettre à la porte? –… Ou dans une maison
De tolérance. – Ou bien de correction? – Mais non!

That?

What?...
SHAKESPEARE.

Essays? – Pooh, I never have essayed!
A study? – Never plagiarized, idle hound.
A tome? – Too behind-hand to be bound...
Articles? – Sadly, no. It's not well-paid.

A poem? – No thanks; I've flogged my lyre.
A book? –... A book still must be read entire!...
Papers? – No, no, thank God. It's stitched up, seems!
Sketches? – Not blank, but without thread, themes.

Fixed rimes? – Fixed noose! And not a pretty sight!
A work? – It's neither polished nor polite!
Song and dance? – My little Muse, I'd love a chance...
Light pieces? – Would I give them a second glance?

– Verse?... You've raised a flood of verse. – It's dammed, no!
– Ah, you've courted Originality, though?
– No... too common a whore she is – *streets... behind* –
She dates whenever she feels up to date – blind.

– A stylist? – Who will show the ropes, strings?
– Grand style? Grand mal? – No death-rasp, no wings!
– Something turned out? – Yes, of doors, to go...
To a house of ill-fame. – Or correction? – No.

– Bon, ce n'est pas classique? – À peine est-ce français!
– Amateur? – Ai-je l'air d'un monsieur à succès?
Est-ce vieux? – Ça n'a pas quarante ans de service...
Est-ce jeune? – Avec l'âge, on guérit de ce vice.

... ÇA c'est naïvement une impudente *pose*;
C'est, ou ce n'est pas *ça*: rien ou quelque chose...
– Un chef-d'œuvre? – Il se peut: je n'en ai jamais fait.
– Mais, est-ce du Huron, du Gagne, ou du Musset?

– C'est du... mais j'ai mis là mon humble nom d'auteur,
Et mon enfant n'a pas même un titre menteur.
C'est un coup de raccroc, juste ou faux, par hasard...
L'Art ne me connaît pas. Je connais pas l'Art.

Préfecture de Police, 20 mai 1873.

– Well, something classic? – Scarcely French, for a start.
– Amateur? – Mr Bestseller, do I look the part?
Then is it old? – Not forty years since its prime...
So, young? – Age cures you of that vice in time.

... THAT, then, is a callow, impudent *pose*;
It is, and isn't *that*; something or nothing as it goes...
– A masterpiece? – Could be; not written one to date.
– But after Huron, Gagne, de Musset? Tell me straight.

– It's after... I've put my humble author's name.
My brainchild has no bogus title to claim.
It's a fluke, and right or wrong, by chance's part...
Art doesn't recognize me. I know no Art.

Police Headquarters, 20th May 1873.

Paris

Bâtard de Créole et Breton,
Il vint aussi là – fourmilière,
Bazar où rien n'est en pierre,
Où le soleil manque de ton.

– Courage! On fait queue… Un planton
Vous pousse à la chaine – derrière! –
… Incendie éteint, sans lumière;
Des seaux passent, vides ou non. –

Là, sa pauvre Muse pucelle
Fit le trottoir en *demoiselle*,
Ils disaient: Qu'est-ce qu'elle vend?

– Rien. – Elle restait là, stupide,
N'entendant pas sonner le vide
Et regardant passer le vent…

                    ★

Là: vivre à coups de fouet! – passer
En fiacre, en correctionnelle;
Repasser à la ritournelle,
Se dépasser, et trépasser!…

– Non, petit, il faut commencer
Par être grand – simple ficelle –
Pauvre: remuer l'or à la pelle;
Obscur: un nom à tout casser!…

Le coller chez les mastroquets,
Et l'apprendre à des perroquets
Qui le chantent ou qui le sifflent…

Paris

Bastard by Creole and Breton got,
He came there, too – ant-hill, bazaar
Where nothing's of stone and that star
The sun lacks style, is not so hot.

– Take heart! You queue... Orderly clot
Shoves you, – last in the chain, you are! –
The fire's out, not a glimmer, char;
The buckets pass, empty or not. –

Here, his chaste Muse, wretched, effete,
Like a fair *damsel* walks the street.
They ask: 'And what has she to sell?'

– Nothing. – Stupid, she hangs around
Not hearing oblivion sound,
Watching the wind pass like a swell...

*

Life goes like whip-lash! – pass the day
In hackney cab or corrective cell;
Pass round again in *ritornelle*,
Pass up your wits, then pass away!...

– No, little one, you start this way:
Be big – a simple dodge, soft sell –
If skint: then rake in gold pell-mell;
Obscure: make a name to say...

In publicans and barmen beat it;
Teach it till parrots can repeat it,
Sing it out or whistle it about...

– Musique! – C'est le paradis
Des mahomets et des houris,
Des dieux souteneurs qui se giflent!

    ★

> *Je voudrais que la rose – Dondaine!*
> *Fût encore au rosier, – Dondé!*

Poète – Après?… il faut *la chose*:
Le Parnasse en escalier,
Les Dégoûteux, et la Chlorose,
Les Bedeaux, les Fous à lier…

L'Incompris couche avec sa pose,
Sous le zinc d'un mancenillier;
Le Naïf « *voudrait que la rose,*
Dondé! fût encore au rosier! »

« *La rose au rosier, Dondaine!* »
– On a le pied fait à sa chaîne.
« *La rose au rosier* »… – Trop tard! –

« *La rose au rosier* »… – Nature!
– On est essayeur, pédicure,
Ou quelqu'autre chose dans l'art!

    ★

J'aimais… – Oh, ça n'est plus de vente!
Même il faut payer: dans le tas,
Pioche la femme! – Mon amante
M'avait dit: « Je n'oublîrai pas »…

… J'avais une amante là-bas
Et son ombre pâle me hante
Parmi des senteurs de lilas…
Peut-être Elle pleure… – Eh bien: chante,

– Start the racket! – It's paradise
For houris and mahomets, vice-
God pimps who give themselves the clout!

★

I'd wish the rose – Hey-ding-a-ding!
Were still upon the briar, – Hey-ho!

Poet – So?... Needs *the thing* to process:
Parnassus up some staircase flight;
Disgustful Ones, the Green with Chlorosis,
Beadles and Madmen straitened tight...

The Misunderstood, reposing his poses
Under the bar of the manchineel's night;
The Naive *'who'd wish the rose is,*
Hey-ho! back on the briar!' all right.

'The rose, hey-ding, on the briar again!'
One has one's foot put in its chain.
'The rose on the briar.' ... – Too late for a start! –

'The rose on the briar.' ... – Idiotist!
– One's a fitter, a pedicurist,
Or either something else in art.

★

I was in love once... – not still for sale!
You even have to pay a fee:
Dig a woman out of the bale!
'I won't forget,' my girl-friend said to me.

... I'd a love back there, and here I see,
I'm haunted by her shadow, pale
In scents of lilac. Maybe She
Is weeping now... – Well, sing a wail

Pour toi tout seul, ta nostalgie,
Tes nuits blanches sans bougie…
Tristes vers, tristes au matin!…

Mais ici: fouette-toi d'orgie!
Charge ta paupière rougie,
Et sors ton grand air de catin!

⋆

C'est la bohème, enfant: Renie
Ta lande et ton clocher à jour,
Les mornes de ta colonie
Et les *bamboulas* au tambour.

Chanson usée et bien finie,
Ta jeunesse… Eh, c'est bon un jour!…
Tiens: – C'est toujours neuf – calomnie
Tes pauvres amours… et l'amour.

Évohé! ta coupe est remplie!
Jette le vin, garde la lie…
Comme ça. – Nul n'a vu le tour.

Et qu'un jour le monsieur candide
De toi dise – Infect! Ah splendide! –
… Ou ne dise rien. – C'est plus court.

⋆

Évohé! fouaille la veine;
Évohé! misère: Éblouir!
En fille de joie, à la peine
Tombe, avec ce mot-là. – Jouir!

For yourself alone, homesickness, night
On sleepless night, no candle light...
Your verse sad, and sadder in the morning!...

But here, whip yourself to orgy's height;
Load you red lids with eye-bright,
Bring out your big appearance of whoring.

★

Here it's bohemia, child: Disown
Your moor-lands, hills a world away,
Your steeple's open-work in stone,
Your drum-mad *bamboula* hey.

That hackneyed song that's long been flown,
Your youth... Hey, good though in its day!...
Hold on: – It's always fresh – your own
Poor loves malign... love, too, betray.

Evoe! Your cup is well and filled!
Slop out the wine, save dregs unspilled...
Like that. – No one's seen the trick.

One day may the gentleman frank
Within you say: 'How foul, and rank! –
Oh splendid!'... Or not. – To keep it quick.

★

Evoe! Flog hard your lucky vein.
Evoe! A drag: to dazzle, vie!
And like a good-time girl, with the strain
Drop with that word: Shag! Or try

Rôde en la coulisse malsaine
Où vont les fruits mal secs moisir,
Moisir pour un quart-d'heure en scène…
– *Voir les planches, et puis mourir!*

Va: tréteaux, lupanars, églises,
Cour des miracles, cour d'assises:
– Quarts-d'heure d'immortalité!

Tu parais! c'est l'apothéose!!!…
Et l'on te jette quelque chose:
– Fleur en papier, ou saleté. –

    ★

Donc, *la tramontane* est montée:
Tu croiras que c'est arrivé!
Cinq-cent-millième Prométhée,
Au roc de carton peint rivé.

Hélas: quel bon oiseau de proie,
Quel vautour, quel *Monsieur Vautour*
Viendra mordre à ton petit foie
Gras, truffé?… pour quoi – Pour le four!…

Four banal!… – Adieu la curée! –
Ravalant ta rate rentrée,
Va, comme le pélican blanc,

En écorchant le chant du cygne,
Bec-jaune, te percer le flanc!…
Devant un pêcheur à la ligne.

    ★

Lurking the sleazy wings, that drain
Where ill-dried fruits go turning high,
For fifteen minutes on stage to reign…
– *To see the boards, and then to die!*

Go on: stage, brothels, churches,
Beggars' sessions, court-sessions; purchase –
Fifteen minutes of immortality.

You appear: it's the apotheosis!!!…
And someone throws you something, throws this –
Flower in paper, or obscenity. –

                    ★

Then, *guiding star* so high on luck,
You will believe the thing is nailed.
Five hundred thousandth Prometheus stuck
On painted-pasteboard rock, impaled.

Good grief! What fine bird of prey,
What vulture, what *Mr Vulture-Louse*,
Will come to peck your liver away,
Truffle stuffed?… For? – Flophouse!…

A flop!… So long the hassle, scene! –
And choking back your long-held spleen,
Go like the pelican white and blank,

And murdering your swan-song, dine,
Yellow-beaked, pierce your own flank!…
Watched by some angler with a line.

                    ★

Tu ris. – Bien! – Fais de l'amertume,
Prends le pli, Méphisto blagueur.
De l'absinthe! et ta lèvre écume...
Dis que cela vient de ton cœur.

Fais de toi ton œuvre posthume,
Châtre l'amour... l'amour – longueur!
Ton poumon cicatrisé hume
Des miasmes de gloire, ô vainqueur!

Assez, n'est-ce pas? va-t'en!
       Laisse
Ta bourse – dernière maîtresse –
Ton revolver – dernier ami...

Drôle de pistolet fini!
... Ou reste, et bois ton fond de vie,
Sur une nappe desservie...

You laugh. – Good. – Out with the bitterness,
Acquire the knack, Mephisto, clown.
Swig absinthe, foam at the mouth … profess
You're speaking from the heart deep down.

Make yourself your posthumous *œuvre* – less
Love … bowdlerize love – that boring noun!
Let your scarred lungs snuff in, yes,
You conqueror, miasmas of renown!

Enough. Isn't it? Get on.
                              And part
With your purse – your final mistress-tart;
Revolver, too – your last friend shed …

Queer son of a gun who've shot your lead!
… Or linger, take your fill of life
From table cleared of food, plate, knife …

Épitaphe

> *Sauf les amoureux commençans ou finis qui veulent*
> *commencer par la fin il y a tant de choses qui finissent*
> *par le commencement que le commencement commence*
> *à finir par être la fin la fin en sera que les amoureux et*
> *autres finiront par commencer à recommencer par ce*
> *commencement qui aura fini par n'être que la fin*
> *retournée ce qui commencera par être égal à l'éternité*
> *qui n'a ni fin ni commencement et finira par être aussi*
> *finalement égal à la rotation de la terre où l'on aura fini*
> *par ne distinguer plus où commence la fin d'où finit le*
> *commencement ce qui est toute fin de tout commence-*
> *ment égale à tout commencement de toute fin ce qui est*
> *le commencement final de l'infini défini par l'indéfini –*
> *Égale une épitaphe égale une préface et réciproquement.*
>
> Sagesse des nations.

Il se tua d'ardeur, ou mourut de paresse.
S'il vit, c'est par oubli; voici ce qu'il se laisse:

– Son seul regret fut de n'être pas sa maîtresse. –

> Il ne naquit par aucun bout,
> Fut toujours poussé vent-de-bout,
> Et fut un arlequin-ragoût,
> Mélange adultère de tout.

> Du *je-ne-sais-quoi*. – Mais ne sachant où;
> De l'or, – mais avec pas le sou;
> Des nerfs, – sans nerf. Vigueur sans force;
> De l'élan, – avec une entorse;
> De l'âme, – et pas de violon;
> De l'amour, – mais pire étalon.
> – Trop de noms pour avoir un nom. –

Epitaph

*Except for lovers beginning or finished who wish to begin
with the end there are so many things that end with the
beginning that the beginning begins to end by being the
end the end of which will be that lovers and others will
end by beginning to re-begin with this beginning which
will have ended by being only the return of the end which
will begin by being equal to eternity which has neither
beginning nor end and which ends by being as finally
equal to the rotation of the earth whereupon one will have
ended by no longer distinguishing where the end begins
from where the start finishes which is every end of every
beginning equal to every beginning of every end which is
the final beginning of the infinite defined by the indefinite
– Equally an epitaph equally a preface and vice versa.*

The wisdom of the nations.

He killed himself with ardour or died of idleness.
If he lives it's by forgetting; here's what he'd confess:

– His one regret, not having been his mistress, no less. –

    Neither head nor heels was he born,
    Head-wind wherever he was drawn;
    Leftovers stewed and simmering,
    Adulterate hash of everything.

    Of *I don't know what*, not knowing where;
    With gold, – but not a penny spare;
    Nerves, – without nerve. With might no main;
    Of sprightliness, – but with a sprain;
    Of sound-post soul, – no fiddle; the flame
    Of love, – but not a stallion's frame;
    – Too many names to bear a name. –

Coureur d'idéal, – sans idée;
Rime riche, – et jamais rimée;
Sans avoir été, – revenu;
Se retrouvant partout perdu.

Poète, en dépit de ses vers;
Artiste sans art, – à l'envers,
Philosophe, – à tort à travers.

Un drôle sérieux, – pas drôle.
Acteur, il ne sut pas son rôle;
Peintre: il jouait de la musette;
Et musicien: de la palette.

Une tête! – mais pas de tête;
Trop fou pour savoir être bête;
Prenant pour un trait le mot *très*.
– Ses vers faux furent ses seuls vrais.

Oiseau rare – et de pacotille;
Très mâle... et quelquefois très *fille*;
Capable de tout, – bon à rien;
Gâchant bien le mal, mal le bien.
Prodigue comme était l'enfant
Du Testament, – sans testament.
Brave, et souvent, par peur du plat,
Mettant ses deux pieds dans le plat.

Coloriste enragé, – mais blême;
Incompris... – surtout de lui-même;
Il pleura, chanta juste faux;
– Et fut un défaut sans défauts.

Ne fut *quelqu'un*, ni quelque chose
Son naturel était la *pose*.

Chaser of ideals, – but idea-less,
Full rhyme, – but blank of all finesse;
Not having lived, – a ghost of thin air;
Finding himself lost everywhere.

Poet, despite his verses' flop;
Artless artist, – arse over top;
Philosopher bull, – in a china-shop.

Serious comic, – not at all droll.
Actor, that never learnt his role;
Painter: he made the bagpipes wince;
Musician: of the palette's tints.

Headstrong! – not strong in the head;
Too wild to be dumb beast led;
His trait the word *outré* – much too;
– His truest lines were out of true…

Rare bird – a *cheep*jack hawk-er, this.
Very male… and often much a*miss*;
All-capable, – for nothing good;
Bodged well the bad; good, ill – he would.
Prodigal he was, as was the child
In the Testament, – intestate filed.
Brave; often scared of a minute
Dull, he put both feet always in it.

Furious colourist, – pale as a ghost;
Misunderstood… – by himself most;
He wept, he sang, perfectly off-key;
– A fault unfaulted would always be.

A *nobody* nor a thing as it goes;
His natural gift was in the *pose*.

Pas poseur, – posant pour *l'unique*;
Trop naïf, étant trop cynique;
Ne croyant à rien, croyant tout.
– Son goût était dans le dégoût.

Trop cru, – parce qu'il fut trop cuit,
Ressemblant à rien moins qu'à lui,
Il s'amusa de son ennui,
Jusqu'à s'en réveiller la nuit.
Flâneur au large, – à la dérive,
Épave qui jamais n'arrive…

Trop *Soi* pour se pouvoir souffrir,
L'esprit à sec et la tête ivre,
Fini, mais ne sachant finir,
Il mourut en s'attendant vivre
Et vécut, s'attendant mourir.

Ci-gît, – cœur sans cœur, mal planté,
Trop réussi, – comme *raté*.

No poser, – posed himself *unique*;
Too naif was his cynical streak;
Believed nil, swallowed hook and line;
– And in distaste his taste was fine.

Too raw, – because too overdone;
Seemed himself more than anyone;
His ennui amused him quite
Enough to wake him up at night;
Idler at sea, – adrift without drive,
A wreck that never will arrive...

A dry spirit but drunken head;
To bear himself too *Selvative*;
Finished, not knowing how to; instead
He died foreboding that he'd live
And lived in hopes of being dead.

Here lies – a heartless heart, ill-grounded,
A *failure* of success unbounded.

Épitaphe

POUR

TRISTAN JOACHIM-ÉDOUARD CORBIÈRE, PHILOSOPHE,
ÉPAVE, MORT-NÉ

Mélange adultère de tout:
De la fortune et pas le sou,
De l'énergie et pas de force,
La Liberté, mais une entorse.
Du cœur, du cœur! de l'âme, non –
Des amis, pas un compagnon,
De l'idée et pas une idée,
De l'amour et pas une aimée,
La paresse et pas le repos.
Vertus chez lui furent défauts,
Âme blasée inassouvie.
Mort, mais pas guéri de la vie,
Gâcheur de vie hors de propos
Le corps à sec et la tête ivre,
Espérant, niant l'avenir,
Il mourut en s'attendant vivre
Et vécut s'attendant mourir.

[Les Amours jaunes, *seconde édition, Vanier, 1891*]

Epitaph

FOR

TRISTAN JOACHIM-ÉDOUARD CORBIÈRE, PHILOSOPHER,
WAIF, STILLBORN

All and nothing's adulterate hash:
Of fortune and not a bit of cash,
Of drive without the might and main,
Of freedom that is just a strain.
Of heart, of heart! but spirit, no –
With friends, but no companion, though;
Of thought with no idea at all,
Of love but not a girl to call,
Of indolence but no repose.
Virtues in him were otiose,
Soul cloyed but never had its fill.
Dead, but of life uncured still,
Beside the point, he trod on toes.
Head drunk, body dry as a sieve,
In hopes, denying a future ahead,
He died foreboding that he'd live
And lived in hopes of being dead.

[Les Amours jaunes, *second edition, Vanier, 1891*]

À l'Éternel Madame

Mannequin idéal, tête-de-turc du leurre,
Éternel Féminin!... repasse tes fichus;
Et viens sur mes genoux, quand je marquerai l'heure,
Me montrer comme on fait chez vous, anges déchus.

Sois pire, et fais pour nous la joie à la malheure,
Piaffe d'un pied léger dans les sentiers ardus.
Damne-toi, pure idole! et ris! et chante! et pleure,
Amante! Et meurs d'amour!... à nos moments perdus.

Fille de marbre! en rut! sois folâtre!... et pensive.
Maîtresse, chair de moi! fais-toi vierge et lascive...
Féroce, sainte, et bête, en me cherchant un cœur...

Sois femelle de l'homme, et sers de Muse, ô femme,
Quand le poète brame en *Âme*, en *Lame*, en *Flamme*!
Puis – quand il ronflera – viens baiser ton Vainqueur!

To Eternity Madam

Ideal lay-figure, aunt-sally of a bait,
Retie your kerchief, Woman, Eternal, Prime!
Come to my knees the moment I indicate,
Show me how you do, angels ex-sublime!

Grow worse, give a bit of zip in a tight strait;
Paw with light foot the hard mounts that climb;
Damn yourself, pure idol; laugh, sing, weep, mate,
Love-bird. Die of love in our spare time.

Marble maiden! on heat, with game and pensive mood;
Mistress, flesh of my flesh; be virgin, lewd...
Crude, saintly, silly, in finding me a heart!...

Oh woman, be feminine of man; to Muse turning
When poet's girning: *Yearning/ Churning/ Burning!*
Then – when he snores – come kiss your Conqueror's part!

Féminin singulier

Éternel Féminin de l'éternel Jocrisse!
Fais-nous sauter, pantins nous payons les décors!
Nous éclairons la rampe... Et toi, dans la coulisse,
Tu peux faire au pompier le pur don de ton corps.

Fais claquer sur nos dos le fouet de ton caprice,
Couronne tes genoux!... et nos têtes dix-cors;
Ris! montre tes dents! mais... nous avons la police,
Et quelque chose en nous d'eunuque et de recors.

... Ah tu ne comprends pas?... – Moi non plus – Fais la belle,
Tourne: nous sommes soûls! Et plats: Fais la cruelle!
Cravache ton pacha, ton humble serviteur!...

Après, sache tomber! – mais tomber avec grâce –
Sur notre sable fin ne laisse pas de trace!...
– C'est le métier de femme et de gladiateur. –

Feminine Singular

Eternal Feminine of the Eternal Dupe! draw
And pull our puppet strings, we fund the do!
We turn on the foot lights, you in the flies thaw
And give the philistine your body freely, you.

Make the crack of your whim lash our backs raw!
Crown your kneecaps!... our ten-horned heads, too;
Laugh! show your teeth! but we've still the law,
Something eunuch in us, and bum-bailiff to sue.

... Ah, don't you understand?... Me, neither. – Be lovely; turn:
And we are drunk! Prat-fallen: Be cruel, stern!
Lash your pasha, your humble servitor and waiter...

After, know how to fall! – but fall with fetching grace –
And on our fine soft sand leave not a single trace!...
– For that's the trade of woman and the gladiator! –

Bohème de chic

Ne m'offrez pas un trône!
À moi tout seul je fris,
Drôle, en ma sauce jaune
De *chic* et de mépris.

Que les bottes vernies
Pleuvent du paradis,
Avec des parapluies...
Moi, va-nu-pieds, j'en ris!

– Plate époque râpée,
Où chacun a du bien;
Où, cuistre sans épée,
Le vaurien ne vaut rien!

Papa, – pou, mais honnête, –
M'a laissé quelques sous,
Dont j'ai fait quelque dette,
Pour me payer des poux!

Son habit, mis en perce,
M'a fait de beaux haillons
Que le soleil traverse;
Mes trous sont des rayons.

Dans mon chapeau, la lune
Brille à travers les trous,
Bête et vierge comme une
Pièce de cent sous!

Modish Bohemia

Don't offer me a throne!
Oddball, I fry unique
In yellow sauce all my own,
Mixed of contempt and *chic*.

Though boots of patent leather
From Paradise rain here,
And umbrellas together...
A barefoot scruff, I jeer!

– The age a shabby, dull one
Where people must possess;
Where, loutish, swordless scullion,
The worthless is worth less!

– A louse but straight, – my dad
Left me a bit of a slice;
I turned it to debt and had
My own back for the lice!

His coat well broached with scags,
Pierced by the sun's blaze,
Gave me my glad rags;
My holes were flashing rays.

Through holes where my hat leaks
The moon shines, ninny-wit
And virginal, it peeks
Like a guinea-bit!

– Gentilhomme!… à trois queues:
Mon nom mal ramassé
Se perd à bien des lieues
Au diable du passé!

Mon blason, – pas bégueule,
Est, comme moi, faquin:
– *Nous bandons à la gueule,*
Fond troué d'arlequin. –

Je pose aux devantures
Où je lis: – DÉFENDU
DE POSER DES ORDURES –
Roide comme un pendu!

Et me plante sans gêne
Dans le plat du hasard,
Comme un couteau sans gaine
Dans un plat d'épinard.

Je lève haut la cuisse
Aux bornes que je vois:
Potence, pavé, suisse,
Fille, priape ou roi!

Quand, sans tambour ni flûte,
Un servile estafier
Au violon me culbute,
Je me sens libre et fier!…

Et je laisse la vie
Pleuvoir sans me mouiller,
En attendant l'envie
De me faire empailler.

– A gent!... with three tails:
My line obscurely cast,
Miles lost for good it trails
To the devil of a past!

My crest – no strait-laced snoblet,
Is like myself a bounder:
– *We bend with gules the gob-let;*
Orts turn-coat pierce the ground. –

I slump in any shop-front
Where I observe this ban:
NO RUBBISH DUMPING! – runt,
Stiff as a hanged man!

Unabashed, I stick my foot
In the crap of chance, image
Of a knife unsheathed and put
Into a plate of spinach.

I cock my leg up high
At any obstacles seen,
Flags, gallows, strong-arm guy,
Game girl or king and queen!

When without fanfare or trumpet
Some lickspittle brawny heel
Kicks me in the drum to lump it,
How proud and free I feel!...

I let life rain on me
And don't get wet. I bide
My time for the urge to be
Well taxi-dermified.

– Je dors sous ma calotte,
La calotte des cieux;
Et l'étoile pâlotte
Clignote entre mes yeux.

Ma Muse est grise ou blonde…
Je l'aime et ne sais pas;
Elle est à tout le monde…
Mais – moi seul – je la bats!

À moi ma Chair-de-poule!
À toi! Suis-je pas beau,
Quand mon baiser te roule
À cru dans mon manteau!

Je ris comme une folle
Et sens mal aux cheveux,
Quand ta chair fraîche colle
Contre mon cuir lépreux!

Jérusalem. – Octobre.

– I kip beneath my cap:
My cap is cut from sky;
The palish star in its lap
Twinkles into my eye.

My Muse is grey or blonde-curled…
I love her – god knows why;
She's open to the world…
Though I'm her beater, I!

For me, my Goose-flesh!
For you! this handsome bloke,
Aren't I, to clasp and thresh
You skin to skin in my cloak!

As I feel it pull my hair,
Like a mad bitch I grin
As your cool limbs stick bare
To my leprous leather skin!

Jerusalem. – October.

Gente Dame

Il n'est plus, ô ma Dame,
D'amour en cape, en lame,
   Que Vous!...
De passion sans obstacle,
Mystère à grand spectacle,
   Que nous!...

Depuis les *Tour de Nesle*
Et les *Château de Presle*,
   Temps frais,
Où l'on couchait en Seine
Les galants, pour leur peine...
   – Après. –

Quand vous êtes *Frisette*,
Il n'est plus de grisette
   Que Toi!...
Ni de rapin farouche,
Pur Rembrandt sans retouche,
   Que moi!

Qu'il attende, Marquise,
Au grand mur de l'église
   Flanqué,
Ton bon coupé vert-sombre,
Comme un bravo dans l'ombre,
   Masqué.

– À nous! – J'arme en croisière
Mon fiacre-corsaire,
   Au vent,
Bordant, comme une voile,

Fair Lady

No longer, oh my lady,
A love, all cape and blady,
      But only You!...
Nor passion without bar,
Mystery spectacular,
      But we, two!...

Since the *Towers of Nesle*
And the *Châteaux of Presle*,
      Chill weather, though,
And bedded in the Seine
The gallants for their pain...
      – After, you know. –

When you are Miss *Frisette*
There's not another grisette
      But only Thee!...
No art-student, moody, smutched,
Pure Rembrandt unretouched,
      But only me!

Oh, Marchioness, let it wait,
Flanked by the church's great
      Walls of stone,
Your classy dark green brougham –
Desperado in shadowdom,
      Masked alone.

– For us! – I arm this trip
My pirate hackney ship,
      I'm tautening
In the wind, just like a sail,

Le store qui nous voile:
    – Avant!…

– Quartier-dolent – tourelle
Tout au haut de l'échelle…
    Quel pas!
– Au sixième – Eh! madame,
C'est tomber, sur mon âme!
    Bien bas!

Au grenier poétique,
Où gîte le classique
    Printemps,
Viens courre, aventurière,
Ce lapin de gouttière:
    Vingt-ans!

Ange, viens pour ton hère
Jouer à la misère
    Des dieux!
Pauvre diable à ficelles,
Lui, joue avec tes ailes,
    Aux cieux!

Viens, Béatrix du Dante,
Mets dans ta main charmante
    Mon front…
Ou passe, en bonne fille,
Fière au bras de ton drille,
    Le pont.

Demain, ô mâle amante,
Reviens-moi Bradamante!
    Muguet!
Eschôlier en fortune,
Narguant, de vers la brune,
    Le guet!

The blind that makes our veil:
       – Forward's the thing!...

Turret – the doleful quarter –
At ladder's height, no shorter...
       What a climb!
– The sixth! – Oh, madam, it's
To fall, on my soul! The splits,
       Down in the grime!

In the poet's garret-room
Where lies that classic bloom,
       Spring, come,
Adventuress, course, prey
Upon this rabbit stray:
       Twenty-some!

Angel, for your *stagg*erer come!
In the gods' misery slum
       In play!
Poor devil on the strings,
He's playing with your wings
       In heaven's ray!

Come, Dante's Beatrice,
In your hand's charming bliss
       Rest my brow...
Or proud on your fellow's arm
Spend like a good girl, ma'am,
       Your French leave now.

Male-volent love, next day,
Bradamante, come my way!
       Dandy, rake!
Sailor of fortune, embark,
Hoodwink the watch through dark
       For my sake.

1 Sonnet

AVEC LA MANIÈRE DE S'EN SERVIR

Réglons notre papier et formons bien nos lettres:

Vers filés à la main et d'un pied uniforme,
Emboîtant bien le pas, par quatre en peloton;
Qu'en marquant la césure, un des quatre s'endorme...
Ça peut dormir debout comme soldats de plomb.

Sur le *railway* du Pinde est la ligne, la forme;
Aux fils du télégraphe: – on en suit quatre, en long;
À chaque pieu, la rime – exemple: *chloroforme.*
– Chaque vers est un fil, et la rime un jalon.

– Télégramme sacré – 20 mots. – Vite à mon aide...
(Sonnet – c'est un sonnet –) ô Muse d'Archimède!
– La preuve d'un sonnet est par l'addition:

– Je pose 4 et 4 = 8! Alors je procède,
En posant 3 et 3! – Tenons Pégase raide:
« Ô lyre! Ô délire! Ô... » – Sonnet – Attention!

Pic de la Maladetta. – Août.

1 Sonnet

WITH THE METHOD OF SERVING

Let's rule up the paper and form our letters properly:

Hand-chiselled verse with feet all uniform,
Platoon in fours, in lock-step marching-time;
One of them drops off at the caesural norm...
Can sleep on foot, like a lead soldier's mime.

On Pindus *railway* is the line, the form;
With telegraph wires: – four running up the climb;
At each post rhyme – example: *ch-loroform.*
– Each verse a plum[b]-line; the pillar, rhyme.

– Sacred telegram – 20 words. – Help, step on it...
O Muse of Archimedes! (Sonnet; it's a sonnet.)
– The proof of any sonnet's adding one:

– I put 4 and 4 = 8! Go on to con it
With 3 and 3! – Let's hold Pegasus strictly on it:
'O lyre, O delyrium, O!...' – Sonnet – 'Shun!

Pic de la Maladetta. – August.

Sonnet à Sir Bob

> *Chien de femme légère, braque*
> *anglais pur sang.*

Beau chien, quand je te vois caresser ta maîtresse,
Je grogne malgré moi – pourquoi? – Tu n'en sais rien...
– Ah! c'est que moi – vois-tu – jamais je ne caresse,
Je n'ai pas de maîtresse, et... ne suis pas beau chien.

– *Bob! Bob!* – Oh! le fier nom à hurler d'allégresse! ...
Si je m'appelais *Bob*... Elle dit Bob si bien!...
Mais moi je ne suis pas *pur sang*. – Par maladresse,
On m'a fait *braque* aussi... mâtiné de chrétien.

– Ô Bob! nous changerons à la métempsycose:
Prends mon sonnet, moi ta sonnette à faveur rose;
Toi ma peau, moi ton poil – avec puces ou non...

Et je serai *sir Bob* – Son seul amour fidèle!
Je mordrai les roquets, elle me mordrait, Elle!...
Et j'aurai le collier portant Son petit nom.

> *British channel. – 15 may.*

Sonnet to Sir Bob

> *Dog of an easy lay, a pure-bred*
> *English hound.*

Fine dog, I watch you nuzzle your mistress, press;
And groan despite myself – why? – Empty head...
– Ah, it's because – d'you see – I never caress,
I have no mistress, and... am no thoroughbred.

– *Bob! Bob!* – Swell name to shout in cheerfulness!...
Were *Bob* my name... So nice the way she said
Bob!... But me, no *pedigree.* – Made by some mess,
A *mutt-hound*, too... but christian-cross instead.

– Oh Bob! by transmigration we'll change place:
Take my jingles; I, your jingler, on its pink lace;
You, skin; I, fur – with or without the fleas...

I'll be *Sir Bob* – Her one faithful love, me!
I'll bite all mongrels; she'll bite me – She!...
I'll wear Her first name on the collar, please.

> *British Channel. – 15th May.*

Steam-Boat

À une passagère.

En fumée elle est donc chassée
L'éternité, la traversée
Qui fit de Vous ma sœur d'un jour,
    Ma sœur d'amour!...

Là-bas: cette mer incolore
Où ce qui fut Toi flotte encore...
Ici: la terre, ton écueil,
    Tertre de deuil!

On t'espère là... Va légère!
Qui te bercera, Passagère?...
Ô passagère [de] mon cœur,
    Ton remorqueur!...

Quel ménélas, sur son rivage,
Fait le pied?... – Va, j'ai ton sillage...
J'ai, – quand il est là voir venir, –
    Ton souvenir!

Il n'aura pas, lui, ma Peureuse,
Les sauts de ta gorge houleuse!...
Tes sourcils salés de poudrain
    Pendant un grain!

Il ne t'aura pas: effrontée!
Par tes cheveux au vent fouettée!...
Ni, durant les longs quarts de nuit,
    Ton doux ennui...

Steam-Boat

To a Lady Passenger.

A puff of smoke on air,
Eternity – that voyage where
My day sister you toured,
 My love-sister aboard!…

There: sea's colourless swill
Where what was You floats still…
Here: land, your grounding reef,
 Shoals of grief.

You're expected there… Go lightly!
Passenger, who'll rock you nightly?…
Passenger in my heart snug,
 Your ocean tug…

What menelaus for your sake
Paces his shore?… – Your wake
I have, – when your coming, he'll see –
 And your memory!

He'll not have, my Fearfullest,
The heave of your swelling breast!…
Your lashes dashed with fall
 Of spray in squall!

Not have you: brazen hussy!
With hair wind-lashed and mussy!…
Nor in the night-watch chores
 Sweet tediums of yours…

Ni ma poésie où: – *Posée,*
Tu seras la mouette blessée,
Et moi le flot qu'elle rasa ...,
    Et cœtera.

– Le large, bête sans limite,
Me paraîtra bien grand, Petite,
Sans Toi!... Rien n'est plus l'horizon
    Qu'une cloison.

Qu'elle va me sembler étroite!
Tout seul, la boîte à deux!... la boîte
Où nous n'avions qu'un oreiller
    Pour sommeiller.

Déjà le soleil se fait sombre
Qui ne balance plus ton ombre,
Et la houle a fait un grand pli...
    – Comme l'oubli! –

Ainsi déchantait sa fortune,
En vigie, au sec, dans la hune,
Par un soir frais, vers le matin,
    Un pilotin.

               10′ long. O.
               40′ lat. N.

Nor my verse where: – *You'll be,*
Put down, the hurt gull; me,
The wave she's skimmed to north
    And so forth.

– The high sea, beast without bound,
Without You, Slight One, around,
Will seem so vast!… And no horizon
    But bulkhead, eyes on.

How cramped it's going to be,
The double bunk… where we
Had just one pillow to share
    And managed there.

The sun now dulls its rays,
Your shadow no more sways,
The swell's raised a great ruck…
    – Like oblivion struck! –

So, lowering his fore-tune a notch,
Atop, high and dry, on watch,
A chill night till dawn, he vents this,
    Pilot apprentice.

10′ long. W.
40′ lat. N.

Pudentiane

Attouchez, sans toucher. On est dévotieuse,
    Ni ne retient à son escient.
Mais On pâme d'horreur d'être: *luxurieuse*
    De corps et de consentement!...

Et de chair... de cette œuvre On est fort curieuse,
    Sauf le vendredi – seulement:
Le confesseur est maigre... et l'extase pieuse
    En fait: *carême entièrement.*

... Une autre se donne. – Ici l'On se damne –
C'est un tabernacle – ouvert – qu'on profane.
Bénitier où le serpent est caché!

Que l'Amour, ailleurs, comme un coq se chante...
CI-GÎT! La *pudeur-d'-attentat* le hante...
C'est la Pomme (cuite) en fleur de péché.

Rome. – 40 ans. – 15 août.

Pudenty-Anne

Contact without touch. One's a devotee,
  Don't hold her from her intent,
But One faints in horror: *at lechery,*
  In body and consent! ...

And of the flesh ... rule kept with propriety,
  Except on Fridays – solitary bent:
The confessor's lean ... it's ecstatic piety
  That does it: *entirely Lent.*

... Another gives herself. – Self-damnation obtains –
It's a tabernacle – open – that one profanes.
The holy water stoup the serpent's hidden in!

May love be crowing like the cock elsewhere ...
HERE LIES! *Modesty-with-intent* haunts the air ...
It is the Apple (cooked) in flower of sin.

    Rome. – 40 years old. – 15th August.

Après la pluie

J'aime la petite pluie
     Qui s'essuie
D'un torchon de bleu troué!
J'aime l'amour et la brise,
     Quand ça frise…
Et pas quand c'est secoué.

– Comme un parapluie en flèches,
     Tu te sèches,
Ô grand soleil! grand ouvert…
À bientôt l'ombrelle verte
     Grand'ouverte!
Du printemps – été d'hiver. –

La passion c'est l'averse
     Qui traverse!
Mais la femme n'est qu'un grain:
Grain de beauté, de folie
     Ou de pluie…
Grain d'orage – ou de serein. –

Dans un clair rayon de boue,
     Fait la roue,
La roue à grand appareil,
– Plume et queue – une Cocotte
     Qui barbote;
Vrai déjeuner de soleil!

– « Anne! ou qui que tu sois, chère…
     Ou pas chère,
Dont on fait, à l'œil, les yeux…

After the Rain

I like a shower of light rain
       That dries again
On a rag of tattered blue!
I like love and the breeze,
       As ruffling tease…
Not kicking up a to-do.

– Like an umbrella shaped of darts
       You dry your parts,
O bright sun, opening wide…
Soon the green sunshade of spring
       Wide-opening!
– And summer of the winter-tide. –

For passion's the cloudburst
       That's traversed!
But woman is a slight spot:
A beauty spot, spot of inane
       Folly or rain…
Squall of storm – or damp nightspot. –

There in a clear and muddy rut
       Off on her strut,
Parades in full display, –
Feather and tail – a game bird who
       Is splashing through…
Flying colours, sweetie tray!

– 'Anne, or whoever you are, dear…
       Or not so dear,
At whom, on tic, one's making eyes…

Hum… Zoé! Nadjejda! Jane!
   Vois: je flâne,
Doublé d'or comme les cieux! »

« *English spoken?* – Espagnole?…
   Batignolle?…
Arbore le pavillon
Qui couvre ta marchandise,
   Ô marquise
D'Amaëgui!… Frétillon!…

« Nom de singe ou nom d'Archange?
   Ou mélange?…
Petit nom à huit ressorts?
Nom qui ronfle, ou nom qui chante?
   Nom d'amante?…
Ou nom à coucher dehors?…

« Veux-tu, d'une amour fidèlle,
   Éternelle!
Nous adorer pour ce soir?…
Pour tes deux petites bottes
   Que tu crottes,
Prends mon cœur et le trottoir!

« N'es-tu pas doña Sabine?
   Carabine?…
Dis: veux-tu le paradis
De l'Odéon? – traversée
   Insensée!…
On emporte des radis. » –

C'est alors que se dégaine
   La rengaine:
« Vous vous trompez… Quel émoi!…

Um… Zoë! Nadezhda! Jane!
       I'm loafing again,
Look: lined with gold like the skies!'

'Spanish? *English spoken?* …
       Batignol… broken?…
Raise up the colours, show
Your goods, you flutteress,
       O marchioness
Of Amaëgui!… No?…

'Your name angel or chimp's?
       Or cross-bred imp's?…
Pet name well-heeled (spring!)?
Handle of mistress? Tuneful?
       Silver-spoonful?
That hums? Or chokes like string?…

'With love faithful evermore
       Shall we adore
Each other this evening?… Sweet,
For your little bootees' sake,
       That you mud-cake,
Take to my heart and the street!

'But donna Sabine, aren't you?
       Carabine, I'd grant you…
Tell me: do you fancy the gods
Atop the Odéon? – crossing,
       A wild tossing!…
You'll take off over the odds.' –

And then it's time to draw
       Out the old saw:
'You are mistaken… Leave me be…

Laissez-moi… je suis honnête…
                    – Pas si bête!
– Pour qui me prends-tu? – Pour moi!…

« … Prendrais-tu pas quelque chose
                    Qu'on arrose
Avec n'importe quoi… du
Jus de perles dans des coupes
                    D'or?… Tu coupes!…
Mais moi? Mina, me prends-tu?

« – Pourquoi pas? ça va sans dire!
                    – Ô sourire!…
Moi, par-dessus le marché!…
Hermosa, tu m'as l'air franche
                    De la hanche!
Un cuistre en serait fâché!

« – Mais je me nomme Aloïse…
                    – Héloïse!
Veux-tu, pour l'amour de l'art,
– Abeilard avant la lettre –
                    Me permettre
D'être un peu ton Abeilard? »

.   .   .   .
.   .   .   .

Et, comme un grain blanc qui crève,
                    Le doux rêve
S'est couché là, sans point noir…
« Donne à ma lèvre apaisée,
                    La rosée
D'un baiser levant – Bonsoir –

I am respectable... What a to-do!...
       – Less nonsense, you!
– Who d'you take me for? – For me!...

'... Wouldn't you like a bite, some snack
       To be knocked back
With no matter what? Spirit of pearl
In golden goblets? You'd water it?...
       But me, admit
You'll take me, Mina, my girl?

– 'Why not? It goes without saying!
       – A smirk playing!...
But, into the bargain, for me!...
Hermosa, to me you seem a cookie
       That wants her nookie!
A yob would react so angrily!

– 'But my name is Aloïse...
       – Heloïse!
For love of art, would you permit –
An Abelard before his day –
       Me now to play,
Your Abelard just for a bit?'

. . . .
. . . .

Like a white squall dying abeam,
       The sweet dream
Set, no black cloud in the sky...
'Put to my lips now quelled and calm
       The rosy charm
Of a rising kiss – Good night. Good bye. –

« C'est le chant de l'alouette,
                    Juliette !
Et c'est le chant du dindon…
Je te fais, comme l'aurore
                    Qui te dore,
Un rond d'or sur l'édredon. »

'It's the song of the lark,
            Juliet, hark!
And the turkey cock's awake ...
Like dawn, that turns you gilt
            Across your quilt,
A chink of gold I'll make.'

À une rose

Rose, rose-d'amour vannée,
　　Jamais fanée,
Le rouge-fin est ta couleur,
　　Ô fausse fleur!

Feuille où pondent les journalistes
　　Un fait-divers,
Papier-Joseph, croquis d'artistes:
　　– Chiffres ou vers –

Cœur de parfum, montant arôme
　　Qui nous embaume…
Et ferait même avec succès,
　　Après décès;

Grise l'amour de ton haleine,
　　Vapeur malsaine,
Vent de pastille-du-sérail,
　　Hanté par l'ail!

Ton épingle, épine-postiche,
　　Chaque nuit fiche
Le hanneton-d'or, ton amant…
Sensitive ouverte, arrosée
De fausses-perles de rosée,
　　En diamant!

Chaque jour palpite à la colle
　　De ta corolle
Un papillon-coquelicot,
　　Pur calicot.

To a Rose

Rose, love's rose, jaded,
                Never faded.
Your colour's wine red,
                False flower-head!

Leaf where journalists lay
                News of the day,
Jewellers' tissue, artist's draught:
                – Numbers, verse-craft –

Heart of scent whose fragrance
                Embalms us vagrants...
And would create a breath
                Of success after death;

Get love pissed with your breath's
                Sick fumes like meths,
Harem's joss-stick pong,
                With garlic strong!

Fake thorn, your pinning pricks
                Each night to fix,
Your golden goose, your dear...
Showered, tender flower you,
In fake pearls of dew,
                Like diamond gear!

Each day flutters in the gum
                Of your corolla, some
Butterfly poppy-cock,
                Pure calico (mock!).

Rose-thé!... – Dans le grog, peut-être! –
                Tu dois renaître
Jaune, sous le fard du tampon,
                Rose-pompon!

Vénus-Coton, née en pelote,
                Un soir-matin,
Parmi l'écume... que culotte
                Le clan rapin!

Rose-mousseuse, sur toi pousse
                Souvent la mousse
De l'Aï... Du BOCK plus souvent
                – À 30 C^{ent}.

– Un coup-de-soleil de la rampe!
                Qui te retrempe;
Un coup de pouce à ton grand air
                Sur fil-de-fer!...

Va, gommeuse et gommée, ô rose
                De couperose,
Fleurir les faux-cols et les cœurs.
                Gilets vainqueurs!

Tea-rose!... – Perhaps in the toddy! –
    Reborn in body,
Yellow, under the rouge you chose,
    Pom-pom rose!

Cotton Venus born in a ball,
    One eve of dawn
Amid the spume... daubed by all
    The art-farts that spawn!

Sparkling moss-rose you show
    A head of l'Aÿ... Though
Oftener of BOCK – a fizz
    – At 30 cents, that is.

– The floodlights' sunstroke!
    Invigorating soak;
A finger deft at your airs: on wire
    There, the high-flier!...

Split, stuck-up and sticky rose,
    Grog-blossomed, acneose;
Make starched collars and hearts strut
    The winning waistcoat's cut!

À la mémoire de Zulma
VIERGE-FOLLE HORS BARRIÈRE
et d'un louis

Bougival, 8 mai.

Elle était riche de vingt ans,
Moi j'étais jeune de vingt francs,
Et nous fîmes bourse commune,
Placée, à fonds perdu, dans une
Infidèle nuit de printemps…

La lune a fait un trou dedans,
Rond comme un écu de cinq francs,
Par où passa notre fortune:
Vingt ans! vingt francs!… et puis la lune!

– En monnaie – hélas – les vingt francs!
En monnaie aussi les vingt ans!
Toujours de trous en trous de lune,
Et de bourse en bourse commune…
– C'est à peu près même fortune!

. . . .

– Je la trouvai – bien des printemps,
Bien des vingt ans, bien des vingt francs,
Bien des trous et bien de la lune
Après – Toujours vierge et vingt ans,
Et… colonelle à la Commune!

. . . .

– Puis après: la chasse aux passants,
Aux vingt sols, et plus aux vingt francs…
Puis après: la fosse commune,
Nuit gratuite sans trou de lune.

Saint-Cloud. – Novembre.

To the Memory of Zulma
FOOLISH VIRGIN BEYOND THE PALE
and of a louis

Bougival, 8th May.

Rich with twenty years was she;
Me, young of twenty francs and we,
Our cash-flow pool at one bank,
Quite unsecured, our savings sank
In one spring night unfaithfully ...

The moon burnt a hole in that, maybe
A five-franc crown in circularity,
And drew our fortune through it – yank:
Twenty years! twenty francs!... the moon's blank!

– 's now small change – twenty francs! – dear me!
Twenty years, too, small currency!
Now hole on hole, moon-flit, out flank,
Share pool and share pool drawing blank...
– Fortune itself, it'd almost rank!

. . . .

– I found her – many springs, post me,
Many score years, score francs in fee,
Many holes burnt, much moonings blank
After – Still virgin and twenty ... rank:
Colonel to the Commune – to be frank!

. . . .

– Much later, chasing passers was she,
For twenty coppers, not francs, the fee ...
And then, a communal grave; the dank
Night free, no moonlight flit to bank on.

Saint-Cloud. – November.

Bonne fortune
et
fortune

Odor della feminita.

Moi, je fais mon trottoir, quand la nature est belle,
Pour la passante qui, d'un petit air vainqueur,
Voudra bien crocheter, du bout de son ombrelle,
Un clin de ma prunelle ou la peau de mon cœur...

Et je me crois content – pas trop! – mais il faut vivre:
Pour promener un peu sa faim, le gueux s'enivre...

Un beau jour – quel métier! – je faisais, comme ça,
Ma croisière. – Métier!... – Enfin, Elle passa
– Elle qui? – La Passante! Elle, avec son ombrelle!
Vrai valet de bourreau, je la frôlai... – mais Elle

Me regarda tout bas, souriant en dessous,
Et... me tendit sa main, et...

                       m'a donné deux sous.

Rue des Martyrs.

Good Fortune
and
a Fortune

Odor della feminita.

Me, I hit the streets, in a fine spell,
For that stroller who, with petty-triumphant look,
Wants, with her sunshade's point, to crotchet well
A wink of mine, or my heart's skin with her hook...

I think I'm content – not too much! – but you must live.
To take their hunger walking, tramps booze like a sieve...

One fine day – what a job! – doing just that,
Cruising – Some job!... – And there at last, pat,
She passed – she who? – The Stroller! Sunshade, too!
Real vice-headsman, I brushed against her... – Who

Glanced me once over, hiding a smile with it...
Held out her hand, and...

                     gave me a tup'ny bit.

Martyrs' Street.

À une camarade

Que me veux-tu donc, femme trois fois fille?...
Moi qui te croyais un si bon enfant!
– De l'amour?... – Allons: cherche, apporte, pille!
M'aimer aussi, toi!... moi qui t'aimais tant.

Oh! je t'aimais comme... un lézard qui pèle
Aime le rayon qui cuit son sommeil...
L'Amour entre nous vient battre de l'aile:
– Eh! qu'il s'ôte de devant mon soleil!

Mon amour, à moi, n'aime pas qu'on l'aime;
Mendiant, il a peur d'être écouté...
C'est un lazzarone enfin, un bohème,
Déjeunant de jeûne et de liberté.

– Curiosité, bibelot, bricole?...
C'est possible: il est rare – et c'est son bien –
Mais un bibelot cassé se recolle;
Et lui, décollé, ne vaudra plus rien!...

Va, n'enfonçons pas la porte entr'ouverte
Sur un paradis déjà trop rendu!
Et gardons à la pomme, jadis verte,
Sa peau, sous son fard de fruit défendu.

Que nous sommes-nous donc fait l'un à l'autre?...
– Rien... – Peut-être alors que c'est pour cela;
– Quel a commencé? – Pas moi, bon apôtre!
Après, quel dira: c'est donc tout – voilà!

To Just a Woman Friend

What d'you want of me, then, woman, thrice chaste?...
I thought to myself you were such a good little kid!
– Love?... – Come now: hunt, forage, lay waste!
You, love me, too!... Me, that loved you as I did?

Oh, I loved you like a sloughing lizard
Loves the ray of sun that cooks him basking...
Love comes between us to beat his wings a blizzard.
– Hoy! beat it out of my sun! That's all I'm asking.

My self love doesn't love itself to be loved.
A beggar it is, scared of being listened to...
Lazzarone, bohemian, pillow to poster shoved,
Fast-feeding on fast and liberty – not you.

– A trinket, knick-knack, bygone, curio?...
Could be: he is a rarity – that's his best suit. –
But broken trinkets can be mended, though;
While, he, come quite unstuck, 's not worth a hoot!...

Enough. Let's not force the door, half-open,
On a paradise already too bushed. Let's retain
The skin on the once-green apple unbroken
Under its make-up of forbidden fruit again.

What have we done to each other? It was
– Nothing... – Perhaps it is because of that?
– Who started it? – Apostle of the double Cross,
Not me. Over, who'll say: finished – that's flat!

– Tous les deux, sans doute… – Et toi, sois bien sûre
Que c'est encor moi le plus attrapé :
Car si, par erreur, ou par aventure,
Tu ne me trompais… je serais trompé !

Appelons cela : *l'amitié calmée*;
Puisque l'amour veut mettre son holà.
N'y croyons pas trop, chère mal-aimée…
– C'est toujours trop vrai ces mensonges-là ! –

Nous pourrons, au moins, ne pas nous maudire
– Si ça t'est égal – le quart-d'heure après.
Si nous en mourons – ce sera de rire…
Moi qui l'aimais tant ton rire si frais !

– Both of us, doubtless… – But this you'd better believe.
It's me still tangled in the worst of it:
For if, by chance or slip, you didn't deceive
Me I'd be deceived, you little chit!

Let's call it: *friendship becalmed*, dutch;
Since love would like to call it finished, through.
Dear ill-beloved, let's not believe too much…
– Those are the lies that always turn out true! –

We could try not cursing each other, at least –
If it's all the same to you – the quarter hour after.
If we die of it – what a scream!… Creased,
I've so much loved the freshness of your laughter!

Un jeune qui s'en va

Morire.

Oh le printemps! – Je voudrais paître!...
C'est drôle, est-ce pas: Les mourants
Font toujours ouvrir leur fenêtre,
Jaloux de leur part de printemps!

Oh le printemps! Je veux écrire!
Donne-moi mon bout de crayon
– Mon bout de crayon, c'est ma lyre –
Et – là – je me sens un rayon.

Vite!... j'ai vu, dans mon délire,
Venir me manger dans la main
La Gloire qui voulait me lire!
– La gloire n'attend pas demain. –

Sur ton bras, soutiens ton poète,
Toi, sa Muse, quand il chantait,
Son Sourire quand il mourait,
Et sa Fête... quand c'était fête!

Sultane, apporte un peu ma pipe
Turque, incrustée en faux saphir,
Celle qui *va bien à mon type*...
Et ris! – C'est fini de mourir;

Et viens sur mon lit de malade;
Empêche la mort d'y toucher,
D'emporter cet enfant maussade
Qui ne veut pas s'aller coucher.

A Youngster on the Way Out

Morire.

Oh, the Spring! – I'd like to graze...
Weird, isn't it? The dying's thing
To have their windows wide, such days,
Anxious for their share of spring!

Oh, Spring! I want to write a quire!
Give me my pencil-stub to bite
– My stub of pencil, that's my lyre –
And – twang – I am a ray of light.

Quick!... In my delirium I've seen,
Coming to eat out of my hand,
Acclaim that wants to read me, keen!
– Acclaim won't wait, d'you understand? –

So raise your poet on your arm,
You, his Muse, when he used to chaunt;
His Smile when he was deathly gaunt,
His Treat... when past all treatment, ma'am!

Sultana, bring my Turkish pipe
A while, studded with sapphires (fake),
The one *that suits so well my type*...
And laugh! – Death ends in a wake;

Come to my sickbed, do as I bid;
Hinder death's drawing to my head,
And carrying off this sulky kid
That doesn't want to go to bed!

Ne pleure donc plus, – je suis bête –
Vois: mon drap n'est pas un linceul…
Je chantais cela pour moi seul…
Le vide chante dans ma tête…

Retourne contre la muraille.
– Là – l'esquisse – un portrait de toi –
Malgré lui mon œil soûl travaille
Sur la toile… C'était de moi.

J'entends – bourdon de la fièvre –
Un chant de berceau me monter:
« *J'entends le renard, le lièvre,*
« *Le lièvre, le loup chanter.* »

… Va! nous aurons une chambrette
Bien fraîche, à papier bleu rayé;
Avec un vrai bon lit honnête
À nous, à rideaux… et payé!

Et nous irons dans la prairie
Pêcher à la ligne tous deux,
Ou bien *mourir pour la patrie!*…
– Tu sais, je fais ce que tu veux.

… Et nous aurons des robes neuves,
Nous serons riches à bâiller
Quand j'aurai revu *mes épreuves!*
– Pour vivre, il faut bien travailler…

– Non! mourir…
                La vie était belle
Avec toi! mais rien ne va plus…
À moi le pompon d'immortelle
Des grands poètes que j'ai lus!

So don't weep on! – I'm a dense biped. –
Look: my cover's not a shroud...
I sang that to myself, unaloud...
The void is singing out in *my* head...

But glance away toward the wall.
– There – that sketch – portrait of you, see –
Despite themselves my drunk eyes scrawl
On the canvas... me again – yours truly.

I hear – burden of the fever's air –
A cradle song rise in my head:
'*I hear the fox, the hare, the hare,
The wolf all singing.*' So it said.

... Come on! We'll have an airy, small
Room, with some blue-striped paper; pick
A good respectable bed, and all
Ours, and with curtains... cash not tick!

And we will wander to the meadow,
Fish, the two of us together,
Or *die for our country!* well and dead, oh...
– You know I do as you want – whatever.

... And we will have fresh gear, all new.
We'll be rich enough to bust
When I've seen my *trial-proof* all through.
– To live, it's work and work you must...

– Never! It's death...
                          Life was fine
With you! But nothing works any more...
I want the everlasting first in line
Of the great poets I've read before!

À moi, *Myosotis! Feuille morte*
De *Jeune malade à pas lent!*
Souvenir de soi… qu'on emporte
En croyant le laisser – souvent!

– Décès: Rolla: – l'Académie –
Murger, Baudelaire: – hôpital, –
Lamartine: – en perdant la vie
De sa fille, en strophes pas mal…

Doux bedeau, pleureuse en lévite,
Harmonieux tronc des *moissonnés*,
Inventeur de la *larme écrite*,
Lacrymatoire d'abonnés!…

Moreau – j'oubliais – Hégésippe,
Créateur de l'art-hôpital…
Depuis, j'ai la phtisie en grippe;
Ce n'est plus même original.

– Escousse encor: mort en extase
De lui; mort phtisique d'orgueil.
– Gilbert: phtisie et paraphrase
Rentrée, en se pleurant *à l'œil.*

– Un autre incompris: Lacenaire,
Faisant des vers en amateur
Dans le goût anti-poitrinaire,
Avec Sanson pour éditeur.

– Lord Byron, gentleman-vampire,
Hystérique du ténébreux;
Anglais sec, cassé par son rire,
Son noble rire de lépreux.

For me: *Forget-me-not! Dead leaf*
Of *sick youngster with step slow*.
Memory of self – one carries the sheaf,
In thinking one leaves it – no go!

– Deaths! Rolla: – The Academy –
Murger, Baudelaire: – the hospital, –
Lamartine: – losing his daughter, he,
In stanzas not too bad at all…

Soft beadle, weepy in his long gear,
Harmonious alms-box of the *reaped*;
Inventor of the *written tear*;
Lachrimatory of subscribers (steeped)!…

Moreau – nearly forgot – Hégésippe,
Creator of the hospital art…
Since then, consumption's given me gyp;
It's hardly now an original start.

– Escousse: dead in ecstasy
At himself; dead of consumptive pride.
– Gilbert: consumption and summary,
Gaunt, self-wept *on tic*, cock-eyed.

Lacenaire – misunderstood again –
Making verses as amateur
In the anti-consumptive vein,
With Sanson as his publisher.

– Byron, gentleman vampire, dry
Englishman, hysterical dark shafter,
By his laughter broken, by
Nobleness of his leper's laughter.

– Hugo: l'Homme apocalyptique,
L'Homme-Ceci-tûra-cela,
Meurt, gardenational épique;
Il n'en reste qu'un – celui-là! –

… Puis un tas d'amants de la lune,
Guère plus morts qu'ils n'ont vécu,
Et changeant de fosse commune
Sans un discours, sans un écu!

J'en ai lus mourir!… Et ce cygne
Sous le couteau du cuisinier:
– Chénier –… Je me sens – mauvais signe! –
De la jalousie. – Ô métier!

Métier! Métier de mourir…
Assez, j'ai fini mon étude.
Métier: se rimer finir!…
C'est une affaire d'habitude.

Mais non, la poésie est: vivre,
Paresser encore, et souffrir
Pour toi, maîtresse! et pour mon livre;
Il est là qui dort
                              – Non: mourir!

. . . .

Sentir sur ma lèvre appauvrie
Ton dernier baiser se gercer,
La mort dans tes bras me bercer…
Me déshabiller de la vie!…

Charenton. – Avril.

– Hugo: apocalyptic Bard,
Dying, the 'This will Bump off That-er',
And the epic nationalguard;
The last one of them left – this latter! –

... And then a heap of moon-lovers,
Scarcely deader than when liver;
And swopping common graves, the duffers
Without a speech, without a fiver!

I've read them to death!... And that swan,
– Chénier – under the head chef's blade –...
A bad omen! – I feel it's coming on –
– Jealousy. – Oh, what a trade!

Some trade! The dying trade... Penned
Enough, my study is complete.
Some trade: rhyme oneself to the end!...
A matter of habits that repeat!

No: poetry is: to live on, while
Time away still, and suffer breath
For you, love; for my book and style.
There, look, it sleeps.
      – No: it's death!

. . . .

To feel your last of kisses chafe
Itself on my impoverished lip,
Death in your arms cradling me safe...
Undressing me of life, to kip!...

Charenton. – April.

Insomnie

Insomnie, impalpable Bête!
N'as-tu d'amour que dans la tête?
Pour venir te pâmer à voir,
Sous ton mauvais œil, l'homme mordre
Ses draps, et dans l'ennui se tordre!...
Sous ton œil de diamant noir.

Dis: pourquoi, durant la nuit blanche,
Pluvieuse comme un dimanche,
Venir nous lécher comme un chien:
Espérance ou Regret qui veille,
À notre palpitante oreille
Parler bas... et ne dire rien?

Pourquoi, sur notre gorge aride,
Toujours pencher ta coupe vide
Et nous laisser le cou tendu,
Tantales, soiffeurs de chimère:
– Philtre amoureux ou lie amère,
Fraîche rosée ou plomb fondu! –

Insomnie, es-tu donc pas belle?...
Eh pourquoi, lubrique pucelle,
Nous étreindre entre tes genoux?
Pourquoi râler sur notre bouche,
Pourquoi défaire notre couche,
Et... ne pas coucher avec nous?

Pourquoi, Belle-de-nuit impure,
Ce masque noir sur ta figure?...
– Pour intriguer les songes d'or?...
N'es-tu pas l'amour dans l'espace,

Insomnia

Insomnia, impalpable Creature!
Is love for you a head feature?
To come and relish standing by
With evil eye, watching one twist
In boredom, chewing sheets as grist!...
Under your black diamond eye.

Say: why, during a restless night,
Like a wet Sunday, d'you invite
Yourself in to lick us like a dog:
Hope or Remorse who keeps good guard,
And at our throbbing ear unbarred
Speak softly... nothing's monologue?

Why tilt towards our parching lips
Always this empty cup that slips
And leaves our necks outstretched to drink,
Like Tantalus, soaks of mirage booze.
– Bitter cheer, love-philtre, dews
Cooling, or molten lead and zinc! –

Insomnia, aren't you a pretty sight?...
So why, you shameless broad, by night,
Clinch us between your legs till blue?
Why heavy breathing at our lips,
Why disturb our beds and kips
And... still we never sleep with you?

Why, impure Eve-ling Lily, this mask
Black on your face, if one may ask?...
– To mystify our golden dreams?...
Aren't you love in air (thin),

Souffle de Messaline lasse,
Mais pas rassasiée encor!

Insomnie, es-tu l'Hystérie…
Es-tu l'orgue de barbarie
Qui moud l'*Hosannah* des Élus?…
– Ou n'es-tu pas l'éternel plectre,
Sur les nerfs des damnés-de-lettre,
Raclant leurs vers – qu'eux seuls ont lus.

Insomnie, es-tu l'âne en peine
De Buridan – ou le phalène
De l'enfer? – Ton baiser de feu
Laisse un goût froidi de fer rouge…
Oh! viens te poser dans mon bouge!…
Nous dormirons ensemble un peu.

Gasps of Messalina, done in
But still unsatisfied, it seems!

Insomnia, you miss Hysterical?...
Are you the barrel organ, clerical,
Wheezing the Chosen Ones' hosannas?...
– Or aren't you the eternal plectrum
On hell-lettrists' nerves, as they confect rum
Verses – themselves their only scanners?

Insomnia, are you Buridan's ass
In two minds on the palliasse –
Or moth of hell? – Your fiery kiss
Leaves the cold taste of red-hot metal...
Come to my hang-out now and settle!...
We'll sleep a bit together, miss.

La pipe au poète

Je suis la Pipe d'un poète,
Sa nourrice, et: j'endors *sa Bête*.

Quand ses chimères éborgnées
Viennent se heurter à son front,
Je fume… Et lui, dans son plafond,
Ne peut plus voir les araignées.

… Je lui fais un ciel, des nuages,
La mer, le désert, des mirages;
– Il laisse errer là son œil mort…

Et, quand lourde devient la nue,
Il croit voir une ombre connue,
– Et je sens mon tuyau qu'il mord…

– Un autre tourbillon délie
Son âme, son carcan, sa vie!
… Et je me sens m'éteindre. – Il dort –

.   .   .   .

– Dors encor: la *Bête* est calmée,
File ton rêve jusqu'au bout…
Mon Pauvre!… la fumée est tout.
– S'il est vrai que tout est fumée…

Paris. – Janvier.

Pipe to the Poet

I am a poet's Pipe, his trim
Nurse, and: I lull the *Beast* in him.

When his one-eyed phantoms fling
Themselves against his forehead reeling,
I smoke ... And he, upon his ceiling,
No longer sees the spiders cling.

... I make him a sky, cloud,
The sea, the desert, mirages crowd;
– He lets his dead eye roam in them ...

And when thick cloud is overlaid
He thinks he sees a familiar shade,
– And I feel him bite my stem ...

Another cloud-puff frees from strife
His soul, his iron collar, his life!
... I feel put out. – He's dozed pro-tem. –

. . . .

– The *Beast* is calmed: sleep on, poor bloke.
Chase your dream right to its pall ...
My poor fellow! ... smoke is all,
– If it's true that all is smoke ...

Paris. – January.

Le Crapaud

Un chant dans une nuit sans air…
La lune plaque en métal clair
Les découpures du vert sombre.

… Un chant; comme un écho, tout vif
Enterré, là, sous le massif…
– Ça se tait: Viens, c'est là, dans l'ombre…

– Un crapaud! – Pourquoi cette peur,
Près de moi, ton soldat fidèle!
Vois-le, poète tondu, sans aile,
Rossignol de la boue… – Horreur! –

… Il chante. – Horreur!! – Horreur pourquoi?
Vois-tu pas son œil de lumière…
Non: il s'en va, froid, sous sa pierre.

. . . .

Bonsoir – ce crapaud-là c'est moi.

Ce soir, 20 Juillet.

The Toad

Some song on an airless night...
The moon tin-plates clear and bright
The cut-outs of gloomy greenery.

... Some song; like an echo dies,
Buried alive in that clump it lies...
– Finished: there in the shadows, see...

– A toad! – Why ever this fear
Of me, your old faithful thing?
Look: a shorn poet, not a wing,
The mud lark... – Horrible to hear! –

... It sings. – Horrible!! – Horrible, why?
Don't you see its eye's bright look?...
No: gone, cold, to its stone nook.

.   .   .   .

Goodnight – that toad is me. Goodbye.

This evening, 20th July.

Femme

La Bête féroce.

Lui – cet être faussé, mal aimé, mal souffert,
Mal haï – mauvais livre … et pire: il m'intéresse. –
S'il est vide après tout … Oh mon dieu, je le laisse,
  Comme un roman pauvre – entr'ouvert.

Cet homme est laid … – Et moi, ne suis-je donc pas belle,
  Et belle encore pour nous deux! –
En suis-je donc enfin aux rêves de pucelle?…
  – Je suis reine: Qu'il soit lépreux!

Où vais-je – femme! – Après… suis-je donc pas légère
  Pour me relever d'un faux pas!
Est-ce donc Lui que j'aime! – Eh non! c'est son mystère …
  Celui que peut-être Il n'a pas.

Plus Il m'évite, et plus et plus Il me poursuit …
  Nous verrons ce dédain suprême.
Il est rare à croquer, celui-là qui me fuit!…
  Il me fuit – Eh bien non!… Pas même.

… Aurais-je ri pourtant! si, comme un galant homme,
  Il avait allumé ses feux …
Comme Ève – femme aussi – qui n'aimait pas la Pomme,
  Je ne l'aime pas – et j'en veux! –

C'est innocent. – Et lui?… Si l'arme était chargée …
  – Et moi, j'aime les vilains jeux!
Et… l'on sait amuser, avec une dragée
  Haute, un animal ombrageux.

Woman

The ferocious She-beast.

Him. That twister, unlovable, so hard to take
    Yet hard to hate – dull book... and worse: he interests me.
What if after all he's hollow... I'll leave him, for God's sake,
    Like a lousy novel – openly.

That man is hideous... – And me? Now aren't I beautiful?
    Enough for both of us, I mean! –
Or am I come to the virgin's dream when gathering wool?...
    – Let him be leper! I am queen.

Where am I off to – woman! – Well... Aren't I light
    Enough to rise from such a blunder?
Am I really in love with Him? – No. His mystique... He might
    Perhaps not have, I shouldn't wonder.

The more He dodges, the more and more He pursues me...
    We'll see about this supreme disdain.
He's a rare nut to crack, this one, he wants to lose me!...
    He's dodging me – Well, no!... Not again.

... Still, wouldn't I have laughed if he'd raked up fire
    To play the gallant with me somehow?...
Like Eve – all woman, too – Apple no real desire –
    I don't love him – and want it now! –

Harmless enough. – But him?... If he'd a loaded gun...
    – But me, I fancy dirty play!
And... with titbits dangled, it's easy to have fun
    And make a moody housedog beg away.

De quel droit ce regard, ce mauvais œil qui touche:
      Monsieur poserait le fatal?
Je suis myope, il est vrai… Peut-être qu'il est louche;
      Je l'ai vu si peu – mais si mal. –

… Et si je le laissais se draper en quenouille,
      Seul dans sa honteuse fierté!…
– Non. Je sens me ronger, comme ronge la rouille,
      Mon orgueil malade, irrité.

Allons donc! c'est écrit – n'est-ce pas – dans ma tête,
      En pattes-de-mouche d'enfer;
Écrit, sur cette page où – là – ma main s'arrête.
      – Main de femme et plume de fer. –

Oui! – Baiser de Judas – Lui cracher à la bouche
      Cet *amour!* – Il l'a mérité –
Lui dont la triste image est debout sur ma couche,
      Implacable de volupté.

Oh oui: coller ma langue à l'inerte sourire
      Qu'il porte là comme un faux pli!
Songe creux et malsain, repoussant… qui m'attire!

    .   .   .   .

      – Une nuit blanche… un drap sali.

                              ★ ★ ★

What right's he got to give me this evil eye?
     Sir would deploy his fatal charm?
– True, I'm short-sighted ... A double-cross-eyed guy?
     I've seen so little of him – and such harm. –

... So if I left him standing there ready to shuttle,
     Tod-rod, in his shamefaced pride! ...
– No. As rust corrodes, I feel myself the subtle
     Corrosion of hurt pride, sick inside.

Come on, then! It's written – isn't it – in my head,
     In a spidery and hellish script.
Written on this sheet where – there my hand stops dead.
     – A woman's hand, a steel pen dipped. –

That's it! – The Judas Kiss. – To spit it in his gob,
     This *love!* – Of that he's deserved his fill,
This jerk whose sorry image stands now on my squab,
     Implacable sensualist spill.

Oh yes: to stick my tongue on that limp smile
     Gawping away like a false pleat!
A filthy, hollow thought ... opposites attract awhile!

    . . . .

     – A sleepless night ... and a soiled sheet.

                                           * * *

Duel aux camélias

J'ai vu le soleil dur contre les touffes
Ferrailler. – J'ai vu deux fers soleiller,
Deux fers qui faisaient des parades bouffes;
Des merles en noir regardaient briller.

Un monsieur en linge arrangeait sa manche;
Blanc, il me semblait un gros camélia;
Une autre fleur rose était sur la branche,
Rose comme... Et puis un fleuret plia.

– Je vois rouge... Ah oui! c'est juste: on s'égorge –
... Un camélia blanc – là – comme Sa gorge...
Un camélia jaune, – ici – tout mâché...

Amour mort, tombé de ma boutonnière.
– À moi, plaie ouverte et fleur printanière!
Camélia vivant, de sang panaché!

Veneris Dies 13 ★ ★ ★

Duel with Camellias

I've seen the harsh sun blade to grass blade
Cross swards. – I've seen two swords flash like suns.
Two flash blades buffoonish on parade;
Blackbirds in mourning watched those gleaming ones.

A gentleman, coatless, got his sleeve settled.
White, a huge camellia, he seemed to me;
Another flower, branched opposite, pink-petalled,
Pink like … And a foil flexed, pulled free.

– I see red … Ah, yes! That's it: you cut throats
For each other –… A white camellia – there – floats …
Like Her breast … A yellowed – here – mutilated …

Dead love, fallen from my buttonhole.
– Mine: open wound, spring flowered! poll
Of living camellia, with red variegated!

Veneris Dies 13 * * *

Fleur d'art

Oui – Quel art jaloux dans Ta fine histoire!
Quels bibelots chers! – Un bout de sonnet,
Un cœur gravé dans ta manière noire,
Des traits de canif à coups de stylet. –

Tout fier mon cœur porte à la boutonnière
Que tu lui taillas, un petit bouquet
D'immortelle rouge – Encor ta manière –
C'est du sang en fleur. Souvenir coquet.

Allons, pas de pleurs à notre mémoire!
– C'est la mâle-mort de l'amour ici –
Foin du myosotis, vieux sachet d'armoire!

Double femme, va!… Qu'un âne te braie!
Si tu n'étais fausse, eh serais-tu vraie?…
L'amour est un duel: – Bien touché! Merci.

★ ★ ★

Paper Flower

Yeah – In Your fine tale what jealous art!
What priceless curios! – A sonnet's stress;
Engraved – in your black style: – one heart,
By penknife strokes with all a stylet's finesse. –

My heart, quite proud, wears in the buttonhole
You carved in it, a dainty spray of flowers –
Red immortelles. – Your style, on the whole –
It's blood in bloom. Trim keepsake of ours.

There, there, now, don't you cry remembering us!
– Manslaughter of love, that's what we have here –
Stuff the forget-me-nots, old pomanders of fuss!

Two-timing whore, split!... An ass bray your shanks!
If you were not false, would you be sincere?...
Love is a duel: – A touch, a touch! Well, thanks.

★ ★ ★

Pauvre garçon

La Bête féroce.

Lui, qui sifflait si haut son petit air de tête,
Était plat près de moi; je voyais qu'il cherchait...
Et ne trouvait pas, et... j'aimais le sentir bête,
Ce héros qui n'a pas su trouver qu'il m'aimait.

J'ai fait des ricochets sur son cœur en tempête.
Il regardait cela... Vraiment, cela l'usait?...
Quel instrument rétif à jouer, qu'un poète!...
J'en ai joué. Vraiment – moi – cela m'amusait.

Est-il mort?... Ah – c'était, du reste, un garçon drôle.
Aurait-il donc trop pris au sérieux son rôle,
Sans me le dire... au moins. – Car il est mort, de quoi?...

Se serait-il laissé fluer de poésie...
Serait-il mort *de chic*, de boire, ou de phtisie,
Ou, peut-être, après tout: de rien...

                             ou bien de Moi.

                                 ★ ★ ★

Poor Kid

The ferocious She-beast.

He whistled his little tune in his head, shrilly,
Boring beside me. I saw how much he sought...
Found nothing and... I liked him feeling silly:
This hero that couldn't twig he loved me, caught.

I glanced things off his storm-tossed heart. And still
He watched me at it... Did it really fag him, thwart?...
A poet's a cussèd fiddle to play with skill!...
Me, I've played some. Really – for me – good sport.

Dead, is he?... He was, besides that, an odd youth.
Would he have played his role too straight like truth
Yet never tell me... at least. – Death from what, could it be?...

Would he have let his vein run out in verse...
Or die *in vogue* or drink, t.b. or worse?
Or, maybe, after all: of nothing...

or Me.

★ ★ ★

Déclin

Comme il était bien, Lui, ce Jeune plein de sève!
Âpre à la vie *Ô Gué!*... et si doux en son rêve.
Comme il portait sa tête ou la couchait gaîment!
Hume-vent à l'amour!... qu'il passait tristement.

Oh comme il était Rien!... – Aujourd'hui, sans rancune
Il a vu lui sourire, au retour, la Fortune;
Lui ne sourira plus que d'autrefois; il sait
Combien tout cela coûte et comment ça se fait.

Son cœur a pris du ventre et dit bonjour en prose.
Il est coté fort cher... ce Dieu c'est quelque chose;
Il ne va plus les mains dans les poches tout nu...

Dans sa gloire qu'il porte en paletot funèbre,
Vous le reconnaîtrez fini, banal, célèbre...
Vous le reconnaîtrez, alors, cet inconnu.

Downer

How fine He was, this Young Man full of sap!
Hard on life with a *Heigh-ho!*... and in his dream, soft pap.
How high he carried his head or rested it in gladness!
He'd got the wind of love!... that he exhaled with sadness.

Oh how Nothing he was!... – Today, without bile,
He's seen, returning, Fortune giving him a smile;
But he'll smile only for things past; he knows
How much it all costs now, and how it all goes.

His heart has put a paunch on, says good day in prose.
He's highly priced... this God is something; and he goes
No longer hands in pockets, naked... How he's grown.

Wearing his glory like a funeral coat, he'll be;
You'll recognize him, finished, trite, celebrity...
You'll recognize him, then and there, this well unknown.

Bonsoir

Et vous viendrez alors, imbécile caillette,
Taper dans ce miroir clignant qui se paillette
D'un éclis d'or, accroc de l'astre jaune, éteint.
Vous verrez un bijou dans cet éclat de tain.

Vous viendrez à cet homme, à son reflet mièvre
Sans chaleur… Mais, au jour qu'il dardait la fièvre,
Vous n'avez rien senti, vous qui – midi passé –
Tombez dans ce rayon tombant qu'il a laissé.

Lui ne vous connaît plus, Vous, l'Ombre déjà vue,
Vous qu'il avait couchée en son ciel toute nue,
Quand il était un Dieu!… Tout cela – n'en faut plus. –

Croyez – Mais lui n'a plus ce mirage qui leurre.
Pleurez – Mais il n'a plus cette corde qui pleure.
Ses chants… – C'était d'un autre; il ne les a pas lus.

Good Evening

You idiotic twit, you'll come to this pass:
Catching the fancy of this blinking looking-glass
That glints with gold, the spent yellow star's trace,
In the flash of the silvering a sparkler you'll face.

You'll come to this man: reflection effete,
Without warmth... But in his day at fever heat
You didn't feel a thing, you that – noon passed –
Fall in the falling ray that he has cast.

He doesn't know You now, Shadow, old hat,
You he'd bedded starkers in his sky. But that
Was when he was a God!... That's – over and done. –

Believe – But he's no mirage to take the eye;
Weep – But he's lost that string, the plangent cry.
His songs... – Someone else's. He hasn't read them. None.

Le Poète contumace

Sur la côte d'ARMOR. – Un ancien vieux couvent,
Les vents se croyaient là dans un moulin-à-vent,
      Et les ânes de la contrée,
Au lierre râpé, venaient râper leurs dents
Contre un mur si troué que, pour entrer dedans,
      On n'aurait pu trouver l'entrée.

– Seul – mais toujours debout avec un rare aplomb,
Crénelé comme la mâchoire d'une vieille,
Son toit à coups-de-poing sur le coin de l'oreille,
Aux corneilles bayant, se tenait le donjon,
Fier toujours d'avoir eu, dans le temps, sa légende…
Ce n'était plus qu'un nid à gens de contrebande,
Vagabonds de nuit, amoureux buissonniers,
Chiens errants, vieux rats, fraudeurs et douaniers.

– Aujourd'hui l'hôte était de la borgne tourelle,
Un Poète sauvage, avec un plomb dans l'aile,
Et tombé là parmi les antiques hiboux
Qui l'estimaient d'en haut. – Il respectait leurs trous, –
Lui, seul hibou payant, comme son *bail* le porte:
Pour vingt-cinq écus l'an, dont: remettre une porte. –

Pour les gens du pays, il ne les voyait pas:
Seulement, en passant, eux regardaient d'en bas,
      Se montrant du nez sa fenêtre;
Le curé se doutait que c'était un lépreux;
Et le maire disait: – Moi, qu'est-ce que j'y peux,
      C'est plutôt un Anglais… un *Être*.

Les femmes avaient su – sans doute par les buses –
Qu'il *vivait en concubinage avec des Muses!*…

Poet by Default

An old monastery once – on the ARMORICAN coast. –
Winds thought they rampaged round a windmill's post,
      And local mules would centre
On its tattered ivy, whet their teeth on what's supposed
To be the wall – so holey that it didn't boast
      A door by which to enter.

– Remote – but upright still, and with a rare nerve,
Crenellated like an agèd widow's gums,
Roof punched over one ear so that the sky comes
Pouring in, and yet the keep could still just serve.
Still proud of having been a legend in its time…
No more than a smugglers' hideout in its prime,
For night-wanderers, stray dogs, the contraband,
Customs-men and bushed lovers, hand in hand.

– The master of the one-eyed tower is today
A wild Poet with one wing shot away,
Fallen among the ancient mope-owls there
Who size him up from above. – But he respects their lair, –
He, the only paying owl, as his *lease* intended:
Twenty-five pounds a year: one door to be mended. –

As for the locals, though, he never saw them pass:
They looked up to him, yes. His window glass
      Their passing noses pointed out.
The priests had long considered he must be a leper.
The mayor opined: – 'Me, I know salt from pepper:
      He must be English… a *VIP*, no doubt.'

And all the women knew – from buzzards, there's no doubt –
He *lived in sin with all the Muses!* a devout

Un hérétique enfin… Quelque *Parisien*
De Paris ou d'ailleurs. – Hélas! on n'en sait rien. –
Il était invisible; et, comme *ses Donzelles*
Ne s'affichaient pas trop, on ne parla plus d'elles.

– Lui, c'était simplement un long flâneur, sec, pâle;
Un ermite-amateur, chassé par la rafale…
Il avait trop aimé les beaux pays malsains.
Condamné des huissiers, comme des médecins,
Il avait posé là, soûl et cherchant sa place
Pour mourir seul ou pour vivre par contumace…

       Faisant, d'un à-peu-près d'artiste,
       Un philosophe d'à peu près,
       Râleur de soleil ou de frais,
       En dehors de l'humaine piste.

Il lui restait encor un hamac, une vielle,
Un barbet qui dormait sous le nom de *Fidèle*;
Non moins fidèle était, triste et doux comme lui,
Un autre compagnon qui s'appelait l'Ennui.

Se mourant en sommeil, il se vivait en rêve.
Son rêve était le flot qui montait sur la grève,
       Le flot qui descendait;
Quelquefois, vaguement, il se prenait attendre…
Attendre quoi… le flot monter – le flot descendre –
       Ou l'Absente… Qui sait?

Le sait-il bien lui-même?… Au vent de sa guérite,
A-t-il donc oublié comme les morts vont vite,
Lui, ce viveur vécu, revenant égaré,
Cherche-t-il son follet, à lui, mal enterré?

– Certe, Elle n'est pas loin, celle après qui tu brames,
Ô Cerf de Saint Hubert! Mais ton front est sans flammes…

Heretic, in short ... *Parisian*, of Paris or
Elsewhere. – Alas, they knew so little to make more. –
He was invisible; and, since his *damsels drew
Scant notice*, no one put together two and two.

– He was just a rangy loafer, withered, pale,
An amateurish hermit, swept in by the gale ...
He'd too much liking for the fine, unhealthy view,
Always condemned by bailiffs, and physicians, too,
He perched there, bored, wanting a place to call a halt
Where he could be alone or hang on by default ...

> Making a philosopher of sorts
> Out of a kind of artist-hack,
> Miles off the usual beaten track,
> Rain or shine, breathing his last snorts.

He still possessed a hammock and a hurdy-gurdy,
A spaniel sleeping with the name of *Fido*; a sturdy
Old Faithful was another bosom-friend he had,
Called Boredom, gentle like him, and very sad.

At death's door when sleeping, he lived off dreams.
His dream the tide that surges up the shore and teems,
> The ebb as back it flows.
And sometimes, waveringly, he set himself to wait ...
To wait for what? ... Tide to rise – tide to abate –
> Or the Absentess? ... Who knows?

Does he know himself? ... In his windswept lookout post
Has he forgotten how soon the dead go? Stray ghost,
And clapped-out libertine, does he really expect
His own ineptly buried sprite to resurrect?

– Indeed, She isn't far, the one for whom you rut,
St Hubert's Stag! But no flames from your forehead jut ...

N'apparais pas, mon vieux, triste et faux déterré…
Fais le mort si tu peux… Car Elle t'a pleuré!

– Est-ce qu'il pouvait, Lui!… n'était-il pas poète…
Immortel comme un autre?… Et dans sa pauvre tête
Déménagée, encor il sentait que les vers
Hexamètres faisaient les cent pas de travers.

– Manque de savoir-vivre extrême – il survivait –
Et – manque de savoir-mourir – il écrivait:
« C'est un être passé de cent lunes, ma Chère,
En ton cœur poétique, à l'état légendaire.
Je rime, donc je vis… ne crains pas, c'est *à blanc*.
– Une coquille d'huître en rupture de banc! –
Oui, j'ai beau me palper: c'est moi! – Dernière faute –
En route pour les cieux – car ma niche est si haute! –
Je me suis demandé, prêt à prendre l'essor:
Tête ou pile… – Et voilà – je me demande encor…

« C'est à toi que je fis mes adieux à la vie,
À toi qui me pleuras, jusqu'à me faire envie
De rester me pleurer avec toi. Maintenant
C'est joué, je ne suis qu'un gâteux revenant,
En os et… (j'allais dire en chair). – La chose est sûre
C'est bien moi, je suis là – mais comme une rature.

« Nous étions amateurs de curiosité:
Viens voir *le Bibelot*. – Moi j'en suis dégoûté. –
Dans mes dégoûts surtout, j'ai des goûts élégants;
Tu sais: j'avais lâché la Vie avec des gants;
L'*Autre* n'est pas même à prendre avec des pincettes…
Je cherche au mannequin de nouvelles toilettes.

« Reviens m'aider: Tes yeux dans ces yeux-là! Ta lèvre
Sur cette lèvre!… Et, là, ne sens-tu pas ma fièvre

Don't haunt, old chap, sad, and so falsely exhumed...
Act dead if you can... She's mourned for you, She's gloomed!

– Couldn't He do so?... Wasn't he a poet, for goodness sake?...
Immortal as any other?... Didn't his poor head ache,
Unhinged by all the hexameters he still feels
Parading up and down his mind with clicking heels?

– Quite lacking life's know-how – he lingered – then,
Lacking the die-how – he took up the pen:
'He's a being passed, after a hundred moons, my Dear,
In your poetic heart, into a legend here.
I rime, therefore I exist... Never fear. It's *blank*.
– A bedless oyster, he is; he makes his bank
Shell out! – Yes, in vain I pinch myself. – Last fault:
It's me all right and skyward bound – so high my vault! –
On point of taking flight, I'm wondering now which:
Heads, tails?... – There – wondering still how it will pitch...

'To you, I make my life's farewells to you!
To you that mourned me till I'm anxious, too,
To stay and mourn myself with you. The die is cast,
And now I'm just a drivelling ghost at last,
Of bones... (I won't say flesh). – Without a doubt,
It's really me. I'm there – like a rubbing-out.

'We're addicts of curiosities, bric-à-brac.
Come and see the *Curio*. – It disgusts me, that tack. –
In my distastes above all, my taste is exquisite.
I've put life off with my gloves, you know that bit.
The *Other* I wouldn't touch with a barge-pole here...
I rummage on the model for the latest gear.

'Come back and help me: Your eyes in these! Your lip
On this lip!... There, do you feel my fever grip?

– Ma *fièvre de Toi?*... – Sous l'orbe est-il passé
L'arc-en-ciel au charbon par nos nuits laissé?
Et cette étoile?... – Oh! va, ne cherche plus l'étoile
      Que tu voulais voir à mon front;
      Une araignée a fait sa toile,
      Au même endroit – dans le plafond.

« Je suis un étranger. – Cela vaut mieux peut-être...
– Eh bien! non, viens encor un peu me reconnaître;
Comme au bon saint Thomas, je veux te voir la foi,
Je veux te voir toucher la plaie et dire: – Toi! –

« Viens encor me finir – c'est très gai: De ta chambre,
Tu verras mes moissons – Nous sommes en décembre –
Mes grands bois de sapin, les fleurs d'or des genêts,
Mes bruyères d'Armor... – en tas sur les chenets.
Viens te gorger d'air pur – Ici j'ai de la brise
Si franche!... que le bout de ma toiture en frise.
Le soleil est si doux... – qu'il gèle tout le temps.
Le printemps... – Le printemps n'est-ce pas tes vingt ans.
On n'attend plus que toi, vois: déjà l'hirondelle
Se pose... en fer rouillé, clouée à ma tourelle. –
Et bientôt nous pourrons cueillir le champignon...
Dans mon escalier que dore... un lumignon.
Dans le mur qui verdoie existe une pervenche
Sèche. –... Et puis nous irons à l'eau *faire* la planche
– Planches d'épave au sec – comme moi – sur ces plages.
La Mer roucoule sa *Berceuse pour naufrages*;
Barcarolle du soir... pour les canards sauvages.

« En *Paul et Virginie*, et virginaux – veux-tu –
Nous nous mettrons au vert du paradis perdu...
Ou *Robinson avec Vendredi* – c'est facile –
La pluie a déjà fait, de mon royaume, une île.

– *You-fever?* ... – The coal scuttled rainbow of our nights
Together has it sunk beneath the globe its deadlights?
And that star?... – Oh, come off it. Don't hunt the star
       That you want to see on my brow;
       A spider's made a web so far
       In that place – on the ceiling now.

'I'm a stranger. – Maybe that's better anyhow ...
– Well, no. – Come closer to recognize me now.
As with the good St Thomas, it's your faith I want to see,
To hear you say: – "It's You!" – and touch the wound in me. –

'Come and finish me off. – What fun! From your room
You'll see my harvests – We're in December bloom –
The golden flowers of broom, the great forests of pine,
Armorican heather... – heaped on the fire-dogs – all mine!
Come and gulp pure air – for here I've wind that swirls
So freely!... that my roof-ridge ends in frizzy curls.
The sun's so nice and warm... – it's always ice and rime.
Spring... – Springtime, isn't it your twenty-year-old prime?
No one's missing but you. The swallow's already back,
Perched... on my tower on rusty iron and a tack. –
And soon there'll be some mushrooms we can pick...
On my staircase, gilded... by the candle wick.
And in the mildewed wall a periwinkle grows
Dry. –... We'll plank ourselves down and float where the tide
    flows.
– Planks dried out – like me – from wrecks this seaboard breaks.
Her *Lullaby for Wrecks* the sea coos in their wakes,
A song and dance in evening rags at ducks and Drakes.

'In *Paul & Virginia* style – and virgin, if you insist –
We'll put ourselves out to grass in paradise missed...
Or *Crusoe & Friday* style – it's easy – the rain
Already makes an island here of my domain.

« Si pourtant, près de moi, tu crains la solitude,
Nous avons des amis, sans fard – Un braconnier;
Sans compter un caban bleu qui, par habitude,
Fait toujours les cent-pas et contient un douanier...
Plus de clercs d'huissier! J'ai le clair de la lune,
Et des amis pierrots amoureux sans fortune.

– « Et nos nuits!... *Belles nuits pour l'orgie à la tour!*...
Nuits à la Roméo! – Jamais il ne fait jour. –
La Nature au réveil – réveil de déchaînée –
Secouant son drap blanc... éteint ma cheminée.
Voici mes rossignols... rossignols d'ouragans –
Gais comme des poinçons – sanglots de chats-huants!
Ma girouette dérouille en haut sa tyrolienne
Et l'on entend gémir ma porte éolienne,
Comme chez saint Antoine en sa tentation...
Oh viens! joli Suppôt de la séduction!

– « Hop! les rats du grenier dansent des farandoles!
Les ardoises du toit roulent en castagnoles!
Les Folles-du-logis...
                    Non, je n'ai plus de Folles!

... « Comme je revendrais ma dépouille à Satan
S'il me tentait avec un petit Revenant...
– Toi – Je te vois partout, mais comme un voyant blême,
Je t'adore... Et c'est pauvre: adorer ce qu'on aime!
Apparais, un poignard dans le cœur! – Ce sera,
Tu sais bien, comme dans *Inès de La Sierra*...
– On frappe... oh! c'est quelqu'un...
                                    Hélas! oui, c'est un rat.

– « Je rêvasse... et toujours c'est *Toi*. Sur toute chose,
Comme un esprit follet, ton souvenir se pose:
Ma solitude – *Toi!* – Mes hiboux à l'œil d'or:

'However, if close to me you fear the solitude,
We have some friends – not made up. – A poacher here;
Not counting a pea-jacket always in the mood
For sentry-go and holds a customs-man, my dear...
No bailiff's clerks! And I've the light of the moon,
Some loving elegant fowl not born with a silver spoon.

– 'And our nights!... *Lovely nights for orgy in the tower!*...
Romeo's nights! – Never again will the day glower. –
Nature awaking – awaking again in the wild state –
Shakes its white sheet... damps the fire in my grate.
Here are my night-in-gales... of squalling and of howls –
Blithe as larks – the long sobs of the screech-owls!
My weathervane, pitched high, derusts its yodelling
And my aeolian door still groans, if anything
Like St Anthony in his temptation... Come!
Come, you pretty imp of seduction, come!

– 'Ha, the granary rats are dancing the farandole!
Like awning blocks over galley slaves, the slates roll!
Mad Fancy women...

          No, no more Fancies, on my soul!

... 'How soon I'd sell the Devil back my husk of skin
If he would tempt me with a little Ghost – and win...
– You – I see you everywhere, but a vision signally dim.
I adore you... And to worship what one loves is grim!
Appear, a dagger in your heart! – For that
Would be like *Inez of the Sierra*, you know it pat...
– A knock... There's someone come...

          Alas! yes, it's a rat.

– 'I daydream... and always of *You*. Over everything
Like a hobgoblin your memory is hovering:
My solitude – *You!* – My owls on the slate: – *You.* – The mill

– *Toi!* – Ma girouette folle: Oh *Toi!*... – Que sais-je encor...
– *Toi*: mes volets ouvrant les bras dans la tempête...
Une lointaine voix: c'est Ta chanson! – c'est fête!...
Les rafales fouaillant Ton nom perdu – c'est bête –
C'est bête, mais c'est *Toi!* Mon cœur au grand ouvert
      Comme mes volets en pantenne,
      Bat, tout affolé sous l'haleine
      Des plus bizarres courants d'air.

« Tiens... une ombre portée, un instant, est venue
Dessiner ton profil sur la muraille nue,
Et j'ai tourné la tête... – Espoir ou souvenir –
Ma sœur Anne, à la tour, voyez-vous pas venir?...

– « Rien! – je vois... je vois, dans ma froide chambrette,
Mon lit capitonné de *satin de brouette*;
Et mon chien qui dort dessus – Pauvre animal –
... Et je ris... parce que ça me fait un peu mal.

« J'ai pris, pour t'appeler, ma vielle et ma lyre.
Mon cœur fait de l'esprit – le sot – pour se leurrer...
Viens pleurer, si mes vers ont pu te faire rire;
      Viens rire, s'ils t'ont fait pleurer...

« Ce sera drôle... Viens jouer à la misère,
D'après nature: – *Un cœur avec une chaumière.* –
... Il pleut dans mon foyer, il pleut dans mon cœur feu.
Viens! Ma chandelle est morte et je n'ai plus de feu... »

      ★

Sa lampe se mourait. Il ouvrit la fenêtre.
Le soleil se levait. Il regarda sa lettre,
Rit et la déchira... Les petits morceaux blancs,
Dans la brume, semblaient un vol de goëlands.

Penmarc'h – jour de Noël.

Of my mad weathervane: *You!*... – All I know still...
– *You:* my shutters, wide-open-armed to wind and rain...
A distant voice: Your signature tune! – it's fetch champagne!...
The gusts lashing Your lost name – it's so inane –
Inane but it is *You!* My heart, wide-open there,
>   Like my shutters in half-mast flap,
>   Beats, maddened by the constant rap
>   Of the weirdest blasts of air.

'Hang on... a shadow cast a moment falls
Tracing your profile over the bare walls,
And it's turned my head... – Memory or hope (some!) –
Sister Anne, in the tower, d'you see anyone come?...

– 'Nothing! – I see... I see in the freezing attic room
My bed, with *hearse-suit satin* quilted, loom;
My dog asleep on it – Poor little beast –
... And I laugh... because it makes me ill at least.

'I've taken up my lyre and hurdy-gurdy to sigh
You back. My heart – fool – cracks... its jokes and fakes awhile...
Come and laugh, if my verse has made you cry.
Come and weep if my verse has made you smile...

'It'll be amusing... Come and slum as large as life: –
Love in a hut. – Come and play at misery's wife...
... It rains in my hearth, it rains in my late heart.
Come on! My candle's dead. I've no fire to restart...'

                    ★

His light was dying. He opened up the window wide.
The sun was rising. He looked his letter over, tried
A laugh and tore it up... The little pieces of white
Seemed, in rising mist, like gulls in flight.

                         Penmarc'h – Christmas Day.

Sonnet de nuit

Ô croisée ensommeillée,
Dure à mes trente-six morts!
Vitre en diamant, éraillée
Par mes atroces accords!

Herse hérissant rouillée
Tes crocs où je pends et mords!
Oubliette verrouillée
Qui me renferme… dehors!

Pour Toi, Bourreau que j'encense,
L'amour n'est donc que vengeance?…
Ton balcon: gril à braiser?…

Ton col: collier de garotte?…
Eh bien! ouvre, Iscariote,
Ton judas pour un baiser!

Night Sonnet

Lattice asleep, detached
From my umpteen deaths! Pane
Of diamonds, scratched
By my atrocious refrain!

Portcullis, spikes all rust,
Hooks where I hang – about!
Oubliette bolted, just
To keep me shut... out!

For You, Hangman I soft-soap,
Is love revenge's old rope?...
Your balcony a grilling, miss?...

Your collar: for my garrotte?...
Well, open your judas slot,
Iscariot, for a kiss!

Guitare

Je sais rouler une amourette
      En cigarette,
Je sais rouler l'or et les plats!
Et les filles dans de beaux draps!

Ne crains pas de longueurs fidèles:
Pour mules mes pieds ont des ailes;
Voleur de nuit, hibou d'amour,
      M'envole au jour.

Connais-tu Psyché? – Non? – Mercure?…
Cendrillon et son aventure?
– Non? –… Eh bien! tout cela, c'est moi:
      Nul ne me voit.

Et je te laisserais bien fraîche
Comme un petit Jésus en crèche,
Avant le rayon indiscret…
      – Je suis si laid! –

Je sais flamber en cigarette,
      Une amourette,
Chiffonner et flamber les draps,
Mettre les filles dans les plats!

One-String Guitar

I know how to roll an affair yet,
      Like a cigarette;
How to roll dupes and cash my way!
And girls in fine linen to lay!

No fear of faithful tediums from me:
No mules, my feet have wings to flee;
The owl of love, thief in the night,
      Wings me to light.

Know Psyche? – No? – Mercury?...
Cinderella and her history?
– No? –... Well! I'm all three, you know:
      No one sees me go.

And I would leave you feeling fresh
Like little Jesus in the crèche,
Before the indiscretion of light...
      – I'm a hideous sight! –

I know how to light up a cig.,
      And the old jig,
Rumple and scorch through linen
And drop them in it, women!

Rescousse

Si ma guitare
Que je répare,
Trois fois barbare:
Kriss indien,

Cric de supplice,
Bois de justice,
Boîte à malice,
Ne fait pas bien...

Si ma voix pire
Ne peut te dire
Mon doux martyre...
– Métier de chien! –

Si mon cigare,
Viatique et phare,
Point ne t'égare;
– Feu de brûler...

Si ma menace,
Trombe qui passe,
Manque de grâce;
– Muet de hurler...

Si de mon âme
La mer en flamme
N'a pas de lame;
– Cuit de geler...

Vais m'en aller!

Here's my Back up

If this guitar
I mend or mar,
Twice barbarous jar:
Malayan *kris*,

Screw of the rack,
Guillotine stack,
Spite's jumping jack,
Plays so amiss...

If my voice, worse,
Can't tell you, terse,
My sweet pang's verse...
– A dog's life, this! –

If my cigar,
Last rite, pole star,
Can't lead you far;
– The stake fire...

If my threats brayed –
A whirlwind raid –
Relentance dissuade
– Let the dumb choir...

If the ocean burning
With all my yearning
Lack tide for turning;
– Frozen by fire...

A goner, I'll go!

Toit

Tiens non! J'attendrai tranquille,
  Planté sous le toit,
Qu'il me tombe quelque tuile,
  Souvenir de Toi!

J'ai tondu l'herbe, je lèche
  La pierre, – altéré
Comme *la Colique-sèche*
  De Miserere!

Je crèverai – Dieu me damne! –
Ton tympan ou la peau d'âne
  De mon bon tambour!

Dans ton boîtier, ô Fenêtre!
Calme et pure, gît peut-être...
  .   .   .   .

    Un vieux monsieur sourd!

Roof

Oh no, I won't. Quiet, I'll wait,
      Stuck under the roof
Till I'm walloped by a slate –
      Memento of You, proof!

I've cut the lawn. I lick the stones
      Clean till I am dry
As the *parched colic* that groans
      The *Miserere* cry!

God damn me! – but I swear I'll burst
Your tympanum in or break first
      My ass-skin drum!

Maybe in your case, Panes, there lies
Chaste and peaceful, gone to bye-byes...

   · · · · · · · · ·

      An old gent, deaf and dumb.

Litanie

Non… Mon cœur te sent là, Petite,
Qui dors pour me laisser plus vite
Passer ma nuit, si longue encor,
Sur le pavé comme un rat mort…

– Dors. La berceuse litanie
Sérénade jamais finie
Sur Ta lèvre reste poser
Comme une haleine de baiser:

– « Nénuphar du ciel! Blanche Étoile!
Tour ivoirine! Nef sans voile!
Vesper, amoris Aurora! »

Ah! je sais les répons mystiques,
Pour le cantique des cantiques
Qu'on chante… au Diable, Señora!

Litany

No ... My heart feels you're there, Dear.
You sleep fast to leave me fast here
Spending my night – longer than that –
On the pavement like a dead rat ...

– All right, sleep. The lullaby's repeat,
Serenade never to be complete,
Lingers to brush, breath of a kiss,
Upon Your lips, a touch of this:

'Lily of Heaven; Star, white and pale;
Ivory Tower; Navel without sail;
Vesper, amoris Aurora!'

The mystic responses to the song
Of songs, ah, I've known all along,
That one hymns ... to the Devil, Señora!

Chapelet

À moi, grand chapelet! pour égrener mes plaintes,
Avec tous les AVE de Sa *Perfeccion*,
Son nom et tous les noms de ses Fêtes et Saintes...
Du Mardi-gras jusqu'à la *Circoncicion*:

– *Navaja-Dolorès-y* – *Crucificcion!*...
– Le Christ avait au moins son éponge d'absinthe... –
Quand donc arriverai-je à ton *Ascencion!*...
– Isaac Laquedem, prête-moi ta complainte.

– *O Todas-las-Santas!* Tes vitres sont pareilles,
Secundum ordinem, à ces fonds de bouteilles
Qu'on casse à coups de trique à la *Quasimodo*...

Mais, ô *Quasimodo*, tu ne viens pas encore;
Pour casse-tête, hélas! je n'ai que ma mandore...
– *Se habla español: Paraque... raquando?*...

Rosary

Your help, great rosary, telling my plaints pieced
With all the AVES made to Her *Perfeccion*.
Her name, and all her Saints' and Days of Feast...
From Mardi Gras up to the *Circoncicion*:

– *Navaja-Dolorès-y – Crucificcion!*...
– Christ had his absinthe sponge at least –
But when shall I come to your *Ascencion!*...
– Wandering Jew, lend your lament unceased.

– *O Todas-las-Santas!* Your windows parallel,
Secundum ordinem, bottle-bottoms well
Smashed with bludgeons on *Quasimodo*... And, oh,

Quasimodo, you're nowhere near; and for
Any brain-cudgelling I've just my mandore...
– *Se habla español: Paraque... raquando?*...

Elizir d'amor

Tu ne me veux pas en rêve,
Tu m'auras en cauchemar!
T'écorchant au vif, sans trêve,
– Pour moi… pour l'amour de l'art.

– Ouvre: je passerai vite,
Les nuits sont courtes, l'été…
Mais ma musique est maudite,
Maudite en l'éternité!

J'assourdirai les recluses,
Éreintant à coups de pieux,
Les Neuf et les autres Muses…
Et qui n'en iront que mieux!…

Répéterai tous mes rôles
Borgnes – et d'aveugle aussi…
D'ordinaire tous ces drôles
Ont assez bon *œil* ici:

– À genoux, haut Cavalier,
À pied, traînant ma rapière,
Je baise dans la poussière
Les traces de Ton soulier!

– Je viens, Pèlerin austère,
Capucin et Troubadour,
Dire mon bout de rosaire
Sur la viole d'amour.

Elizir d'Amor

You do not want me in your dreams;
You'll have me in nightmare start
Flaying you without mercy – screams,
– For me... and for the love of art.

– Open up. I'll pass like a bee-line.
These summer nights are summary...
But cursèd is this racket of mine,
Accursed to all eternity!

I'll deafen the reclusive shes,
Religiously bludgeon under my beat
The Nine and other Muses... these
Will be the better for the feat!...

I'll replay all my roles, cock-eyed
And vulgar – and the blind ones, too...
Usually, all these skits, well-tried,
Have drawn a good *look-out*, view:

– Kneeling, my haughty Cavalier
On foot, trailing my rapier through,
I kiss the very dust down here,
The foot-prince of Your shoe!

– Next, frugal Pilgrim-bloke, I come,
Capuchin or Troubadoury,
To tell my rosary with a strum
On the *viola d'amore.*

– Bachelier de Salamanque,
Le plus simple et le dernier…
Ce fonds jamais ne me manque:
– Tout vœux! et pas un denier! –

– Retapeur de casseroles,
Sale Gitan vagabond,
Je claque des castagnoles
Et chatouille le jambon…

– Pas-de-loup, loup sur la face,
Moi chien-loup maraudeur,
J'erre en offrant de ma race:
– Pur-Don-Juan-du-Commandeur. –

Maîtresse peut me connaître,
Chien parmi les chiens perdus:
Abeilard n'est pas mon maître,
Alcibiade non plus!

– And now, my squire of Salamanca,
The simplest and the very last of …
Capital fellow, backed like a banker,
– All speculations – not a penny, brassed off. –

– My Keeper of cookware in good nick,
My Dirty Gypsy Roameo,
My castanets I click and click,
I tickle up the hams, heel, toe …

– With lupine stealth, mask looped on face,
Me, wolfhound, marauding chancer,
I wander, offering my line and race:
– Pure Don Juan, Knight Commander. –

Mistress can recognize me faster,
Among the mangy curs, a stray;
Abelard is not my master,
Neither Alcibiades! No way.

Vénerie

Ô Vénus, dans ta Vénerie,
Limier et piqueur à la fois,
Valet-de-chiens et d'écurie,
J'ai vu l'Hallali, les Abois!…

Que Diane aussi me sourie!…
À cors, à cris, à pleine voix
Je fais le pied, je fais le bois;
Car on dit que: *bête varie*…

– Un pied de biche: Le voici,
Cordon de sonnette sur rue;
– Bois de cerf: de la porte aussi;
– Et puis un pied: un pied-de-grue!…

Ô Fauve après qui j'aboyais,
– Je suis fourbu, qu'on me relaie! –
Ô Bête! es-tu donc une laie?
.   .   .   .
Bien moins sauvage te croyais!

Venery

O Venus, in your Venery,
Staghound and hunter both, am I,
Kennel- and stable-boy – all me.
I've seen the Mort, the Bay, oh my!...

Diana, look on smilingly!...
In fullest voice, with horn and cry
I start afoot, the horn-beams try,
Since *wildlife varies*, all agree...

– Track of a deer, end of the spore:
A belle-pull giving on the street;
– Beams of the dear, beams of the door;
– A foot in, kicking heels in heat!...

O Fawny Beast for which I bayed,
– It's someone else's stint. I'm creased. –
Are you a sow-ride, then, you Beast?
. . . .
Thought you less savage, I'm afraid!

Vendetta

Tu ne veux pas de mon âme
Que je jette à tour de bras:
Chère, tu me le payeras!...
Sans rancune – je suis femme! –

Tu ne veux pas de ma peau:
Venimeux comme un jésuite,
Prends garde!... je suis ensuite
Jésuite comme un crapaud,

Et plat comme la punaise,
Compagne que j'ai sur moi,
Pure... mais, – ne te déplaise, –
Je te préférerais, Toi!

– Je suis encor, Ma très-Chère,
Serpent comme le Serpent
Froid, coulant, poisson rampant
Qui fit pécher ta grand'mère...

Et tu ne vaux pas, Pécore,
Beaucoup plus qu'elle, je croi...
Vaux-tu ma chanson encore?...
Me vaux-tu seulement moi!...

Vendetta

You want none of my soul I throw
At you with all my might and main.
Dearest, I'll pay you back again!...
– I'm woman in that, no rancour, though. –

You want no hide nor hair of mine:
Venomous as a jesuit – take care! –
I am and then some and to spare...
Jesuitical as a toad's malign,

And dull and boring as the bug –
Lady-friend that grows on me –
Pure... but, – don't take on so, spug, –
I do prefer You to that flea!

– I'm still, My dearest Darling wish,
A serpent like the Serpent: thin,
Cold, slippery, grovelling fish
That made your grandma angle sin...

And you're not worth, I dare to say,
You silly Goose, much more than she...
Are you even worth my lay?...
Or worthy of me, even to me?...

Heures

Aumône au malandrin en chasse!
Mauvais œil à l'œil assassin!
Fer contre fer au spadassin!
– Mon âme n'est pas en état de grâce! –

Je suis le fou de Pampelune,
J'ai peur du rire de la Lune,
Cafarde, avec son crêpe noir…
Horreur! tout est donc sous un éteignoir.

J'entends comme un bruit de crécelle…
C'est la male heure qui m'appelle.
Dans le creux des nuits tombe: un glas… deux glas.

J'ai compté plus de quatorze heures…
L'heure est une larme – Tu pleures,
Mon cœur!… Chante encor, va – Ne compte pas.

Hours

Alms to the highwayman in chase!
To dead-eyed shot the evil eye!
Sword for sword the swashbuckler defy!
– My soul, it isn't in a state of grace! –

I'm Pamplona's idiot here.
I'm scared of the Moon's laughing jeer,
In mourning hatband, a creeping nark...
Horror! The lot is in the snuffer's dark.

A sort of rattle's racket I hear...
The evil hour that strikes my ear.
And in the trough of nights: a knell... a second.

I've counted the strikes, fourteen gone by...
Each hour's a tear. – My heart, you cry...
Come, sing on. Don't count too much. – Leave unreckoned.

Chanson en *Si*

Si j'étais noble Faucon,
Tournoîrais sur ton balcon…
– Taureau: foncerais ta porte…
– Vampire: te boirais morte…
   Te boirais!

– Geôlier: lèverais l'écrou…
– Rat: ferais un petit trou…
Si j'étais brise alizée,
Te mouillerais de rosée…
   Roserais!

Si j'étais gros Confesseur,
Te fouaillerais, ô Ma Sœur!
Pour seconde pénitence,
Te dirais ce que je pense…
   Te dirais…

Si j'étais un maigre Apôtre,
Dirais: « Donnez-vous l'un l'autre,
Pour votre faim apaiser:
Le pain-d'amour: Un baiser. »
   Si j'étais!…

Si j'étais Frère-quêteur,
Quêterais ton petit cœur
Pour Dieu le Fils et le Père,
L'Église leur Sainte Mère…
   Quêterais!

If-Key Song

If be I were a noble falcon
Your balcony I'd land and stalk on...
– A bull, I'd force your door instead...
– Vampire, and I would suck you dead...
        Suck you, I would!

– Your jailer: your locks I would undo...
– Rat: and a little hole I'd chew...
If I were a tradewind, too,
I'd moisten you with morning dew...
        Dew you, I would!

If a fat Confessor-priest
I'd lash you, Sister, not the least!
A further penance you would pay:
To take in everything I'd say...
        Say it I would...

If an Apostle, all skin and bone,
'Take each other,' I'd intone,
'To ease your hunger-pains with bliss.
The bread of love: It is a kiss.'
        If I were, I would...

If I were a begging Friar
I'd beg your little heart entire
For God the Father and the Son,
The Church, their Mother – dearest one...
        Beg it I would!

Si j'étais Madone riche,
Jetterais bien, de ma niche,
Un regard, un sou béni
Pour le cantique fini…
  Jetterais!

Si j'étais un vieux bedeau,
Mettrais un cierge au rideau…
D'un goupillon d'eau bénite,
L'éteindrais, la vespre dite,
   L'éteindrais!

Si j'étais roide pendu,
Au ciel serais tout rendu:
Grimperais après ma corde,
Ancre de miséricorde,
   Grimperais!

Si j'étais femme… Eh, la Belle,
Te ferais ma Colombelle…
À la porte les galants
Pourraient se percer des flancs…
  Te ferais…

Enfant, si j'étais la duègne
Rossinante qui te peigne,
Señora, si j'étais Toi…
J'ouvrirais au pauvre Moi.
  – Ouvrirais! –

If I were a Madonna, rich,
I'd throw a glance out from my niche,
And two blessèd penny pieces
As soon as the canticle ceases...
   Throw them, I would!

If agèd beadle I had been,
I'd put a candle to the screen...
With holy water I would souse it;
After vespers I would douse it,
   Douse it, I would!

If a hanged stiff on gibbet high
About to surrender to the sky;
I'd go climbing up the rope,
Sheet anchor of mercy and hope,
   Climb it, I would!

If I were a woman – Ah, my Lovely!
I'd take you as my Little Dovey...
And let the gallants at your door
Pierce each other, stab and gore...
   Take you, I would...

Child, if I were the duenna mare,
Rossinante, to deck you there,
Señora, if You I were to be...
I'd open up to poor old Me.
   – Open, I would! –

Portes et Fenêtres

N'entends-tu pas? – Sang et guitare! –
Réponds!… je damnerai plus fort.
Nulle ne m'a laissé, Barbare,
Aussi longtemps me crier mort!

Ni faire autant de purgatoire!…
Tu ne vois ni n'entends mes pas,
Ton œil est clos, la nuit est noire:
Fais signe – Je ne verrai pas.

En enfer j'ai pavé ta rue.
Tous les damnés sont en émoi…
Trop incomparable Inconnue!
Si tu n'es pas là… préviens-moi!

À damner je n'ai plus d'alcades,
Je n'ai fait que me damner moi,
En serinant mes sérénades…
– Il ne reste à damner que Toi!

Doors and Windows

Can't you hear? – Blood and guitar! –
Answer!... I'll damn still louder, I said!
No woman – savage that you are –
Left me so long to bawl myself dead!

Nor stretched so long on purgatory's rack!...
You neither see nor hear me coming.
Your eye is closed; the night is black:
Beckon. – I wouldn't see you thumbing.

In Hell now I have paved your way
And all the damned are buzzing, stirred...
Too peerless mystery Woman, say,
If you're not there... give me the word!

For damning I've run out of alcaides;
I've only damned myself till blue,
Through drumming up my serenades...
– All that remains is to damn You!

Grand Opéra

Ier ACTE *(Vêpres).*

Dors sous le tabernacle, ô Figure de cire!
　　　Triple Châsse vierge et martyre,
　　　Derrière un verre, sous le plomb,
Et dans les siècles des siècles... Comme c'est long!

Portes-tu ton cœur d'or sur ta robe lamée,
Ton âme veille-t-elle en la lampe allumée?...

　　　　　　Elle est éteinte
　　　　　　Cette huile sainte...
　　　　　　Il est éteint
　　　　　　Le sacristain!...

L'orgue sacré, ses flots et ses bruits de rafale
Sous les voûtes, font-ils frissonner ton front pâle?...

Dans ton éternité sais-tu la barbarie
De mon orgue infernal, *orgue de Barbarie?*

Du prêtre, sous l'autel, n'ouïs-tu pas les pas
Et le mot qu'à l'Hostie il murmure tout bas?...

– Eh bien! moi j'attendrai que sur ton oreiller,
La trompette de Dieu vienne te réveiller!

. . . .

Châsse, ne sais-tu pas qu'en passant ta chapelle,
　　　De par le Pape, tout fidèle,
Évêque, publicain ou lépreux, a le droit
De t'entr'ouvrir sa plaie et d'en toucher ton doigt?...

Grand Opera

ACT ONE *(Vespers)*

Under the tabernacle, you waxwork Figure, sleep!
   Triply Enshrined virgin and martyr, deep
   Behind the glass, beneath the leaden lattices,
For century after century ... How long it is!

D'you wear a heart of gold on that cloth of gold robe?
Does your soul keep vigil in the lighted globe? ...

     Extinguished, damp,
     The holy lamp ...
     Extinguished man
     The sacristan! ...

The sacred organ roll, its swell and squalling gale,
Under the vaulting, does it make you shudder pale? ...

D'you hear in your eternity the barbarous bars
Of my hellish organ, my *barrel organ's* jars?

D'you hear the priest's steps beneath the altar go;
The words to the raised Host he's murmuring low? ...

– Oh well! Myself, I'll wait until across your bed,
The blast of the Last Trumpet comes to wake your head!

. . . .

Shrine, don't you know, that those of faith and hope,
   Who pass your chapel by leave of the Pope,
Bishop, publican, or leper, each one has the right
To half-open his wound and put your finger on its site? ...

À Saint-Jacques de Compostelle
J'en ai bien fait autant pour un bout de chandelle.
À ce prix-là je dois baiser la blanche hostie
Qui scelle, sur ta bouche en or, ta chasteté
Close en odeur de sainteté

. . . .

Cordieu! Madame est donc sortie?...

IIe ACTE *(Sabbat).*

Je suis un bon ange, ô bel Ange!
Pour te couvrir, doux gardien...
La terre maudite me tient.
Ma plume a trempé dans la fange...

Hâ! je ne bats plus que d'une aile!...
Prions... l'esprit du Diable est prompt...
– Ah! si j'étais lui, de quel bond
Je serais sur toi, la Donzelle!

... Ma blanche couronne à ma tête
Déjà s'effeuille; la tempête
Dans mes mains a brisé mon lys...

Par Belzébuth! contre la borne
Je viens de me rompre la corne!

. . . .

Comme les trucs sont démolis!

At St James of Compostella's shrine
I've done indeed as much for a bit of candle shine!
For that price there I must kiss the white host
Which seals, on your mouth in gold, your chastity
    Shut in the odour of sanctity.

    .   .   .   .

    Good God! Madame's gone off – out... post!

ACT TWO *(Sabbath)*

I'm a good angel, to cover you,
Beautiful Angel, your gentle guard...
The cursèd earth holds me back hard,
My quill is clagged down with clay, too...

Hah! I can only beat one wing!...
Let's pray... The Devil's spirit is prompt...
– If I were he how I'd have romped
On you, you Tart, no dithering!

... The white crown on my head is dropping
Petals already; the storm sopping
My hands has broken my lily off...

By Beelzebub! against this bourn
I have gaffed – and snapped my horn!

.   .   .   .

How all these ploys are wiped out, duff!

IIIe ACTE *(Sereno)*.

Holà!... je vois poindre un fanal oblique
       – Flamberge au vent, joli Muguet!
      Sangre Dios! rossons le guet!...

     Un bonhomme mélancolique
Chante: – Bonsoir Señor, Señor Caballero,
     Sereno... – *Sereno* toi-même!
     Minuit: second jour de carême,
     Prêtez-moi donc un cigaro...

     Gracia! La Vierge vous garde!
– La Vierge?... grand merci, vieux! Je sens la moutarde!...
– Par Saint-Joseph! Señor, que faites-vous ici? –
     – Mais... pas grand'chose et toi, merci.
– C'est pour votre plaisir?... – Je damne les alcades
     De Tolose au Guadalété!
– Il est un violon, là-bas sous les arcades...
     – Çà: n'as-tu jamais arrêté
     Musset... musset pour sérénade?

     – *Santos!*... non, sur la promenade,
     Je n'ai jamais vu de mussets...
     – Son page était en embuscade...
– *Ah Carambah!* Monsieur est un señor Français
     Qui vient nous la faire à l'aubade?...

ACT THREE *(Evening)*

Hold it!... I catch off beam a lantern's shine.
        – Draw sword, my Dandy, fine and dashing!
        Sangre Dios! let's give the watch a thrashing!...

A melancholy fellow begs in a whine:
– Good evening, Señor, Señor Cabellero, ah.
        Sereno... – And *Sereno* back to you!
        Midnight. And Lent, day two.
        Could you just lend me a cigar...

        Gracia! The Virgin keep you well.
– The Virgin?... many thanks, old boy! My dander's up,
                     I tell you!...
– By St Joseph! Señor, what are you hoping to do?
        – Well: nothing much, thank you; and you?
– Come for some fun?... – To damn and blast all alcaides
        From Tolose to Guadalété, all the way!
– There're bars – for bird – underneath the arcades...
        – I say, did you ever arrest Musset...
        Musset for bird serenades?

        – *Santos!*... No, on the parade
        I've never seen mussets here before...
        – His page was waiting in an ambuscade...
– *Ah Carambah!* Monsieur's a French señor
        Who comes to cuff our ears with an aubade?...

Pièce à carreaux

Ah! si Vous avez à Tolède,
        Un vitrier
Qui vous forge un vitrail plus raide
        Qu'un bouclier!…

À Tolède j'irai ma flamme
        Souffler, ce soir;
À Tolède tremper la lame
        De mon rasoir!

Si cela ne vous amadoue:
        Vais aiguiser,
Contre tous les cuirs de Cordoue,
        Mon dur baiser:

– Donc – À qui rompra: votre oreille,
        Ou bien mes vers!
Ma corde-à-boyaux sans pareille,
        Ou bien vos nerfs?

– À qui fendra: ma castagnette,
        Ou bien vos dents…
L'Idole en grès, ou le Squelette
        Aux yeux dardants!

– À qui fondra: vous ou mes cierges,
        Ô plombs croisés!…
En serez-vous beaucoup plus vierges,
        Carreaux cassés?

Room with Lattice Windows

Ah, if You've a glazing man
      Forges you lattices
In Toledo tougher than
      A buckler is?...

I'm off this evening to Toledo
      To blow on my ardour,
Toledo, to whet the blade of
      My razor much sharper.

If that doesn't win you altogether,
      I'll slope off, miss,
And strop smooth on Cordovan leather
      My rough harsh kiss.

– Right! – Which of us breaks? Your ear,
      Or my verse first?
My catgut strings without a peer?
      Or your nerves burst?

– My castanets, or else your teeth
      First split apart!...
Stoneware Idol, or Skeleton beneath
      With eyes that dart!

– Which melt: you, or my candle-wax,
      O criss-cross lead!...
Will you be more virgin for cracks,
      Smashed panes, instead?

Et Vous qui faites la cornue,
   Ange là-bas!…
En serez-vous un peu moins nue,
   Les habits bas?

– Ouvre! fenêtre à guillotine:
   C'est le bourreau!
– Ouvre donc porte de cuisine!
   C'est Figaro.

… Je soupire, en vache espagnole,
   Ton numéro
Qui n'est, en français, Vierge molle!
   Qu'un grand ZÉRO.

       Cadix. – Mai.

And you who play the 'ornery,
  Angel up there...
Less full confrontal will you be,
  Your clothes off, bare?

– Open up, window-guillotine,
  The headsman draws near!
– The kitchen-door, I'd rather mean.
  Figaro's here.

... Murdering the tongue like a Spanish cow,
  Your number here, O
Soft virgin, I sigh; in French it's now
  A great big ZERO.

Cadix. – May.

Laisser-courre

Musique de ISAAC LAQUEDEM.

J'ai laissé la potence
Après tous les pendus,
Andouilles de naissance,
Maigres fruits défendus;
Les plumes aux canards
Et la queue aux renards...

Au Diable aussi sa queue
Et ses cornes aussi,
Au ciel sa chose bleue
Et la Planète – ici –
Et puis tout: n'importe où
Dans le désert au clou.

J'ai laissé dans l'Espagne
Le reste et mon château;
Ailleurs, à la campagne,
Ma tête et son chapeau;
J'ai laissé mes souliers,
Sirènes, à vos pieds!

J'ai laissé par les mondes,
Parmi tous les frisons
Des chauves, brunes, blondes
Et rousses... mes toisons.

Letting Slip

Set by ISAAC LAQUEDEM.

I've left the noose's girth,
To all its hanging mutes,
The rubber necks of birth,
Skinny forbidden fruits;
Left ducks, feather and plume;
Foxes left brush – and broom...

Left Devil his tail, too,
And his horns as well; left clear
Sky its thingy, blue,
And the Planet – this here –
The whole caboodle: somewhere
In hock out in thin air.

I've left abroad in Spain
Remains, my airborne château;
Elsewhere in a country lane
My head still in its hat; O
Sirens, I've left – and right –
My shoes at your feet! 'Night.

Through worlds and much beyond
Among the locks of baldicoot,
Of ginger, brown and blond,
I've left my fleeces – most hirsute.

Mon épée aux vaincus,
Ma maîtresse aux cocus...

Aux portes les portières,
La portière au portier,
Le bouton aux rosières,
Les roses au rosier,
À l'huys les huissiers,
Créance aux créanciers...

Dans mes veines ma veine,
Mon rayon au soleil,
Ma dégaine en sa gaine,
Mon lézard au sommeil;
J'ai laissé mes amours
Dans les tours, dans les fours...

Et ma cotte de maille
Aux artichauts de fer
Qui sont à la muraille
Des jardins de l'Enfer;
Après chaque oripeau
J'ai laissé de ma peau.

J'ai laissé toute chose
Me retirer du nez
Des vers, en vers, en prose...
Aux bornes, les bornés;
À tous les jeux partout,
Des rois et de l'atout.

J'ai laissé la police
Captive en liberté,
J'ai laissé La Palisse
Dire la vérité...

My sword, to those who've truckled;
My mistress to the cuckold...

To wards, locks – wardeness;
And wardeness to warder;
Bud on the rose-girl press,
And rose to briar and border.
The bailiff, to the door;
To creditors the score...

My vein in veins to run;
My chest I leave its trunk;
My own lights to the sun,
My basking to the bunk.
I've left my loves a drop
In their towers – and their flop...

My coat of mail I settle
On the arti-chokey spikes
Of iron that top and nettle
Hell's garden walls like pikes;
To every bit of tinsel,
I've left a scrap of skin-cell.

I've left to everything
To worm from me by the nose
Verse and prose on a string;
Bounds on the hidebound pose;
The sport of kings to all
And the last trump's call!

I've left all the coppers,
Captive at liberty,
Peter, wolf-crying whoppers,
To speak truth honestly...

Laissé courre le sort
Et ce qui court encor.

J'ai laissé l'Espérance,
Vieillissant doucement,
Retomber en enfance,
Vierge folle sans dent.
J'ai laissé tous les Dieux,
J'ai laissé pire et mieux.

J'ai laissé bien tranquilles
Ceux qui ne l'étaient pas;
Aux pattes imbéciles
J'ai laissé tous les plats;
Aux poètes la foi…
Puis me suis laissé moi.

Sous le temps, sans égides
M'a mal mené fort bien
La vie à grandes guides…
Au bout des guides – rien –
… Laissé, blasé, passé,
Rien ne m'a rien laissé…

Let slip the dogs of fate,
And what's the going rate.

I've left to Hope, that gently
Lapses old and youthless,
A second childhood entry,
A foolish virgin, toothless.
I've left every God first;
I've left the best and worst.

I've left most peaceful those
Who never were a minute;
Idiot mitts, to pose
Their hoofs serenely in it.
Faith to poets I leave be...
And then I'm left with me.

No aegis, under the weather,
Life's led me, supremely muffing
At the very end of the tether
In dashing style – to nothing –
... Left, blasé, has-been, for
Nothing's left me nothing more...

À ma jument souris

Pas d'éperon ni de cravache,
N'est-ce pas, Maîtresse à poil gris…
C'est bon à pousser une vache,
Pas une petite Souris.

Pas de mors à ta pauvre bouche:
Je t'aime, et ma cuisse te touche.
Pas de selle, pas d'étrier:
J'agace, du bout de ma botte,
Ta patte d'acier fin qui trotte.
Va: je ne suis pas cavalier…

– Hurrah! c'est à nous la poussière!
J'ai la tête dans ta crinière,
Mes deux bras te font un collier.
– Hurrah! c'est à nous le hallier!

– Hurrah! c'est à nous la barrière!
– Je suis emballé: tu me tiens –
Hurrah!… et le fossé derrière…
Et la culbute!… – Femme tiens!!

To My Mousy Mare

It's neither spur nor horsewhip now,
Eh, Mistress in your coat of grey...
They're good enough to drive a cow;
But a little Mousy, no way.

No bit at your poor little lip:
I love you, your flank to my hip.
No saddle, stirrup: I am pricking
With the end of my boot *instanter*
Your fine steel pins into a canter.
Hup! I'm no whoresy type... We're kicking

Up – hurrah! – a dust! My brain
I have tangled in your mane!
My two arms have collared you.
– Hurrah! The thicket's ours. We're through!

– Hurrah! The final hurdle's near,
– I'm hell for leather: you've got the pull
Of me – Hurrah!... Last ditch to clear...
Arse over tits!... – Right, womanful!!

À la douce amie

Çà: badinons – J'ai ma cravache –
Prends ce mors, bijou d'acier gris;
– Tiens: ta dent joueuse le mâche…
En serrant un peu: tu souris…

– Han!… C'est pour te faire la bouche…
– V'lan!… C'est pour chasser une mouche…
Veux-tu sentir te chatouiller
L'éperon, honneur de ma botte?…
– Et la *Folle-du-Logis* trotte… –
Jouons à l'Amour-cavalier!

Porte-beau ta tête altière,
Laisse mes doigts dans ta crinière…
J'aime voir ton beau col ployer!…
Demain: je te donne un collier.

– Pourquoi regarder en arrière?…
Ce n'est rien: c'est une étrivière…
Une étrivière… et – je te tiens!

. . . .

Et tu m'as aimé… – rosse, tiens!

To the Docile Girl Friend

So: let's play! – My horsewhip now. –
Take the bit, this gem steel-grey.
– Here: your game teeth chew, and how!...
Your champing's forced a smile to play...

– Houf!... That's to curl a smiling lip!...
– Thwack!... for chasing flies... Your hip,
Would you like to feel my spur pricking,
Courtesy of my boot – *instanter*?...
– My *Fancy Madam* at a canter... –
Let's get some loving horseplay kicking!

Carry your head high with disdain.
Leave my fingers in your mane...
Your fine neck bowed I like to view!...
Tomorrow: I will collar you.

– Why are you looking round?... This, here,
's nothing: a stirrup leather... a sheer
Leathering... and – I've got the pull!

. . . .

And you've loved me... – jade! No bull!

À mon chien Pope

– GENTLEMAN-DOG FROM NEW-LAND –

mort d'une balle.

Toi: ne pas suivre en domestique,
Ni lécher en fille publique!
– Maître-philosophe cynique:
N'être pas traité comme un chien,
Chien! tu le veux – et tu fais bien.

– Toi: rester toi; ne pas connaître
Ton écuelle ni ton maître.
Ne jamais marcher sur les mains,
Chien! – c'est bon pour les humains.

… Pour l'amour – qu'à cela ne tienne:
Viole des chiens – Gare la Chienne!

Mords – Chien – et nul ne te mordra.
Emporte le morceau – Hurrah! –

Mais après, ne fais pas la bête;
S'il faut payer – paye – Et fais tête
Aux fouets qu'on te montrera.

– Pur ton sang! pur ton chic sauvage!
         – Hurler, nager –
Et, si l'on te fait enrager…
         Enrage!

Île de Batz. – Octobre.

To my Dog Pope

— GENTLEMAN-DOG FROM NEW-LAND —

shot dead.

Don't dog my heels like a lackey, cur;
Nor fawn as do the street-girls, sir!
– Master Cynic Philosopher:
Not to be treated like a dog,
Dog! you want – go the whole hog!

– So you stay you. Don't be constrained,
To your own dish or master chained.
Never go on your hands and knees,
Dog! – that's for humans, if you please!

… Amour! – May you never get the itch!
Go to the dogs! – Beware the Bitch.

Bite – Dog – and none will bite you back.
Snaffle the titbit. – Splendid tack! –

But after, don't be a dumb beast.
If you must pay – pay – And fight at least
Against the lash they'll make to thwack.

– Pure your blood. Pure your savage flair!
        – Swimming, howling. –
If someone maddens you when prowling…
            Drive him rabid there.

Île de Batz. – October.

À un Juvénal de lait

Incipe, parve puer, risu cognoscere...

À grands coups d'avirons de douze pieds, tu rames
En vers... et contre tout – Hommes, auvergnats, femmes. –
Tu n'as pas vu l'endroit et tu cherches l'envers.
Jeune renard en chasse... Ils sont trop verts – tes vers.

C'est le *vers solitaire*. – On le purge. – *Ces Dames*
Sont le remède. Après tu feras de tes nerfs
Des cordes-à-boyau; quand, guitares sans âmes,
Les vers te reviendront déchantés et soufferts.

Hystérique à rebours, ta Muse est trop superbe,
Petit cochon de lait, qui n'as goûté qu'en herbe,
L'âcre saveur du fruit encore défendu.

Plus tard, tu colleras sur papier tes pensées,
Fleurs d'herboriste, mais, autrefois ramassées...
Quand il faisait beau temps au paradis perdu.

To a Suckling Juvenal

Incipe, parve puer, risu cognoscere ...

With mighty sweeps of twelve-foot oars, you row and row
In-verse ... to all – Men, Auvergnats, women, and flow. –
You haven't seen the place and seek out the reverse.
Foxcub out hunting ... Too green – your hex-amateurs.

They're *worming out*, your lines. You're purging. – *Those
    Women*, though,
The pick-you-up. After, you'll make catgut of your nerves;
When like guitars unsouled, for lack of sound-post, so
Decried and put-up-with, worms back to you your verse.

Your Muse, hysterical when crossed, in pride unmatched,
Suckling piglet that simply tasted, before it's hatched,
The bitterness of fruit it's still forbidden to eat.

Later you'll stick your thoughts, your posies down on pages,
Herbalists' simples but gathered up in bygone ages ...
Of paradise lost when the weather always was a treat!

À une demoiselle

Pour Piano et Chant.

La dent de ton Érard, râtelier osanore,
Et scie et broie à cru, sous son tic-tac nerveux,
La gamme de tes dents, autre clavier sonore…
Touches qui ne vont pas aux cordes des cheveux!

– Cauchemar de meunier, ta: *Rêverie agile!*
– Grattage, ton: *Premier amour à quatre mains!*
Ô femme transposée en *Morceau difficile,*
Tes croches sans douleur n'ont pas d'accents humains!

Déchiffre au clavecin cet accord de ma lyre;
Télégraphe à musique, il pourra le traduire:
Cri d'os, dur, sec, qui plaque et casse – Plangorer…

Jamais! – La *clef-de-Sol* n'est pas la clef de l'âme,
La *clef-de-Fa* n'est pas la syllabe de *Femme,*
Et deux *demi-soupirs*… ce n'est pas soupirer.

To a Young Lady

For Piano and Voice.

The teeth of your Érard, ivory dentures in,
It rawly chops and grinds with nervous plink-plonk there
The scale off your teeth, a secondary keyboard's din...
With touches never sending a quaver through the hair!

– A miller's nightmare, your 'Nimble Reverie'!
– Grating, your 'First Love for Four Hands' choice!
Woman, transposed to 'Difficult Piece', for me,
Your crotchets without sorrow have no human voice!

Sight-read at the harpsichord these notes of my lyre:
Musical telegraph; translation would require:
Bone shriek, hard, dry, that thumps and breaks. – Plangorize...

Never! – The treble-clef's no *key* to the soul;
The F- no *intro* to the Female; two whole
Semi-quavers resting... no wrested sighs.

Décourageux

Ce fut un vrai poète: Il n'avait pas de chant.
Mort, il aimait le jour et dédaigna de geindre.
Peintre: il aimait son art – Il oublia de peindre…
Il voyait trop – Et voir est un aveuglement.

– Songe-creux: bien profond il resta dans son rêve;
Sans lui donner la forme en baudruche qui crève,
Sans *ouvrir le bonhomme*, et se chercher dedans.

– Pur héros de roman: il adorait la brune,
Sans voir s'elle était blonde… Il adorait la lune;
Mais il n'aima jamais – Il n'avait pas le temps. –

– Chercheur infatigable: Ici-bas où l'on rame,
Il regardait ramer, du haut de sa grande âme,
Fatigué de pitié pour ceux qui ramaient bien…

Mineur de la pensée: il touchait son front blême,
Pour gratter un bouton ou gratter le problème
        Qui travaillait là – Faire rien. –

– Il parlait: « Oui, la Muse est stérile! elle est fille
D'amour, d'oisiveté, de prostitution;
Ne la déformez pas en ventre de famille
Que couvre un étalon pour la production!

« Ô vous tous qui gâchez, maçons de la pensée!
Vous tous que son caprice a touchés en amants,
– Vanité, vanité – La folle nuit passée,
Vous l'affichez *en charge* aux yeux ronds des manants!

Uncouraged

A true poet he was. He'd not a song, lineless.
Dead, he loved the light, disdaining all complaint.
Painter, he loved his art – he forgot to paint…
He saw too much – And seeing is a blindness.

– Day-dreamer: in dream he stayed too deep in it,
Not making it like a goldbeater's skin that split,
Nor *opened up the good bloke* to look within.

– A pure romantic hero; he adored the brunette
Not seeing she was blond… adored the moon, yet
He never loved. – He'd never had the time to begin. –

– A tireless quester: Down there where they galley-slaved,
From his great soul's height, he watched, and waived,
Tired with pity for those who slaved at the long haul…

Prospector of saws: he touched his pallid brow
To scratch a spot or scratch at the problem how –
        That struggled there – to do nothing at all. –

– He'd say: 'Yes. The Muse is barren; daughter, she
Of love, of idleness and of the game. Fine.
Don't disfigure her to stomach a family,
Mounted by some stud for a production line!

'Oh all you botchers, thought's jerry-builders, you;
All you her fantasies have turned to lovers.
– Vanity, vanity! – The night of madness through
And you will *send her up* before the round-eyed duffers!

« Elle vous effleurait, vous, comme chats qu'on noie,
Vous avez accroché son aile ou son réseau,
Fiers d'avoir dans vos mains un bout de plume d'oie,
Ou des poils à gratter, en façon de pinceau ! »

– Il disait : « Ô naïf Océan ! Ô fleurettes,
Ne sommes-nous pas là, sans peintres, ni poètes !…
Quel vitrier a peint ! quel aveugle a chanté !…
Et quel vitrier chante en raclant sa palette,

« Ou quel aveugle a peint avec sa clarinette !
– Est-ce l'art ?… »
                        – Lui resta dans le Sublime Bête
Noyer son orgueil vide et sa virginité.

Méditerranée.

'She'd brush against you, just like cats you go and drown.
And by her hair or wing you've grabbed her in a rush,
Proud to hold a goose quill, not just down,
Or hairs to scrape by with, like a painter's brush!'

– He'd say, 'Naive Ocean, Sweet nothings! Yet.
Don't we exist without poet or painter's fret!…
What glazier has painted, what blind man's sung in time!
What glazier sings with his palette a scraping duet,

'Or what blind man has painted with his clarinet!
– Is that art?…'
                              – It's left to him to drown his wet
And empty pride and virginity in the Fatuous Sublime.

The Mediterranean.

Rapsodie du sourd

À Madame D ✶ ✶ ✶.

L'homme de l'art lui dit: – Fort bien, restons-en là.
Le traitement est fait: vous êtes sourd. Voilà.
Comme quoi vous avez l'organe bien perdu. –
Et lui comprit trop bien, n'ayant pas entendu.

– « Eh bien, merci Monsieur, vous qui daignez me rendre
        La tête comme un bon cercueil.
Désormais, à crédit, je pourrai tout entendre
        Avec un légitime orgueil...

À *l'œil* – Mais gare à l'œil jaloux, gardant la place
De l'oreille au clou!... – Non – À quoi sert de braver?
... Si j'ai sifflé trop haut le ridicule en face,
En face, et bassement, il pourra me baver!...

Moi, mannequin muet, à fil banal! – Demain,
Dans la rue, un ami peut me prendre la main,
En me disant: vieux pot..., ou rien, en radouci;
Et je lui répondrai – Pas mal et vous, merci! –

Si l'un me corne un mot, j'enrage de l'entendre;
Si quelqu'autre se tait: serait-ce par pitié?...
Toujours, comme un *rebus*, je travaille à surprendre
Un mot de travers... – Non – On m'a donc oublié!

– Ou bien – autre guitare – un officieux être
Dont la lippe me fait le mouvement de paître,
Croit me parler... Et moi je tire, en me rongeant,
Un sourire idiot – d'un air intelligent!

– Bonnet de laine grise enfoncé sur mon âme!
Et – coup de pied de l'âne... Hue! – Une bonne-femme

Rhapsody of the Deaf Man

*For Mrs D * * * .*

The expert told him: 'Well now, that's your lot.
The treatment's done: you're deaf. The upshot
Is clearly that your hearing's gone for good.' –
And, hearing not a word, he fully understood.

– 'Well, thank you, doctor, since you deign to make
        A coffin of my head.
With proper pride, from now on, I can take
        On trust whatever's said ...'

– It's *eye-credit* now! – Beware the jealous eye
Replacing the banged-up ear: – Why brazen it out?
... If, facing ridicule, I've hissed a bit too high,
Full in my face, to show me stupid, it will spout! ...

Dumb puppet, I am, on obvious string. – Today,
In town, some friend could take my arm to say:
'Deaf ... as a post.' – Or, nothing, on kinder view,
And I'd reply: – 'Not bad, thanks; how about you?'

If someone bellows in my ear, I go mad to hear;
If someone's mum: is it in pity for me? ...
Always, as with a *rebus*, I must persevere
To sort a word out ... – Fail – Ignored, a vacancy!

– Or else – to play another string – some officious gink,
Whose blubber-lips are grazing, seems to think
That he's addressing me ... An inane grin I wear
To give him the appearance that – I am all there!

– Grey woollen headgear pulled down over my soul,
And – worst kick up the ass ... Gee up! Roll! –

Vieille Limonadière, aussi, de la Passion!
Peut venir saliver sa sainte compassion
Dans ma *trompe-d'Eustache*, à pleins cris, à plein cor,
Sans que je puisse au moins lui marcher sur un cor!

– Bête comme une vierge et fier comme un lépreux,
Je suis là, mais absent… On dit: Est-ce un gâteux,
Poète muselé, hérisson à rebours?… –
Un haussement d'épaule, et ça veut dire: un sourd.

– Hystérique tourment d'un Tantale acoustique!
Je vois voler des mots que je ne puis happer;
Gobe-mouche impuissant, mangé par un moustique,
Tête-de-turc gratis où chacun peut taper.

Ô musique céleste: entendre, sur du plâtre,
Gratter un coquillage! un rasoir, un couteau
Grinçant dans un bouchon!… un couplet de théâtre!
Un os vivant qu'on scie! un monsieur! un rondeau!…

– Rien – Je parle sous moi… Des mots qu'à l'air je jette
De chic, et sans savoir si je parle en indou…
Ou peut-être en canard, comme la clarinette
D'un aveugle bouché qui se trompe de trou.

– Va donc, balancier soûl affolé dans ma tête!
Bats en branle ce bon tam-tam, chaudron fêlé
Qui rend la voix de femme ainsi qu'une sonnette,
Qu'un coucou!… quelquefois: un moucheron ailé…

– Va te coucher, mon cœur! et ne bats plus de l'aile.
Dans la lanterne sourde étouffons la chandelle,
Et tout ce qui vibrait là – je ne sais plus où –
Oubliette où l'on vient de tirer le verrou.

That good woman, old soft drink seller to the Passion! she
Can come and drool on me her blessèd sympathy
In my *Eustachian tube*; in full cry, full horn-blaster
And me without the chance to tread on her corn-plaster!

– Stupid as a virgin; unapproachable as a leper,
I'm all there and I'm not. They say: Dribbling decrepit
Is he, a muzzled poet, cussèd, crabbed old coot?…
– They shrug their shoulders, meaning 'deaf as a root!'

– Hysterical torment of an acoustic Tantalus!
I see words flying past and miss them on the wing;
Stung by mosquitoes, useless flycatcher, cantankerous,
A free aunt-sally where anyone has a fling.

O music of the spheres! to hear a shell engage
And scrape on plaster; a razor, knife-blade go
Squealing across the boozer!… a couplet hammed on stage,
Sawing of living bone! a gentleman! a rondeau!…

– Nothing. – I talk beneath my usual self… Let fly
Words *out of con-text*, not knowing if I speak Hindu…
Or mallardies a blind man's clarinet will cry
When so sealed off his fingers switch a hole or two.

– Pendulum, sloshed and crazy in my cranium, sway!
Beat with a swing this fine tom-tom, this cracked pot
That makes a woman's voice either a cuckoo's lay,
A doorbell's clatter… or a gnat, more often than not!…

– Go to bed, heart! Don't flap your wings about.
The candle mute in the dark lantern let's put out,
And all that flickered there – its whereabouts unknown –
An oubliette on which the bolt has just been thrown.

– Soyez muette pour moi, contemplative Idole,
Tous les deux, l'un par l'autre, oubliant la parole,
Vous ne me direz mot: je ne répondrai rien…
Et rien ne pourra dédorer l'entretien.

Le silence est d'or (Saint Jean Chrysostome).

Frère et Sœur jumeaux

Ils étaient tous deux seuls, oubliés là par l'âge…
Ils promenaient toujours tous les deux, à longs pas,
Obliquant de travers, l'air piteux et sauvage…
Et deux pauvres regards qui ne regardaient pas.

Ils allaient devant eux essuyant les risées,
– Leur parapluie aussi, vert, avec un grand bec –
Serrés l'un contre l'autre et roides, sans pensées…
Eh bien, je les aimais – leur parapluie avec! –

Ils avaient tous les deux servi dans les gendarmes:
La Sœur à la *popote*, et l'Autre sous les armes;
Ils gardaient l'uniforme encor – veuf de galon:
Elle avait la barbiche, et lui le pantalon.

Un Dimanche de Mai que tout avait une âme,
Depuis le champignon jusqu'au paradis bleu,
Je flânais aux bois, seul – à deux aussi: la femme
Que j'aimais comme l'air… m'en doutant assez peu.

– But as for me, be dumb, contemplative Idol, each
Of us, one after the other, forgetting speech,
Don't say a word to me: and I'll not answer you...
And nothing can dis-aurient our intercourse of two.

Silence is golden (St John Chrysostom).

Mixed Twins

Two loners, forgotten by the times, they were...
They always went together with their long stride,
Leaning sideways with wild and pitiful air...
Two sorry looks that saw nothing they eyed.

They forged straight through the jeering squalls that flew.
– As did – green, its handle huge – their gamp. –
Clasped together, stiff, no thought between the two...
Well, I liked them – and their umbrella, a champ! –

They had both served in their time as gendarmes,
The Sister in the mess, the Other in arms.
They kept to uniform still – no braid any more.
She had the goatee, the trousers he still wore.

One Sunday in May when everyone had a soul,
From mushroom to the paradisal blue,
Alone, I loafed – with a partner, too, on a stroll –
Whom I loved like the air... doubtful enough, too.

– Soudain, au coin d'un champ, sous l'ombre verdoyante
Du parapluie éclos, nichés dans un fossé,
Mes Vieux Jumeaux, tous deux, à l'aube souriante,
Souriaient rayonnants… quand nous avons passé.

Contre un arbre, le vieux jouait de la musette,
Comme un sourd aveugle, et sa sœur dans un sillon,
Grelottant au soleil, écoutait un grillon
Et remerciait Dieu de son beau jour de fête.

– Avez-vous remarqué l'humaine créature
Qui végète loin du vulgaire intelligent,
Et dont l'âme d'instinct, au trait de la figure,
Se lit… – N'avez-vous pas aimé de chien couchant?…

Ils avaient de cela – De retour dans l'enfance,
Tenant chaud l'un à l'autre, ils attendaient le jour
Ensemble pour la mort comme pour la naissance…
– Et je les regardais en pensant à l'amour…

Mais l'Amour que j'avais près de moi voulut rire;
Et moi, pauvre honteux de mon émotion,
J'eus le cœur de crier au vieux duo: Tityre! –

. . . .

Et j'ai fait ces vieux vers en expiation.

– Suddenly in the corner of a field in the green shade
Of the blooming gamp, nestled in a ditch,
My Old Twins together, at smiling aubade,
Were beaming smiles... when we passed their pitch.

The old man played the bagpipes, leant on a tree
Like a deaf-blind man; in a furrow shivering away,
In the sun, his sister heard a cricket and she
Thanked God for fine weather on the holiday

– Have you ever noticed odd human creatures
That vegetate away from the commonly clever,
And whose soul of instinct shows on their features?...
– Haven't you loved a setter dog sleeping, ever?...

They had just that. – In second childhood, he and she,
Warming each other, waiting for the day to share
Their death together, just as they had nativity...
– I thought of love as I was looking on them there...

The Love I had with me was verging on laughter;
I, wretch, ashamed of my emotional state,
Had nerve to call the poor dears 'Tityrus!'

. . . .

– After,
I knocked up these old lines to expiate.

Litanie du sommeil

J'ai scié le sommeil!
MACBETH.

Vous qui ronflez au coin d'une épouse endormie,
Ruminant! savez-vous ce soupir: l'Insomnie?
– Avez-vous vu la Nuit, et le Sommeil ailé,
Papillon de minuit dans la nuit envolé,
Sans un coup d'aile ami, vous laissant sur le seuil,
Seul, dans le pot-au-noir au couvercle sans œil?
– Avez-vous navigué?... La pensée est la houle
Ressassant le galet: ma tête... votre boule.
– Vous êtes-vous laissé voyager en ballon?
– Non? – bien, c'est l'insomnie. – Un grand coup de talon
Là! – Vous voyez cligner des chandelles étranges:
Une femme, une Gloire en soleil, des archanges...
Et, la nuit s'éteignant dans le jour à demi,
Vous vous réveillez coi, sans vous être endormi.

                    ★

Sommeil! écoute-moi: je parlerai bien bas:
Sommeil. – Ciel-de-lit de ceux qui n'en ont pas!

Toi qui planes avec l'Albatros des tempêtes,
Et qui t'assieds sur les casques-à-mèche honnêtes!
Sommeil! – Oreiller blanc des vierges assez bêtes!
Et Soupape à secret des vierges assez faites!
– Moelleux Matelas de l'échine en arête!
Sac noir où les chassés s'en vont cacher leur tête!
Rôdeur de boulevard extérieur! Proxénète!
Pays où le muet se réveille prophète!
Césure du vers long, et Rime du poète!

Sommeil! – Loup-Garou gris! Sommeil Noir de fumée!
Sommeil! – Loup de velours, de dentelle embaumée!

The Litany of Sleep

I've bored sleep to…!

MACBETH.

YOU, sleeping in the angle of your partner, snoring,
RUMINANT! D'you hear this sigh: 'INSOMNIA', boring?
– Have you ever seen the Night and Sleep's winged flight?
The midnight butterfly that soars off in the night
With never a friendly flutter, slamming the door on you,
Alone, in the black pot with holeless lid, to stew?
Have you ever been sailing?… Thought is the running squall
Rehashing the shingle: my headpiece… your float ball;
– Or let yourself go up ballooning, know what that feels?
No! – Okay. That's insomnia. – A great kicking of heels,
There! – You see weird candles blinking. A woman, a Glory,
Halo'd in the sun, and archangels, storey after storey…
And the dark wasted away in the day's first light,
You wake up muted, having never slept tight.

*

SLEEP! Listen to me; I'll speak very quietly:
Sleep. – For those without, a bed with canopy.

YOU who with the albatross of storms glide and luff
And settle on the night-cap of the honest buff!
SLEEP! – White pillow for virgins slow enough!
Furtive safety valve for virgins well-maid enough!
– For those with spine in ridges, mattress of softest stuff!
Black sack where the hunted hide their head and scruff!
Prowler of the outer boulevard; procurer of fluff!
Land where the dumb wake up with prophet's huff and puff!
The long line's caesura; the poet's rhyme – not duff!

SLEEP! Grey werewolf. Sleep black with fumes!
SLEEP! – That wolfish mask the scented lace assumes!

Baiser de l'Inconnue, et Baiser de l'Aimée!
– SOMMEIL! Voleur de nuit! Folle-brise pâmée!
Parfum qui monte au ciel des tombes parfumées!
Carrosse à Cendrillon ramassant *les Traînées!*
Obscène Confesseur des dévotes mort-nées!

TOI qui viens, comme un chien, lécher la vieille plaie
Du martyr que la mort tiraille sur sa claie!
Ô sourire forcé de la crise tuée!
SOMMEIL! Brise alizée! Aurorale buée!

TROP-PLEIN de l'existence, et Torchon neuf qu'on passe
Au CAFÉ DE LA VIE, à chaque assiette grasse!
Grain d'ennui qui nous pleut de l'ennui des espaces!
Chose qui court encor, sans sillage et sans traces!
Pont-levis des fossés! Passage des impasses!

SOMMEIL! – Caméléon tout pailleté d'étoiles!
Vaisseau-fantôme errant tout seul à pleines voiles!
Femme du rendez-vous, s'enveloppant d'un voile!
SOMMEIL! – Triste Araignée, étends sur moi ta toile!

SOMMEIL auréolé! féerique Apothéose,
Exaltant le grabat du déclassé qui pose!
Patient Auditeur de l'incompris qui cause!
Refuge du pêcheur, de l'innocent qui n'ose!
Domino! Diables-bleus! Ange-gardien rose!

VOIX mortelle qui vibre aux immortelles ondes!
Réveil des échos morts et des choses profondes,
– Journal du soir: TEMPS, SIÈCLE et REVUE DES DEUX MONDES!

FONTAINE de Jouvence et Borne de l'envie!
– Toi qui viens assouvir la faim inassouvie!

Kiss of the mystery woman; the darling's kiss that blooms!
SLEEP! Thief of the Night; the mad breeze that swoons!
Perfume rising skyward from the perfumed tombs!
Picking up *streetwalkers, Cinderella's coach* – and *grooms!*
Obscene confessor of the pious stillborn's dooms!

YOU who slink like a dog to lick the old wound
Of martyrs stretched on death's rack to be tuned!
Forced smile of those that death by stroke marooned!
SLEEP! Trade wind! Dawn condensation on the windows runed!

EXISTENCE in excess! And a fresh cloth to race,
In LIFEY'S CAFE, over every greasy place!
Squall of tedium poured from tedium of space!
Ongoing thingummy that leaves no wake or trace!
Bypass of impasse. Bridge for leaps-in-the-dark's embrace!

SLEEP! Time-server chameleon in starry scales!
Ghost ship that roves about with billowed sails!
Call-girl to meet you, wrapping herself in veils!
SLEEP! – Sad Spider, stretch your webs on me like jails!

SLEEP halo'd! magical Apotheosis,
Uplifting the pallet where the dropout re-poses!
For every misjudged whinger, ear that never closes!
Angler's refuge; retreat where each who daren't opposes!
Domino! Blue fiends! Guardian-angels in pinks and roses.

MORTAL voice vibrating with immortal tides! You,
Waker of dead echoes and profundities, too;
Evening paper: TIMES; CENTURY; TWO WORLDS REVIEW!

FOUNT of eternal Youth; and Envy's border-control!
– You come to satisfy insatiable Hunger on a roll!

Toi qui viens délier la pauvre âme ravie,
Pour la noyer d'air pur au large de la vie!

Toi qui, le rideau bas, viens lâcher la ficelle
Du Chat, du Commissaire, et de Polichinelle,
Du violoncelliste et de son violoncelle,
Et la lyre de ceux dont la Muse est pucelle!

Grand Dieu, Maître de tout! Maître de ma Maîtresse
Qui me trompe avec toi – l'amoureuse Paresse –
Ô Bain de voluptés! Éventail de caresse!

Sommeil! Honnêteté des voleurs! Clair de lune
Des yeux crevés! – Sommeil! Roulette de fortune
De tout infortuné! Balayeur de rancune!

Ô corde-de-pendu de la Planète lourde!
Accord éolien hantant l'oreille sourde!
– Beau Conteur à dormir debout: conte ta bourde?...
Sommeil! – Foyer de ceux dont morte est la falourde!

Sommeil – Foyer de ceux dont la falourde est morte!
Passe-partout de ceux qui sont mis à la porte!
Face-de-bois pour les créanciers et leur sorte!
Paravent du mari contre la femme-forte!

Surface des profonds! Profondeur des jocrisses!
Nourrice du soldat et Soldat des nourrices!
Paix des juges-de-paix! Police des polices!
Sommeil! – Belle-de-nuit entr'ouvrant son calice!
Larve, Ver-luisant et nocturne Cilice!
Puits de vérité de monsieur La Palisse!

Soupirail d'en haut! Rais de poussière impalpable,
Qui viens rayer du jour la lanterne implacable!

You come to rescue from its transport the poor soul
And in fresh air on life's broad main to sink his poll!

Curtains once drawn, You who turn up to undo
The strings of Cat, Chief Constable, Punch, the 'cellist, too,
And of his 'cello also; the lyre of anybody who
Has for his muse a chased maid with the odd loose screw!

God! Master of all! Master of my Mistress who betrays
Me with you – me caught napping! – loving Miss Laze!
Warm bath for sensualists; fan with caressing ways!

Sleep! Honour among thieves! Light of the moon
To eyes put out! – Sleep! Wheel of Fortune, boon
To all unfortunates. Rancour's sweeping new broom!

Devil's own… lynch for the earth's ponderous Sphere!
Aeolian harmony that haunts the stone-deaf ear!
– Spinner of knockout yarns: won't you let us hear?…
– Sleep! – Hearth of those whose lantern's out… bum steer!

Sleep – Hearth of those whose lantern's out, so… late!
Skeleton key for those locked out of cupboard, gate!
Door slammed upon all creditors and their rate!
Shield from the battle-axe for every husband prostrate!

Surfacings of the depths! For idiots the deep!
Nurse to the private; privates to the nurses; Sleep!
Policer of police; peace for J.P.s to keep!
Sleep: Bella Donna half-opening for a peep!
Larva; Glow-worm; night Hair-shirt where the flesh can creep!
To Peter crying wolf the well of truth so steep!

Ventilator from above! Dust's impalpable ray
That comes to scotch the lantern of the day!

★

SOMMEIL – Écoute-moi, je parlerai bien bas:
Crépuscule flottant de l'*Être ou n'Être pas!*…

SOMBRE lucidité! Clair-obscur! Souvenir
De l'Inouï! Marée! Horizon! Avenir!
Conte des *Mille-et-une-nuits* doux à ouïr!
Lampiste d'*Aladin* qui sais nous éblouir!
Eunuque noir! muet blanc! Derviche! Djinn! Fakir!
Conte de Fée où *le Roi* se laisse assoupir!
Forêt-vierge où *Peau-d'Âne* en pleurs va s'accroupir!
Garde-manger où l'*Ogre* encor va s'assouvir!
Tourelle où *ma sœur Anne* allait voir rien venir!
Tour où *dame Malbrouck* voyait page courir!…
Où *Femme Barbe-Bleue* oyait l'heure mourir!…
Où *Belle-au-Bois-Dormant* dormait dans un soupir!

CUIRASSE du petit! Camisole du fort!
Lampion des éteints! Éteignoir du remord!
Conscience du juste, et du pochard qui dort!
Contre-poids des poids faux de l'épicier de Sort!
Portrait enluminé de la livide Mort!

GRAND fleuve où Cupidon va retremper ses dards
SOMMEIL! – Corne de Diane, et corne du cornard!
Couveur de magistrats et Couveur de lézards!
Marmite d'*Arlequin!* – bout de cuir, lard, homard –
SOMMEIL! – Noce de ceux qui sont dans les beaux-arts.

BOULET des forcenés, Liberté des captifs!
Sabbat du somnambule et Relais des poussifs! –
SOMME! Actif du passif et Passif de l'actif!
Pavillon de *la Folle* et *Folle* du poncif!…
– Ô viens changer de patte au cormoran pensif!

★

SLEEP – Listen to me; I'll murmur quietly:
Drifting twilight of *To Be or not to Be!* ...

DARK lucidity! Chiaroscuro; Memory's supply
Of the unheard-of! Horizon! Future! Low tide and high!
Tale of *the Arabian Nights*, sweet to hear! The sly
Aladdin's maker of lamps that dazzles every eye!
Black eunuch; white mute; fakir, genie, dervish, hi!
Fairy-tale where the *King* goes to bye-bye!
Virgin forest where *Mother Goose* sinks down to cry!
Larder where the *Giant* stuffs himself with pie!
Turret where *Sister Anne* saw nobody draw nigh!
Tower where *Lady Marlborough* saw a page run by! ...
Where *Blackbeard's wife* heard tell the hour to die! ...
Where *Sleeping Beauty* was sleeping in a sigh!

BREASTPLATE of the puny! Straitjacket of the forceful!
Fairy-lights on lines extinct! snuffer of the remorseful!
Conscience of the just – and drunks who're lying dorsal!
For Grocer Fate's false measure the counter morsel!
Limned portrait of livid Death, the whole corseful!

WIDE river where Cupid goes to dip his dart!
SLEEP! Diana's horn, horn in the cuckold's heart!
Brooder for magistrates; brooder where loafers start!
Di Jester's hash! – scrag-end of skin, pork, lobster, tart –
SLEEP! – Has-been-feast for all of those mixed up in art.

MANACLES of the manic, the prisoner's liberty!
Sabbath of sleepwalkers; for the gasping, hostelry! –
NAP! and in-purse for disburse; impers. from pers. v.!
Blazon of the mad *Fancy*; *Fancy* out of plagiary! ...
– Come, change foot for the cormorant stood so pensively!

Ô brun Amant de l'Ombre! Amant honteux du jour!
Bal de nuit où Psyché veut démasquer l'Amour!
Grosse Nudité du chanoine en jupon court!
Panier-à-salade idéal! Banal four!
Omnibus où, dans l'Orbe, on fait pour rien un tour!

SOMMEIL! Drame hagard! Sommeil, molle Langueur!
Bouche d'or du silence et Bâillon du blagueur!
Berceuse des vaincus! Perchoir des coqs vainqueurs!
Alinéa du livre où dorment les longueurs!

DU jeune homme rêveur Singulier Féminin!
De la femme rêvant pluriel masculin!

SOMMEIL! – Râtelier du Pégase fringant!
SOMMEIL! – Petite pluie abattant l'ouragan!
SOMMEIL! – Dédale vague où vient le revenant!
SOMMEIL! – Long corridor où plangore le vent!

NÉANT du fainéant! Lazzarone infini!
Aurore boréale au sein du jour terni!

SOMMEIL! – Autant de pris sur notre éternité!
Tour du cadran *à blanc!* Clou du Mont-de-Piété!
Héritage en Espagne à tout déshérité!
Coup de rapière dans l'eau du fleuve Léthé!
Génie au nimbe d'or des grands hallucinés!
Nid des petits hiboux! Aile des déplumés!

IMMENSE Vache à lait dont nous sommes les veaux!
Arche où le hère et le boa changent de peaux!
Arc-en-ciel miroitant! Faux du vrai! Vrai du faux!
Ivresse que la brute appelle le repos!
Sorcière de Bohême à sayon d'oripeaux!
Tityre sous l'ombrage essayant des pipeaux!

Dusky Lover of the Shade! Lover ashamed of light!
Mask ball where Psyche wants Eros unmasked that night!
Gross canon nude in mini-slip! – Side-salad, raw sight!
Communal cookhouse flop! Black Maria just right!
Bus in which you tour the Orbit in free flight!

SLEEP! Haggard drama! Sleep, flabby Languorous sag!
Golden mouth of silence, and for the joker, Gag!
Roost of cocks in conquest! Lay of the conquered flag!
Indentations in a book where tediums drag!

For the young man in a dream the feminine singular!
For the dreamy young woman the plural mascular!

SLEEP! – Frisky Pegasus's rack and pain!
SLEEP! – Drizzle that lays the hurricane!
SLEEP! – Vague labyrinth, revenant's venue again!
SLEEP! – Long passage where the wind plangores in vain!

WASTE for the wastrel! Lazzaroni's endless laze!
Northern lights at very heart of tarnished days!

SLEEP! – So much purchase on our eternity!
Point-*blank*, white-hot clock round! Pawn of hockshop and
    pledgee!
Redemption on the Nail! And Spanish castlery
For all the dispossessed! Sword-thrust in Lethe, absently!
Genie with golden halo of the great hallucinatory!
Moping 'owlets' nest; Wing of the fleeced to flee!

HUGE milch Cow whose calves we are and low!
Ark where boa changes skin with the buck lacking dough!
False at the truth, true at the false! rainbow's shimmery glow!
Drunkenness the brute considers rest from go!
Bohemian sorceress glittering in tawdry show!
Tityrus in shadows testing reed-pipes – ray; doh!

Temps qui porte un chibouck à la place de faux!
Parque qui met un peu d'huile à ses ciseaux!
Parque qui met un peu de chanvre à ses fuseaux!
Chat qui joue avec le peloton d'Atropos!

SOMMEIL! – Manne de grâce au cœur disgracié!

. . . .

LE SOMMEIL S'ÉVEILLANT ME DIT: TU M'A SCIÉ.

. . . .

       ★

TOI qui souffles dessus une épouse enrayée,
RUMINANT! dilatant ta pupille éraillée;
Sais-tu?... Ne sais-tu pas ce soupir – LE RÉVEIL! –
Qui bâille au ciel, parmi les crins d'or du soleil
Et les crins fous de ta Déesse ardente et blonde?...
– Non?... – Sais-tu le réveil du philosophe immonde
– Le Porc – rognonnant sa prière du matin;
Ou le réveil, extrait-d'âge de la catin?...
As-tu jamais sonné le réveil de la meute;
As-tu jamais senti l'éveil sourd de l'émeute,
Ou le réveil de plomb du malade fini?...
As-tu vu s'étirer l'œil des Lazzaroni?...
Sais-tu?... ne sais-tu pas le chant de l'alouette?
– Non – Gluants sont tes cils, pâteuse est ta luette,
Ruminant! Tu n'as pas L'INSOMNIE, éveillé;
Tu n'as pas LE SOMMEIL, ô Sac ensommeillé!

(Lits divers – Une nuit de jour)

Father Time with hookah, not a scythe to mow!
One Fate that oils her scissors, silent, slow!
The Second winding hemp on her spindle, row on row!
A cat that plays the ball of Atropos to and fro!

SLEEP! – Manna to the heart in its disgrace!

. . . .

SLEEP SAID, AWAKENED: 'YOU'VE BORED ME TO MY FACE.'

. . . .

★

YOU, on board a shafted wife panting and puffing,
RUMINANT; your bloodshot pupils wide as nothing,
D'you know?... Not really know this sigh – TIME TO WAKE! –
Yawning to the sky as sun gives golden locks a shake?
The wild locks of your Goddess, blonde and smouldering?...
– No?... – D'you know the filthy philosopher's awakening
– The Porker – oinking out his morning prayers, then; – or
The waking – age certificate – for the old whore?...
Have you ever sounded the waking of the pack?
Have you felt the sluggish riot rising to attack,
Or the leaden rising of the terminally ill?...
Nor the Lazzaroni's distended eyes that mill?...
D'you know them?... Don't you know the song trilled by
    the lark?
– No. – Your tongue is furred, your eyes are stuck to the dark,
Ruminant! You don't have INSOMNIA when awake.
You don't have SLEEP, you dozy old Bag, for its own sake.

(Various beds – One night of day)

Idylle coupée

Avril.

C'est très parisien dans les rues
Quand l'Aurore fait le trottoir,
De voir sortir toutes les Grues
Du violon, ou de leur boudoir…

Chanson pitoyable et gaillarde:
Chiffons fanés papillotants,
Fausse note rauque et criarde
Et petits traits crus, turlutants:

Velours ratissant la chaussée;
Grande-duchesse mal chaussée,
Cocotte qui court becqueter
Et qui dit bonjour pour chanter…

J'aime les voir, tout plein légères,
Et, comme en façon de prières,
Entrer dire – Bonjour, gros chien –
Au *merlan*, puis au pharmacien.

J'aime les voir, chauves, déteintes,
Vierges de seize à soixante ans,
Rossignoler pas mal d'absinthes,
Perruches de tout leur printemps;

Et puis *payer le mannezingue*,
Au *Polyte* qui sert d'Arthur,
Bon jeune homme né *brandezingue*,
Dos-bleu sous la blouse d'azur.

Romance Gone Flat

April.

It's most Parisian on the streets
When Aurora's on the gad
To watch game Birds as each retreats
From jug, or issues from her pad...

Ribald, pitiful, the old song:
Tawdry finery shimmering;
Shrill, raucous chirpy note and wrong,
And sharp raw features hey-ding-a-ding:

With velvet gown sweeping the flags,
Grand duchess down-at-heel drags,
A tart trots for a peck and grope;
She bids good day to kill your hope...

I like to watch them, loose and free,
As if for prayers, pop in to see
Mopflourer, chemist just to say: –
'You grubby old dog, good day.' –

I like to watch them, bald and dingy,
Virgins from sixteen to sixty prime,
Halffinching absinthe, no way stingy,
Parrots of their abs'nt-green time;

Then *settling with the demi John*,
Blackguard who does for Prince Charming, here,
Born *brandy-legged*, a nice young con,
Pimply beneath his pimpernel gear.

– C'est au boulevard excentrique,
Au – *BON RETOUR DU CHAMP DU NORD* –
Là: toujours vert le jus de trique,
Rose le nez des Croque-mort…

Moitié panaches, moitié cire,
Nez croqués vifs au demeurant,
Et gais comme un enterrement…
– Toujours le petit *mort* pour rire! –

Le voyou siffle – vilain merle –
Et le poète de charnier
Dans ce fumier cherche la perle,
Avec le peintre chiffonnier.

Tous les deux fouillant la pâture
De leur art… à coups de groins;
Sûrs toujours de trouver l'ordure.
– C'est le fonds qui manque le moins.

C'est toujours un fond chaud qui fume,
Et, par le soleil, lardé d'or…
Le rapin nomme ça: bitume;
Et le marchand de lyre: accord.

– Ajoutez une pipe en terre
Dont la spirale fait les cieux…
Allez: je plains votre misère,
Vous qui trouvez qu'on trouve mieux!

C'est le *Persil* des gueux sans poses,
Et des riches sans un radis…
– Mais ce n'est pas pour vous, ces choses,
Ô provinciaux de Paris!…

– On the eccentric boulevard the scene –
The *WELCOME HOME FROM THE NORTHERN WAR.* –
There: cudgel saps are always green;
The Hearsemen's conks red roar…

Part dander up, part beak as wax,
Conks cracklingly sketched from life after all
And merry as a funeral…
– The little *corpse* is good for cracks. –

The blackguard whistles – villainous git –
The poet of the charnel seeks
The pearl within this heap of shit;
The totting painter also peeks.

Both browse the pasture for a scrap
To serve their art… snouting and snortage;
Always a dead cert to find the crap.
Spoil heaps – toil rich, never a shortage!

Rich background, warm and steaming, then,
And larded golden by the sun…
The paintster calls it: bitumen;
Harmony – the lyre-flogging one.

– And add to that just a clay pipe's
Spirals that wrap a heaven round…
I pity you your dumps, types
Who find there's better to be found!

There's *scoring* with tramps of no pretence,
And of the rich without a sou…
– But things like that not you, you dense,
Rustics of Paris, not for you!…

Ni pour vous, essayeurs de sauces,
Pour qui l'azur est un ragoût!
Grands empâteurs d'emplâtres fausses,
Ne fesant rien, fesant partout!

– Rembranesque! Raphaélique!
– Manet et Courbet au milieu –
… Ils donnent des noms de fabrique
À la pochade du bon Dieu!

Ces *Galimard cherchant la ligne,*
Et ces *Ducornet-né-sans-bras,*
Dont la blague, de chic, vous signe
N'importe quoi… qu'on ne peint pas.

Dieu garde encor l'homme qui glane
Sur le soleil du promenoir,
De flairer jamais la soutane
De la vieille dame au bas noir!

… On dégèle, animal nocturne,
Et l'on se détache en vigueur;
On veut, aveugle taciturne,
À soi tout seul être blagueur.

Savates et chapeau grotesque
Deviennent de l'antique pur;
On se colle comme une fresque
Enrayonnée au pied d'un mur.

Il coule une divine flamme,
Sous la peau; l'on se sent avoir
Je ne sais quoi qui fleure l'âme…
Je ne sais – mais ne veux savoir.

And, testers of sauces, not for you
For whom the azure is a hash!
Dab pasters of fake plaster, who
Make nothing on the make for cash!

– Rembrandtesque or Raphaelite!
– Manet and Courbet, centre, stand –
... They're mocking up makers' names to write
On the rough sketch in God's own hand!

These *Galimards*, '*Hunt-the-Line*':
And all these *Ducornets, born handless,*
Whose con, unique, is they will sign
Anything... what none would stick on canvas.

God keeps the gleaning scavenger,
That down the sunny arcade pegs,
From ever sniffing the cassock of her,
The old crone with black-stockinged legs!

... Creature nocturnal in your kind,
You thaw out, fan out with all vigour;
You'd like, though taciturn and blind,
As your own laughing-stock to figure.

Slippers, and the grotesque hat
Antiquated beyond recall;
Like a fresco you stick yourself flat,
Beam end, at the base of the wall.

A divine flame flows under your skin;
You feel you have – I don't know what
That's redolent of soul within...
I don't know – and I'd rather not.

La Muse malade s'étire…
Il semble que l'huissier sursoit…
Soi-même on cherche à se sourire,
Soi-même on a pitié de soi.

Volez, mouches et demoiselles!…
Le gouapeur aussi vole un peu
D'idéal… Tout n'a pas des ailes…
Et chacun vole comme il peut.

– Un grand pendard, cocasse, triste,
Jouissait de tout ça, comme moi,
Point ne lui demandais pourquoi…
Du reste – une gueule d'artiste –

Il reluquait surtout la tête
Et moi je reluquais le pié.
– Jaloux… pourquoi? c'eut été bête,
Ayant chacun notre moitié. –

Ma béatitude nagée
Jamais, jamais n'avait bravé
Sa silhouette ravagée
Plantée au milieu du pavé…

– Mais il fut un Dieu pour ce drille:
Au soleil loupant comme ça,
Dessinant des yeux une fille…
– Un omnibus vert l'écrasa.

The Muse stretches in poor health...
It seems the bailiff still delays...
Yourself, you try smiling at yourself;
Yourself, you pity yourself and ways.

Fly away, painted ladies, flies!...
The loafer also flies away
A bit in fancy... Not all can rise,
Wingless... each steals off as he may.

– Glum gallows-cheat, a hulking rogue
Revelled in all of this like me.
I never asked why this should be...
– Besides – a smack of artist – he ogled

The head especially, but me
I went for leg. – Jealous?... But why?
That would have been stupidity.
Each had our better half, aye aye. –

My flustered bliss had never yet,
Never had dared, not once, the braving
Of her ravaged silhouette
Slap in the middle of the paving...

– But there was a God for this guy
Loafing in the sun like that,
Tracing a girl out with his eye...
– A green bus crushed him flat.

Le Convoi du pauvre

Paris, le 30 avril 1873,
Rue Notre-Dame-de-Lorette.

Ça monte et c'est lourd – Allons, Hue!
– Frères de renfort, votre main?...
C'est trop!... et je fais le gamin;
C'est mon Calvaire cette rue!

Depuis Notre-Dame-Lorette...
– Allons! *la Cayenne* est au bout,
Frère! du cœur! encor un coup!...
– Mais mon âme est dans la charrette:

Corbillard dur à fendre l'âme.
Vers en bas l'attire un aimant;
Et du piteux enterrement
Rit la Lorette notre dame...

C'est bien ça – Splendeur et misère! –
Sous le voile en trous a brillé
Un bout du tréteau funéraire;
Cadre d'or riche... et pas payé.

La pente est âpre, tout de même,
Et les stations sont des *fours*,
Au tableau remontant le cours
De l'Élysée à la Bohème...

– Oui, camarade, il faut qu'on sue
Après son harnais et son art!...
Après les ailes: le brancard!
Vivre notre métier – ça tue...

The Cortège of the Poor Bloke

Paris, 30th April 1873,
Rue Notre-Dame-de-Lorette.

Stiff climb, and heavy, this. – Hup! Gee!
– More muscle, men, a hand? It's crippling…
Too much… And I play the stripling.
This street is Calvary to me!

And rising from Our Lady the Tart…
– Come on! The *bone-tip*'s at the end!
One more heave! Take heart, my friend!…
– But mine, I know, is in the cart:

Hearse hard enough to break the heart.
A loving loadstone draws it below.
She watches the wretched burial show
And laughs at it, Our Lady the Tart…

That's it. – Splendour and wretchedness! –
From under the tatty pall there rayed
The funeral trestle's tip – excess
Of gilt-rich frame… the bill unpaid.

But still, the rise is steep to boot,
Each station is a bakehouse *flop*,
For the picture, climbing back on top:
The Élysée to Bohemia route…

– Yes, partner, you have to sweat
Over your harness and your art!…
From wings: to shafts – that horse, that cart!
To follow our calling'll kill us yet…

Tués l'idéal et le râble!
Hue!... Et le cœur dans le talon!

. . . .

– Salut au convoi misérable
Du peintre écrémé du Salon!

– Parmi les martyrs ça te range;
C'est prononcé comme l'arrêt
De Rafaël, peintre au nom d'ange,
Par le Peintre au nom de... courbet!

Done in: one's back and one's ideals!
Gee up!... Heart in your boots! Get on!
. . . .
– Bless the wretched cortège at heels
Of a painter skimmed by the Salon!

– Among the martyrs that places you;
Pronounced – like Rafael's judgement (who took
The angel's name) – by Courbet who
Was painted with the name ... bill hook!

Déjeuner de soleil

Bois de Boulogne, 1ᵉʳ mai.

Au Bois, les lauriers sont coupés,
Mais le *Persil* verdit encore;
Au *Serpolet*, petits coupés
Vertueux vont lever l'Aurore...

L'Aurore brossant sa palette:
Kh'ol, carmin et poudre de riz;
Pour faire dire – la coquette –
Qu'on fait bien les ciels à Paris.

Par ce petit-lever de Mai,
Le Bois se croit à la campagne:
Et, fraîchement trait, le champagne
Semble de la mousse de lait.

Là, j'ai vu les *Chère Madame*
S'encanailler avec le frais...
Malgré tout prendre un vrai bain d'âme!
– Vous vous engommerez après. –

... La voix à la note expansive:
– Vous comprenez; voici mon truc:
Je vends mes Memphis, et j'arrive...
– Cent louis!... – Eh, Eh! Bibi... – Mon duc?...

On presse de petites mains:
– Tiens... assez pur cet attelage. –
Même les cochers, au dressage,
Redeviennent simples humains.

Al Frisko

Bois de Boulogne, 1st May.

The laurels are cut down in the Wood.
Acacia Walk still flowers with *Birds' Eyes*.
In the *Wild Thyme*, the broughams go, good
And virtuous, to make Dawn rise...

Her broad palette now Dawn applies,
Kohl, carmine, powder, to tell –
Impudent little flirt – that skies
Of Paris are made up very well.

Since this petty-levee of May
The Wood thinks it's country again,
And, freshly drawn now, the champagne
Seems milk-froth bubbling away.

I've seen, here, *dear Madams* Well-To-Do
Bumming it with the cool of the day...
And taking a real soul-bath, too,
Despite it. – You'll get stuck up after play. –

... The voice takes an effusive air:
– You understand... That's my approach:
I'll sell my Memphis and I'll be there!...
– A hundred louis!... – Eh, eh, chick... – My coach?...

Tiny hands are squeezed just then.
– Hold on... this is a pure-bred pair –
At the breaking-in even the coachmen there
Become just simply human again.

– Encor toi! vieille *Belle-Impure!*
Toujours, les pieds au plat, tu sors,
Dans ce déjeuner de nature,
Fondre un souper à huit ressorts... –

Voici l'école buissonnière:
Quelques maris jaunes de teint,
Et qui *rentrent dans la carrière*
D'assez bonne heure... le matin.

Le lapin inquiet s'arrête,
Un sergent-de-ville s'assied,
Le sportsman promène sa bête,
Et le rêveur la sienne – à pied. –

Arthur même a presque une tête,
Son faux-col s'ouvre matinal...
Peut-être se sent-il poète,
Tout comme *Byron* – son cheval.

Diane au petit galop de chasse
Fait galoper les papillons
Et caracoler sur sa trace,
Son Tigre et les vieux beaux Lions.

Naseaux fumants, grand œil en flamme,
Crins d'étalon: cheval et femme
Saillent de l'avant!...
                              – Peu poli.
– Pardon: *maritime*... et joli.

– You *dirty old Looker*, still around!
You're always out, foot into things,
In this al frisko nibble bound
To melt a supper on eight springs … –

The hedgerow school of truants here.
Several husbands yellow of hue
Head back home *at a career*
Early enough … in morning dew.

The nervy buck is pulled up short.
A constable sits and stays put.
His bitch is walked beside the sport;
The dreamer taking his – on foot. –

Arthur, even, nearly has his head,
Stiff collar loose, for morning larger …
Perhaps he feels a poet bred
Just as *Byron* is – his charger!

Diana, cantering in chase
Makes gamecocks gallop round and go
Wheeling in her tracks apace,
Her Tiger and old dandy-lions in tow.

Nostrils smoking, great eyes aflame,
Stallion manes; the horse and dame
Lead the *fleet* on! …
                                    – That's coarse of you.
– Sorry: *seaman* … and nice, too.

Veder Napoli poi mori

Voir *Naples et*... – Fort bien, merci, j'en viens. – Patrie
D'Anglais en vrai, mal peints sur fond bleu-perruquier!
Dans l'indigo l'artiste en tous genres oublie
Ce *Ne-m'oubliez-pas* d'outremer: le douanier.

– Ô Corinne!... ils sont là déclamant sur ma malle...
Lasciate speranza, mes cigares dedans!
– Ô Mignon!... ils ont tout éclos mon linge sale
Pour le passer au bleu de l'éternel printemps!

Ils demandent *la main*... et moi je la leur serre!
Le portrait de ma Belle, avec *morbidezza*
Passe de mains en mains: l'inspecteur sanitaire
L'ausculte, et me sourit... trouvant *que c'est bien ça!*

Je venais pour chanter leur illustre guenille,
Et leur chantage a fait de moi-même un haillon!
Effeuillant mes faux-cols, l'un d'eux m'offre sa fille...
Effeuillant le faux-col de mon illusion!

– Naples! panier percé des Seigneurs *Lazzarones*
      Riches d'un doux ventre au soleil!
Polichinelles-Dieux, Rois pouilleux sur leurs trônes,
Clyso-pompant l'azur qui bâille leur sommeil!...

Ô Grands en rang d'oignons! Plantes de pieds en lignes!
Vous dont la parure est un sac, un aviron!
Fils réchauffés du vieux Phœbus! Et toujours dignes
Des chansons de Musset, du mépris de Byron!...

Veder Napoli poi mori

To see *Naples and*... – Very well, thanks. I'm back. – Land
Of the English, poorly painted in deep-blue master-wigger!
In that indigo any artist would forget, out of hand,
The ultra-marine *forget-me-not*, this customs-figure.

– O Corinna!... They're inveighing on my trunk...
Abandon hope all my cigars that lurk in crime!
My dirty linen – O Mignon!... they waft in public, dunk
It in the blue of this eternal vernal time!

They ask a *hand* so I shake theirs. Scot-free,
They pass the portrait of my girl in *morbidezza* round
From hand to hand: the health-inspector smiles at me,
Sounding her chest and says that *all round it was sound*.

And I was coming to extol their illustrious gear!
Their crooked extra toll has brought me down to rags.
Plucking my loose collars out, one offers his daughter – dear...
Plucking my illusion's loose collars from my bags!

– Naples: prodigal with Signior Lazzaroni,
         Rich with a soft belly in the sun's caress;
Lousy kings enthroned; Punch-gods force-fed with only
The azure that yawns on them the gift of drowsiness!...

The nobs in wrap scallion rows! sprout lines of soles of feet!
O you whose finery is just a sack, an oar!
Offspring warmed up by Phoebus' fustian heat,
Worthy of Musset's songs, of Byron's scornful roar!...

– Chœurs de *Mazanielli*, Torses de mandolines!
Vous dont le métier est d'être toujours dorés
De rayons et d'amour… et d'ouvrir les narines,
Poètes de plein air! Ô frères adorés!

Dolce Farniente…! – Non! c'est mon sac!… il nage
Parmi ces asticots, comme un chien crevé;
Et ma malle est hantée aussi… comme un fromage!
Inerte, ô Galilée! et… *e pur si muove…*

– Ne ruolze plus ça, toi, grand Astre stupide!
Tas de pâles voyous grouillant à se nourrir;
Ce n'est plus le lézard, c'est la sangsue à vide…
– Dernier *lazzarone* à moi la bon Dormir!

Napoli. – Dogana del porto.

– Torsos of mandolins, *Mesoniello's* choirs
Whose job's to be forever gilded by the sun
And love ... to flair your nostrils wide, the air inspires
You poets of the open! Adored brothers everyone!

Dolce Farniente ...! – Never! that's my bag! ... drifting
Among the maggots like a putrefying cur:
My trunk is haunted, too, just like ... a cheese, unshifting!
Inert, Galileo! and ... *e pur si muove* – astir! ...

– Don't ruolz them anymore, you stupid great Star!
These pallid yobs that swarm to feed, heap on heap.
They're not your basking lizards; starving leech they are ...
– The latest *lazzarone* me, I'm after the good Sleep!

Napoli. – Dogana del porto.

Vésuves et Cie

Pompeïa-station – Vésuve, est-ce encor toi?
Toi qui fis mon bonheur, tout petit, en Bretagne,
– Du bon temps où la foi transportait la montagne –
Sur un bel abat-jour, chez une tante à moi:

Tu te détachais noir, sur un fond transparent,
Et la lampe grillait les feux de ton cratère.
C'était le confesseur, dit-on, de ma grand'mère
Qui t'avait rapporté de Rome tout flambant…

Plus grand, je te revis à l'Opéra-Comique.
– Rôle jadis créé par toi: *Le Dernier Jour*
De Pompeï. – Ton feu s'en allait en musique,
On te soufflait ton rôle, et… tu ne fis qu'un four.

– Nous nous sommes revus: devant-de-cheminée,
À Marseille, en congé, sans musique, et sans feu:
Bleu sur fond rose, avec ta Méditerranée
Te renvoyant pendu, rose sur un champ bleu.

– Souvent tu vins à moi la première, ô Montagne!
Je te rends ta visite, exprès, à la campagne.
Le Vrai vésuve est toi, puisqu'on m'a *fait* cent francs!

. . . .

Mais les autres petits étaient plus ressemblants.

Pompeï, aprile.

Flukes · 237

Vesuviuses & Co.

Pompeii stop – Vesuvius! That really you? It can't
Be you who made me happy in Brittany as a child?
– In the good old times when faith moved mountains, piled –
On a lovely lamp-shade at the house of an aunt:

On a transparent background you rose up black
And the lamp set off the fires in your crater.
My grandmother's confessor, so they told me later,
Returning from Rome brought you red-hot back…

Older, I saw you again at the Comic-Op.
– A role created first by you: *The Last
Days of Pompeii*. – To music faded your fiery blast.
You needed prompting… ended a half-baked flop.

– We met again: you were on a fire-screen,
Me on holiday, Marseilles, no fire, no racket, sound,
Blue on deep rose, in your Mediterranean seen
Reflected upside-down, rose on blue background.

– Often you've visited me first, O Mountain Brow!
So I return your visit, in the country now;
You're the Very vesuvius – I've been had for two
Quid!

. . . .

But the little ones looked more like you.

Pompeï, aprile.

Soneto a Napoli

ALL'SOLE, ALL'LUNA
ALL'SABATO, ALL'CANONICO
E TUTTI QUANTI

CON PULCINELLA

Il n'est pas de Samedi
Qui n'ait soleil à midi;
Femme ou fille soleillant,
Q ui n'ait midi sans amant!...

Lune, Bouc, Curé cafard
Qui n'ait tricorne cornard!
– Corne au front et corne au seuil
Préserve du mauvais œil. –

... *L'Ombilic du jour* filant
Son macaroni brûlant,
Avec la tarentela:

Lucia, Maz'Aniello,
Santa-Pia, Diavolo,
– CON PULCINELLA. –

Mergelina – Venerdi, aprile 15.

Soneto a Napoli

ALL'SOLE, ALL'LUNA
ALL'SABATO, ALL'CANONICO
E TUTTI QUANTI

CON PULCINELLA

No Saturday, not one
Without noonday sun;
No girl sunning away
Without beau at mid-day!...

No man, goat, canting priest
Not horny, times three at least:
– Horn on head, horn over door
Wards off the evil eye for sure. –

... *The day's navel* churning,
Its macaroni burning,
With the tarantella:

Lucia, Maz'Aniello,
Santa-Pia, Diavolo,
– CON PULCINELLA. –

Mergelina – Venerdì, aprile 15.

À l'Etna

Sicelides Musæ, paulo majora canamus.

VIRGILE.

Etna – j'ai monté le Vésuve...
Le Vésuve a beaucoup baissé:
J'étais plus chaud que son effluve,
Plus que sa crête hérissé...

– Toi que l'on compare à la femme...
– Pourquoi? – Pour ton âge? ou ton âme
De caillou cuit?... – Ça fait rêver...
– Et tu t'en fais rire à crever! –

– Tu ris jaune et tousses: sans doute,
Crachant un vieil amour malsain;
La lave coule sous la croûte
De ton vieux cancer au sein.

– Couchons ensemble, Camarade!
Là – mon flanc sur ton flanc malade:
Nous sommes frères, par Vénus,
Volcan!...
       Un peu moins... un peu plus...

Palerme. – Août.

To Etna

Sicelides Musae, paulo majora canamus.
VERGIL.

Etna – I've climbed Vesuvius' height…
Vesuvius was a bit of a let-down:
Hotter than its effluvium, a sight
Me, bristlier than its crater-crown…

– You they compare to womankind…
– Why? – For your age? or soul calcined
Of baked flint?… – Makes you wonder a bit…
– You're a butt for laughter fit to split! –

– You force a wry laugh, cough: you must
Be retching a sick old flame off the chest;
The lava flows beneath the crust
Of your old cancer of the breast.

– Partner, let's sleep together! There –
My side to your sickly side, a pair:
By Venus, we are brothers. Yes,
Vulcanists!…
                    Or more… or less.

Palermo. – August.

Le Fils de Lamartine et de Graziella

*C'est ainsi que j'expiai par ces larmes écrites la
dureté et l'ingratitude de mon cœur de dix-huit ans.
Je ne puis jamais relire ces vers sans adorer cette
fraîche image que rouleront éternellement pour moi
les vagues transparentes et plaintives du golfe de
Naples… et sans me haïr moi-même; mais les âmes
pardonnent là-haut. La sienne m'a pardonné.
Pardonnez-moi aussi, vous!!! J'ai pleuré.*

LAMARTINE, *Graziella.*

(1 fr. 25 c. le vol.)

À l'île de Procide, où la mer de Sorrente
Scande un flot hexamètre à la fleur d'oranger,
Un Naturel se fait une petite rente
      En *Graziellant* l'Étranger…

L'Étrangère surtout, confite en Lamartine,
Qui paye pour fluer, vers à vers, sur les lieux…
– Du *Cygne-de-Saint-Point* l'Homme a si bien la mine,
Qu'on croirait qu'il va rendre un vers… harmonieux.

C'est un peintre inspiré qui lui trouva sa balle,
Sa balle de profil: – Oh mais! dit-il, voilà!
Je te baptise, au nom de la couleur locale:
– LE FILS DE LAMARTINE ET DE GRAZIELLA! –

Vrai portrait du portrait du Rafaël fort triste,*…
Fort triste, pressentant qu'il serait décollé
De sa toile, pour vivre en la peau du *Harpiste*
Ainsi que de son fils, rafaël raffalé.

------

* Lamartine avoue quelque part qu'un seul portrait lui ressemblait alors:
celui de Raphael peint par lui-même.

The Son of Lamartine and Graziella

*Thus it is that I expiated with these written tears
the hardness and ingratitude of my heart at the age
of eighteen years. I am unable to re-read these lines
without adoring the fresh image that the transpar-
ent and plaintive waves of the Bay of Naples will
roll eternally before me nor without hating myself;
but the spirits above forgive. Her spirit has forgiven
me. Forgive me also, you!!! I have wept.*

LAMARTINE, *Graziella.*

(per cop.: 1 fr. 25 c.)

On the island of Procida where the sea of Sorrento
Scans a hexameter tide scented with orange-flower,
A Natural Child raises an income, a cash memento,
    *Graziell*ing the Tourist of his allowance ...

It's most often a Woman, steeped in Lamartine,
Who pays to gush on, line by line, over each place ...
– So closely has the Chap the *Bard of St Point*'s mien
You'd think he's about to spout a line ... of harmonious grace.

His mug was found out for him by a painter truly inspired:
His mug in profile: 'But my!' he said, 'the spit-image bean!
I baptize thee – in the name of local colour, sired –
– THE SON OF GRAZIELLA AND HER LAMARTINE! –

True portrait of the portrait of Rafael,* most sad ...
Most sad, presaging that he might become detached,
From his canvas chopped, to live in the skin of the Harpist clad,
As well as in his son's – a rafael, wreck-raffle unmatched.

---

* Lamartine asserts somewhere that only one portrait truly resembles
him: a self-portrait of Raphael.

– *Raphaël-Lamartine et fils!* – Ô Fornarine-
Graziella! Vos noms font de petits profits;
L'écho dit pour deux sous: *Le Fils de Lamartine!*
Si Lamartine eût pu jamais avoir un fils!

– Et toi, Graziella… Toi, Lesbienne Vierge!
Nom d'amour, que, sopran' il a tant déchanté!…
Nom de joie!… et qu'il a pleuré – Jaune cierge –
Tu n'étais vierge que de sa virginité!

– Dis: moins éoliens étaient, ô Grazielle,
Tes Mâles d'Ischia?… que ce pieux Jocelyn
Qui tenait, à côté, la lyre et la chandelle!…
Et, de loin, t'enterrait en chants de sacristain…

Ces souvenirs sont loin… – Dors, va! Dors sous les pierres
        Que voit, n'importe où, l'étranger,
Où fait paître ton Fils des familles entières
– Citron prématuré de ta Fleur d'Oranger –

Dors – l'Oranger fleurit encor… encor se fane;
Et la rosée et le soleil ont eu ses fleurs…
Le Poète-apothicaire en a fait sa tisane:
        Remède à vers! remède à pleurs!

– Dors – L'Oranger fleurit encor… et la mémoire
Des jeunes d'autrefois dont l'ombre est encor là,
Qui ne t'ont pas pêchée au fond d'une écritoire…
Et n'en pêchaient que mieux! – dis, ô *picciola!*

– Mère de l'Antechrist de Lamartine-Père,
Aurore qui mourus sous un coup d'éteignoir,
Ton Orphelin, posthume et de père et de mère,
Allait – quand tu naquis – déjà comme un vieux Soir.

– *Raphael-Lamartine and Son!* – O Fornarine-
Graziella! Your names are taken for petty profits. Done!
The echo answers, for tenpence: *The Son of Lamartine!*
As if Lamartine could ever have managed to have a son!

– As for you, Graziella... You, Lesbian Virgin! your handle,
Love-name, that he, *false*tto, sang, in *desk-cant* so high!...
And then your pet-name... he bewept. – Yellow candle –
It's only his old-maidenhead that you were virgin by!

– Tell me: were they less aeolian, the Ischaian Men?...
Than that pi-jawed Jocelyn who kept so ready to hand
The lyre and candle!... and, from a distance then,
To the chanting of a sexton, buried you in this land?...

Such memories are distant... – Sleep, under the stones, sleep!
        Everywhere the tourist looks they're strewn
Where your Son sets grazing whole families like sheep.
– Lemon, gathered from your Orange blossom too soon –

Sleep – the Orange blossoms still... and withers, too.
And the dew and the sun have taken its flowers for years...
Now the Quack Poet has made his linctus of its brew:
        Vermifuge, versifugal, drench for tears!

– Sleep – The Orange blossoms, is still orangesque...
And memories rise in those once young whose shadows still are;
They haven't fished you up from the bottom of a desk...
And have fished the better of it! – *Picciola* – and by far.

– Mother of the Antichrist of Father Lamartine,
Dawn who underneath the candle-snuffer died,
Your Waif, posthumous of mother and father, had been
Turning – when you were born – into an ancient Eventide. –

Graziella! – Conception trois fois immaculée…
D'un platonique amour, Messie et Souvenir,
Ce Fils avait vingt ans quand, Mère inoculée,
Tu mourus à seize ans!… C'est bien tôt pour nourrir!

– Pour toi: c'est ta seule œuvre mâle, ô Lamartine,
Saint-Joseph de la Muse, avec elle couché,
Et l'aidant à vêler… par la grâce divine:
Ton fils avant la lettre est conçu sans péché!…

– Lui se souvient très peu de ces scènes passées…
Mais il *laisse le vent et le flot murmurer,*
Et l'Étranger, plongeant dans ses tristes pensées…
          En tirer un franc – pour pleurer!

Et, tout bas, il vous dit, de murmure en murmures:
Que sa fille ressemble à l'Autre… et qu'elle est là,
Qu'on peut pleurer, à l'heure, avec des rimes pures,
Et… – *pour cent sous, Signor* – nommer Graziella!

Isola di Capri. – Gennaio.

Graziella! – Of thrice immaculate Conception, Bride...
Messiah and Keepsake of a platonic love affair,
This Son was twenty when, inoculated Mother, you died
At sixteen!... That's a bit young to be suckling an heir!

– For you: he's your one and only masculine work, Lamartine,
St Joseph of the Muse, you slept with her and in
Her calving helped... by grace divine: your son has been,
Conceived in deed before the letter, without sin!...

– HE remembers so little of that vanished scene...
But *leaves the wind and the tide to murmur deep*
And the Tourist, plunging in melancholy in between...
   To fork up a franc for a good weep!

And, quite low, in a murmur of murmurs, he says to you:
His daughter resembles THE GIRL ... that she's there on the
  shore;
That one could weep right now, and in pure rhyme, too,
And... – call her Graziella – *Signor, for a hundred sous more!*

     Isola di Capri. – Gennaio.

Libertà*

À LA CELLULE IV BIS
(PRISON ROYALE DE GÊNES)

> *Lasciate ogni…*
>
> DANTE.

Ô belle hospitalière
Qui ne me connais pas,
Vierge publique et fière
Qui m'as ouvert les bras!…
Rompant ma longue chaîne,
L'eunuque m'a jeté
Sur ton sein royal, Reine!…
– Vanité, vanité! –

Comme la Vénus nue,
D'un bain de lait de chaux
Tu sors, blanche Inconnue,
Fille des noirs cachots
Où l'on pleure, d'usage…
– Moi: jamais n'ai chanté
Que pour toi, dans ta cage,
Cage de la gaîté!

La misère parée
Est dans le grand égout;
Dépouillons la livrée
Et la chemise et tout!
Que tout mon baiser couvre
Ta franche nudité…
Vraie ou fausse, se rouvre
Une virginité!

––––––––

* Libertà. Ce mot se lit au fronton de la prison de Gênes (?)

Libertà*

TO CELL IV/A
(ROYAL PRISON OF GÊNES)

Lasciate ogni ...

DANTE.

Oh, fine hospitaller,
You don't know me from Adam,
Street virgin – haughtier –
But you enfold me, madam! ...
My long chain broken clean,
Your eunuch's bundled me
On your royal breast, O Queen! ...
– Vanity, O vanity! –

Like Venus naked you start
From a bath of white lime,
You step, white stranger, tart
Of the oubliettes of crime
Where grizzles the usual mug! ...
– But me? Not sung, me, dumb
Except for you, your jug,
Your nook so mettlesome!

True well-decked misery
Is in the open gutter;
Let's peel off livery,
The shirt and all and utter!
So all my kiss may cover
Your frankest nudity ...
Re-open, true or bluffer,
A virginity!

---

* Liberty. This word can be read on the fronton of Genoa Prison (?)

– Plus ce ciel louche et rose
Ni ce soleil d'enfer!…
– Ta paupière mi-close,
Tes cils, barreaux de fer!
Ta ceinture-dorée,
De fer! – Fidélité –
Et ta couche encastrée
Tombeau de volupté!

À nos cœurs plus d'alarmes:
Libres et bien à nous!…
Sens planer les gendarmes,
Pigeons du rendez-vous;
Et Cupidon-Cerbère
À qui la sûreté
De nos amours est chère…
Quatre murs! – Liberté!

Ho! l'Espérance folle
– Ce crampon – est au clou.
L'existence qui colle
Est collée à l'écrou.
Le souvenir qui hante
À l'huys est resté;
L'huys n'a pas de fente…
– Oh le carcan ôté! –

Laissons venir la Muse,
Elle osera chanter;
Et, si le jeu t'amuse,
Je veux te la prêter…
Ton petit lit de sangle,
Pour nous a rajouté
Les *trois bouts du triangle*:
Triple amour! – Trinité!

– No shifty sky of rose,
No more this sun of hell's!...
– Your eye-lids half close,
Your lashes bars like a cell's!
Your belt of gilt iron
– Or rather chastity –
Your fitted bed, to lie on
The tomb of luxury!

No more shocks to our heart:
Well with ourselves, we two!...
Sense gendarmes hover, dart,
Gulls to the rendezvous;
And Cupid-Cerberus
Whose watch on the surety
Of our loves is scrupulous...
Four walls! – and Liberty!

Huh! that stupid Hope,
– Leech drag – is under screws;
Existence that sticks, the dope,
Is stuck in clink, his dues.
Inside closed doors awaits
The haunting of memory;
But no chink in the gates...
– Take off the pillory! –

Let's have the Muse come, too.
She has the nerve to sing.
If her game amuses you
I'll lend you her for a fling...
That folding bed of yours
Has made us up to *three*
Points of the triangle: the score's
A threesome love! – Trinity!

Plus d'huissiers aux mains sales!
Ni mains de chers amis!
Ni menottes banales!...
– Mon nom est *Quatre-Bis*. –
Hors la terrestre croûte,
Désert mal habité,
Loin des mortels je goûte
Un peu d'éternité.

– Prison, sûre conquête
Où le poète est roi!
Et boudoir plus qu'honnête
Où le sage est chez soi,
Cruche, au moins ingénue,
Puits de la vérité!
Vide, quand on l'a bue...
– Vase de pureté! –

– Seule est ta solitude,
Et béats tes ennuis
Sans pose et sans étude...
Plus de jours, plus de nuits!
C'est tout le temps dimanche,
Et le far-niente
Dort pour moi sur la planche
De l'idéalité...

... Jusqu'au jour de misère
Où, condamné, je sors
Seul, ramer ma galère...
Là, n'importe où,... dehors,
Laissant emprisonnée
À perpétuité
Cette fleur cloisonnée,
Qui fut ma liberté...

No bailiffs with grubby grasp!
Nor dear friends' hands, no way!
No common hand cuffs clasp!...
– My name is *4 stroke A*. –
From earth's crust displaced,
A desert people-free,
Away from mortals, I taste
A bit of eternity.

– Prison, certain conquest
Where the poet is crowned;
Bedroom more than honest
Where the wise are homebound.
Jug to the lesser twerp,
Well of veracity!
Empty once you slurp...
– Jerry-mire of purity! –

– Lone is your solitude,
Your tediums a blessing,
Unposed, unstudied mood...
No days or nights progressing!
The only day's the Lord's
And far-niente for me
Is sleeping on the boards
Of ideality...

... Till that day, wretched, blue,
When, once condemned, I'm sent
To paddle my own canoe...
Alone wherever I'm bent!
And leave in prison's bower
In perpetuity,
That cloisonné flower
Which was my liberty...

– Va: reprends, froide et dure,
Pour le captif oison,
Ton masque, ta figure
De porte de prison…
Que d'autres, basse race
Dont le dos est voûté,
Pour eux te trouvent basse,
Altière déité!

Cellule 4 *bis.* – *Genova-la-Superba.*

– Go on: put on, once more,
Stern, cold, your mask, your look
For fronting the prison-door
For the noodlum brought to book…
So others, that low race
Whose backs are bent, may see
You low down in their place,
You high and mighty deity!

Cell *IV/a. – Genova-la-Superba.*

Hidalgo!

Ils sont fiers ceux-là!... comme poux sur la gale!
C'est à la don-juan qu'ils vous *font* votre malle.
Ils ne sentent pas bon, mais ils fleurent le preux:
Valeureux vauriens, crétins chevalereux!
Prenant sans demander – toujours suant la race, –
Et demandant un sol, – mais toujours pleins de grâce...

Là, j'ai fait le croquis d'un mendiant à cheval:
– Le Cid... un cid par un *été* de carnaval:

– Je cheminais – à pied – traînant une compagne;
Le soleil craquelait la route en blanc-d'Espagne;
Et *le cid* fut sur nous en un temps de galop...
Là, me pressant entre le mur et le garrot:
– Ah! seigneur *Cavalier*, d'honneur! sur ma parole!
Je mendie à genoux: un oignon... une obole?... –
(Et son cheval paissait mon col.) – Pauvre animal,
Il vous aime déjà! Ne prenez pas à mal...
– Au large! – Oh! mais: au moins votre bout de cigare?...
La Vierge vous le rende. – Allons: au large! ou: gare!...
(Son pied nu prenait ma poche en étrier.)
– Pitié pour un infirme, ô seigneur-cavalier...
– Tiens donc un sou... – Señor, que jamais je n'oublie
Votre Grâce! Pardon, je vous ai retardé...
Señora: Merci, toi! pour être si jolie...
Ma Jolie, et: Merci pour m'avoir regardé!

(Cosas de España.)

Hidalgo!

Haughty they are!... like fleas upon a regular pest!
And like don juans they *pack* the case for you west.
They don't smell good but have the air of gallant knights:
Derring-do ne'er-do-wells, cretinous chivalry-ites.
Take without asking – always with a whiff of breeding, –
Begging a penny, – but always with such graceful wheedling...

See, I've sketched the beggar on horseback, what a bummer:
– *El Cid* – Lord Sid out of a carnival in summer.

– I'd strolled off – on foot – a girl friend towed.
The sun had cracked, like whiting, all the road.
And at the gallop came *Lord Sid* upon us both...
Squashed me between wall and withers. 'By my troth,
Honoured, signior *Cavalier*. Upon my knee,
I beg: a turnip... penny, two or three?'... –
(His horse was grazing my neck by now.) – 'Poor brute,
He likes you already. Don't take offence.'... – 'Scoot!'
'Oh but: at least the butt of your cigarette...
The Virgin'll repay you.' – 'Vanish. Sheer off or I'll get...'
(He picked my pocket – stirrup for his barefaced foot.)
'Pity an invalid, sir knight!'... so touchingly put!
– 'Well, here's a penny...' – 'Señor, may I never forget
Your Grace! For causing this delay my apology...
And thanks to you, señora, for being so pretty... Well met,
My Beauty, and: Thank you once again for seeing me!'

(Cosas de España.)

Paria

Qu'ils se payent des républiques,
Hommes libres! – carcan au cou –
Qu'ils peuplent leurs nids domestiques!…
– Moi je suis le maigre coucou.

– Moi, – cœur eunuque, dératé
De ce qui mouille et ce qui vibre…
Que me chante leur Liberté,
À moi? toujours seul. Toujours libre.

– Ma Patrie… elle est par le monde;
Et, puisque la planète est ronde,
Je ne crains pas d'en voir le bout…
Ma patrie est où je la plante:
Terre ou mer, elle est sous la plante
De mes pieds – quand je suis debout.

– Quand je suis couché: ma patrie
C'est la couche seule et meurtrie
Où je vais forcer dans mes bras
Ma moitié, comme moi sans âme;
Et ma moitié: c'est une femme…
Une femme que je n'ai pas.

– L'idéal à moi: c'est un songe
Creux; mon horizon – l'imprévu –
Et le mal du pays me ronge…
Du pays que je n'ai pas vu.

Que les moutons suivent leur route,
De Carcassonne à Tombouctou…
– Moi, ma route me suit. Sans doute
Elle me suivra n'importe où.

Pariah

Their republics? They can keep 'em,
Free men! – Their necks stuck in a yoke! –
And their snug nests, they can people'm!...
– I'm the scrawny cuckoo, bloke

With the eunuch heart – that's me. –
Nothing to cast, nor to pulsate...
What's it to me, their Liberty?
Always alone. Always my free state.

– My Country's anywhere... on the ground
And, since the planet is quite round,
Seeing the edge gives me no fright...
My country's where on land or sea
I stand her up – and solely she
Beneath my sole – while I'm upright.

– When I am lying down: my land's
My bruised lone bed in which my hands
Will take my other half, like me
Without a soul; my other half's:
A woman... and the last laugh's
That I haven't one, not she.

– My ideal is an empty dream;
My horizon – unforeseen –
Homesickness eats me to extreme...
For a land where I have never been.

Let the sheep follow their way about
From Carcassonne to Timbuctoo...
My way follows – me. No doubt
It'll go whatever place I do.

Mon pavillon sur moi frissonne,
Il a le ciel pour couronne:
C'est la brise dans mes cheveux…
Et, dans n'importe quelle langue;
Je puis subir une harangue;
Je puis me taire si je veux.

Ma pensée est un souffle aride:
C'est l'air. L'air est à moi partout.
Et ma parole est l'écho vide
Qui ne dit rien – et c'est tout.

Mon passé: c'est ce que j'oublie.
La seule chose qui me lie
C'est ma main dans mon autre main.
Mon souvenir – Rien – C'est ma trace.
Mon présent, c'est tout ce qui passe…
Mon avenir – Demain… demain…

Je ne connais pas mon semblable;
Moi, je suis ce que je me fais.
– *Le Moi humain est haïssable* …
– Je ne m'aime ni ne me hais.

– Allons! la vie est une fille
Qui m'a pris à son bon plaisir…
Le mien, c'est: la mettre en guenille,
La prostituer sans désir.

– Des dieux?… – Par hasard j'ai pu naître;
Peut-être en est-il – par hasard…
Ceux-là, s'ils veulent me connaître,
Me trouveront bien quelque part.

My standard shudders up and down
Above me, with the sky for crown:
It is the breeze that's in my hair...
In any language, any slang,
I can suffer a harangue;
I'm silent if I want, and where.

My thought is just an arid puff:
It's air. Belongs to me, the air.
My word's the echo empty enough.
It says nothing – it's all that's there.

My past: it's everything I forget.
The only thing that holds me yet,
One hand in the other. Memory?
– Nothing. – It's just the way I've gone.
My present? All that passes on...
– Tomorrow and... tomorrow, the future for me...

I've never met an identical;
I make myself; I self create.
– *The human Self's detestable*...
– Myself I neither love nor hate.

– So what! Life is a girl that took
Me for her own good pleasure... mine's:
To put her in rags, and work her nook
Without desire, a pimp's designs.

– Gods?... – I was born by some fluke;
By chance – perhaps there are some then...
So if they want to know this gook
They'll find me somewhere some when.

– Où que je meure: ma patrie
S'ouvrira bien, sans qu'on l'en prie,
Assez grande pour mon linceul…
Un linceul encor: pour que faire?…
Puisque ma patrie est en terre
Mon os ira bien là tout seul…

– Wherever I die: my native spot
Will open, without being pressed a lot,
Wide enough for a shroud to wear...
Why even shroud: what good's that for?...
Since my country's earth, I'm sure
My bones will go without one there...

Paysage mauvais

Sables de vieux os – Le flot râle
Des glas: crevant bruit sur bruit…
– Palud pâle, où la lune avale
De gros vers, pour passer la nuit.

– Calme de peste, où la fièvre
Cuit… Le follet damné languit.
– Herbe puante où le lièvre
Est un sorcier poltron qui fuit…

– La Lavandière blanche étale
Des trépassés le linge sale,
Au *soleil des loups*… – Les crapauds,

Petits chantres mélancoliques
Empoisonnent de leurs coliques,
Les champignons, leurs escabeaux.

Marais de Guérande. – Avril.

Ill-Boding Landscape

Sands of old bones – And the tide coughs
Up death-knells, kicking buckets of noisy spray …
– Pallid salt marsh where the moon scoffs
Fat worms to while the night away.

– The calm of pestilence which brews
Fever … Damned jack-o'-lantern's dying.
– Stinking grass where the hare who's
The coward wizard is off and flying …

– The white Laundress now has spread
The dirty linen of the dead
Out in *the wolves' sun* … – And gloom's

Melancholy little bards, the toads,
Poison with colic their abodes,
The stools made by the mushrooms.

Guérande Marsh. – April.

Nature morte

Des coucous l'*Angelus* funèbre
A fait sursauter, à ténèbre,
Le coucou, pendule du vieux,

Et le chat-huant, sentinelle,
Dans sa carcasse à la chandelle
Qui flamboie à travers ses yeux.

– Écoute se taire la chouette…
– Un cri de bois: C'est *la brouette
De la Mort*, le long du chemin…

Et, d'un vol joyeux, la corneille
Fait le tour du toit où l'on veille
Le défunt qui s'en va demain.

Bretagne. – Avril.

Still Life

The cuckoos' mournful *Angelus* tolled
Has made the cuckoo in the old
Man's ticker jump at twilight,

And the owl, too, on sentry go
In his carcass's candle-glow
Beaming out its eye-light.

– Hark, the screech-owl ceases... – Squeal
From the wood: It is *Death's wheel
Barrow*, coming along the way ...

And the crow with joyful flight
Circles the roof where they watch all night
Around the corpse that leaves next day.

Brittany. – April.

·Un riche en Bretagne

O fortunatos nimium, sua si...
VIRGILE.

C'est le bon riche, c'est un vieux pauvre en Bretagne,
Oui, pouilleux de pavé sans eau pure et sans ciel!
– Lui, c'est un philosophe-errant dans la campagne;
Il aime son pain noir sec – pas beurré de fiel...
S'il n'en a pas: bonsoir. – Il connaît une crèche
Où la vache lui prête un peu de paille fraîche,
Il s'endort, rêvassant planche-à-pain au milieu,
Et s'éveille au matin en bayant au Bon-Dieu.
– *Panem nostrum*... – Sa faim a le goût d'espérance...
Un *Benedicite* s'exhale de sa panse;
Il sait bien que pour lui l'œil d'en haut est ouvert
Dans ce coin d'où tomba la manne du désert
Et le pain de son sac...
Il va de ferme en ferme.
Et jamais à son pas la porte ne se ferme,
– Car sa venue est bien. – Il entre à la maison
Pour allumer sa pipe en soufflant un tison...
Et s'assied. – Quand on a quelque chose, on lui donne;
Alors, il se secoue et rit, tousse et rognonne
Un *Pater* en hébreu. Puis, son bâton en main,
Il reprend sa tournée en disant: à demain.
Le gros chien de la cour en passant le caresse...
– Avec ça, peut-on pas se passer de maîtresse?...
Et, – qui sait, – dans les champs, un beau jour, la beauté
Peut s'amuser à faire aussi la charité...

– Lui, n'est pas pauvre: il est *Un Pauvre*, – et s'en contente.
C'est un petit rentier, moins l'ennui de la rente.
Seul, il se chante vêpre en berçant son ennui...

A Rich Man in Brittany

O fortunatos nimium, sua si...
VERGIL.

He's good and rich, a poor old wretch in Brittany,
Yes, this lousy tramp, without wash or sheet-anchor!
– An errant-philosopher he is, as free as can be.
He likes his bread black, dry – not spread thick with rancour...
If he has none: good night. – He knows where there's a shed
In which the cow will lend him fresh hay for a bed.
He sleeps recurrent dreams of breadboard doorsteps, nightly.
Wakes in the morning gaping at the Almighty.
– *Panem nostrum...* – His hunger tastes of Hope...
Stomach rumbles *Benedicite* like a pope.
And well he knows the Eye is open overhead,
From whose corner desert manna drops and bread
Into his sack...
                        From farm to farm he comes and goes
And not a door is ever slammed upon his nose.
– His coming's seen as a good thing. – He enters houses
To light his pipe, he blows a spill to flame, then douses...
And sits him down. – What can be spared is given him.
He shakes himself, he laughs, coughs, and growls a grim
Our Father in Hebrew. Then, stick in hand, he goes his way
Off on his rounds, just saying: till another day.
The massive yard dog rubs him as he passes through...
– With that, you could do without a mistress, couldn't you?...
And – who knows, – some beauty in the fields one day
May well amuse herself and part her alms his way...

– Him, he's not poor: he is a *Pauper*, – and content.
Small stockholder without tediums of percent.
Alone, sings vespers, nursing his boredoms to sleep...

– Travailler – Pour que faire?... On travaille pour lui.
Point ne doit déroger, il perdrait la pratique;
Il doit garder intact son vieux blason mystique.
– Noblesse oblige. – Il est saint: à chaque foyer
Sa niche est là, tout près du grillon familier.
Bon messager boiteux, il a plus d'une histoire
À faire froid au dos, quand la nuit est bien noire...
N'a-t-il pas vu, rôdeur, durant les clairs minuits
Dans la lande danser les *cornandons* maudits...

– Il est simple... peut-être. – Heureux ceux qui sont simples!...
À la lune, n'a-t-il jamais cueilli des simples?...
– Il est sorcier peut-être... et, sur le mauvais seuil,
Pourrait, en s'en allant, jeter le mauvais œil...
– Mais non: mieux vaut porter bonheur; dans les familles,
Proposer ou chercher des maris pour les filles.
Il est de noce alors, très humble desservant
De *la part du bon-dieu.* – Dieu doit être content:
Plein comme feu Noé, son Pauvre est ramassé
Le lendemain matin au revers d'un fossé.

Ah, s'il avait été senti du doux Virgile...
Il eût été traduit par monsieur Delille,
Comme un « *trop fortuné s'il connût son bonheur...* »

– Merci: ça le connaît, ce marmiteux seigneur!

Saint-Thégonnec.

– Work? – What for? –... People work for him, his keep.
He must preserve his mystic ancient crest from taint,
Unsmirched. – *Noblesse oblige*. – He is a saint:
He has his special niche beside each fire place
Next to the household cricket's chirring space.
Good halting messenger with more than a tale to tell
To chill the spine with ice when night is black as Hell...
Hasn't he had on clear midnights a good glimpse
Upon the moor-land of the dance of cursed *imps*...

– Simple too... perhaps. – And blessèd are the simple! Loon,
Hasn't he picked off simples by the light of the moon?...
– A sorcerer, perhaps... and over the wicked sill
Could, as he's leaving, cast the evil eye at will...
– But no: it's better bringing good luck in; a spouse
Suggest or find for daughters of the house.
Of weddings, then, he is the very lowly priest
Of the *Lord's piece of cake*. – God should be pleased: feast-
Drunk, like the late Noah, his Poor man (rich!)
Is pulled the morning after from the bottom of a ditch.

Ah, if he'd been imagined by sweet Vergil's skill...
He would have been translated by M. Delille
As 'too fortunate if he had known his happiness...'

– Thank you: tattered king of the road, he knew it! Oh yes.

St Thégonnec.

Saint Tupetu de Tu-pe-tu

C'est au pays de Léon. – Est une petite chapelle à saint Tupetu. (En breton: *D'un côté ou de l'autre.*)

Une fois l'an, les croyants – fatalistes chrétiens – s'y rendent en pèlerinage, afin d'obtenir, par l'entremise du Saint, le dénoûment fatal de toute affaire nouée: la délivrance d'un malade tenace ou d'une vache pleine; ou, tout au moins, quelque signe de l'avenir: tel que c'est écrit là-haut. – *Puisque cela doit être, autant que cela soit de suite … d'un côté ou de l'autre.* – *Tu-pe-tu.*

L'oracle fonctionne pendant la grand'messe: l'officiant fait faire, pour chacun, un tour à la *Roulette-de-chance*, grand cercle en bois fixé à la voûte et manœuvré par une longue corde que Tupetu tient lui-même dans sa main de granit. La roue, garnie de clochettes, tourne en carillonnant; son point d'arrêt présage l'arrêt du destin: – *D'un côté ou de l'autre.*

Et chacun s'en va comme il est venu, quitte à revenir l'an prochain … *Tu-pe-tu* finit fatalement par avoir son effet.

Il est, dans la vieille Armorique,
Un saint – des saints le plus pointu –
Pointu comme un clocher gothique
Et comme son nom: TUPETU.

Son petit clocheton de pierre
Semble prêt à changer de bout…
Il lui faut, pour tenir debout,
Beaucoup de foi… beaucoup de lierre…

Et, dans sa chapelle ouverte, entre
– Tête ou pieds – tout franc Breton
Pour lui tâter l'œuf dans le ventre,
L'œuf du destin: C'est oui? – c'est non?

Saint Ivor Orr of Eitherore

It is in the countryside of Léon. – A little chapel to St Tupetu
(In the Breton tongue: *On one side or the other.*)

Once a year, the believers – fatalistic Christians – go there on a
pilgrimage, in order to learn through the intervention of the Saint,
the destined outcome of any knotty problem: the release from a
persistent illness, of a full cow; or at the least some forecast for the
future: such as is written above. – *Since it must be in as much as that
it may follow ... on one hand or the other. – Tu-pe-tu.*

The oracle occurs during mass: the officiating priest for each
one provides a turn at the *Wheel of Chance* – a great wooden rim
fixed to the vault and worked by a long rope that St Tupetu him-
self holds in his granite hand. The wheel, hung with little bells,
turns and rings; its stopping point presages that of fate: – *on one
side or the other.*

And each leaves as he has come, goes to return next year ... *Tu-
pe-tu* ends in destined fashion by taking its effect.

In old Armorica's a saint
– Most pointed of saints, none more –
Pointed as gothic spires, and quaint
Just like his name of IVOR ORR.

His little bell-tower of stone
Is just about to change its end ...
To stay upright and to perpend
It needs much faith ... and ivy grown ...

And to his open chapel legs
Every true Breton – head first or toe –
To taste before they're laid the eggs,
The eggs of fate: It's yes? – It's no?

– Plus fort que sainte Cunégonde
Ou Cucugnan de Quilbignon…
Petit prophète au pauvre monde,
Saint de la veine ou du guignon,

Il tient sa *Roulette-de-chance*
Qu'il vous fait aller pour cinq sous;
Ça dit bien, mieux qu'une balance,
Si l'on est dessus ou dessous.

C'est la roulette sans pareille,
Et les grelots qui sont parmi
Vont, là-haut, chatouiller l'oreille
Du coquin de Sort endormi.

Sonnette de la Providence,
Et serinette du Destin;
Carillon faux, mais argentin;
Grelottière de l'Espérance…

Tu-pe-tu – D'un bord ou de l'autre!
Tu-pe-tu – Banco – Quitte-ou-tout!
Juge-de-paix sans patenôtre…
Tupetu, saint valet d'atout!

Tu-pe-tu – Pas de milieu!…
Tupetu, sorcier à musique,
Croupier du tourniquet mystique
Pour les macarons du Bon-Dieu!…

Médecin héroïque, il pousse
Le mourant à sauter le pas:
Soit dans la vie à la rescousse…
Soit, à pieds joints, en plein trépas:

– More potent than St Cunégonde
Or Cucugnan of Quilbignon still …
To the wretched world beyond,
Minor prophet of well or ill,

He holds his *Roulette Wheel* of chance;
For five sous he will make it spin;
It tells you better than scales adance
If you are down, or up to win.

Roulette without parallel or peer;
The jingles that are all around
Go up to rattle on the ear
Of the rogue Fate who's dozing sound.

It's Providence's doorbell rope.
Destiny's bird-organ, sorry singer;
Silver-toned but tuneless ringer;
Chatterer in the teeth of Hope …

Eitherore – From one side or other!
Eitherore. – Banco – Double or Quit!
J.P. without an Our Father … brother
Ivor Orr, saint knave of trumping it.

Eitherore – No middle ground! …
Ivor Orr, musical enchanter bod;
Croupier of the mystic merry-go-round
For lackeys of Almighty God! …

Heroic doctor who will make
The dying jump to a decision:
Into life and rallying to his shake …
Or, feet together, death's collision:

– *Tu-pe-tu!* cheval couronné!
– *Tu-pe-tu!* qu'on saute ou qu'on butte!
– *Tu-pe-tu!* vieillard obstiné!…
Au bout du fossé la culbute!

TUPETU, saint tout juste honnête,
Petit Janus chair et poisson!
Saint confesseur à double tête,
Saint confesseur à double fond!…

– Pile-ou-face de la vertu,
Ambigu patron des pucelles
Qui viennent t'offrir des chandelles…
Jésuite! tu dis: – *Tu-pe-tu!*…

– *Eitherore!* old broken-kneed hack!
– *Eitherore!* stumble or jump!
– *Eitherore!* pighead old jack!...
The joyride then the Cropper's dump!

IVOR ORR, saint straight and honest;
Titchy Janus, flesh and fish!
Saint confessor, two-faced connist;
Saint confessor, false-bottomed bish!...

– Heads or tails with virtue you play,
Ambiguous patron of virgins who
Come to offer their candles to you...
Jesuit! *Either or* – you say!...

La Rapsode foraine
et
le pardon de Sainte-Anne

La Palud, 27 Août, jour du Pardon.

Bénite est l'infertile plage
Où, comme la mer, tout est nud.
Sainte est la chapelle sauvage
De Sainte-Anne-de-la-Palud...

De la Bonne Femme Sainte Anne
Grand'tante du petit Jésus,
En bois pourri dans sa soutane
Riche... plus riche que Crésus!

Contre elle la petite Vierge,
Fuseau frêle, attend l'*Angelus*;
Au coin, Joseph tenant son cierge,
Niche, en saint qu'on ne fête plus...

.   .   .   .

C'est le *Pardon*. – Liesse et mystères –
Déjà l'herbe rase a des poux...
– *Sainte Anne, Onguent des belles-mères!*
Consolation des époux!...

Des paroisses environnantes:
De Plougastel et Loc-Tudy,
Ils viennent tous planter leurs tentes,
Trois nuits, trois jours – jusqu'au lundi.

Trois jours, trois nuits, la palud grogne,
Selon l'antique rituel,
– Chœur séraphique et chant d'ivrogne –
Le *CANTIQUE SPIRITUEL*.

The Wandering Minstrel
and
the Pardon of St Anne

La Palud, 27th August, day of the Pardon.

Blessèd are the barren sands
Where all, just like the sea, is bare.
Hallowed the crude chapel that stands
To Saint Anne of the Marshes, there...

The Good-Hearted woman, Saint Anne,
Great-Aunt of the little Jesus;
Wood rotten in cloth richer... than
All the riches of Croesus!

The little Virgin, frail spindly mite,
For the *Angelus* awaits;
Joseph, in a nook with his light,
Nestles, a saint none invocates...

. . . .

It's the *Pardon*. – Mysteries; celebrations! –
Already lice in the trampled sward...
– *Saint Anne: for husbands, consolations;*
For mothers-in-law, a Potion poured!...

From parishes all round they tramp:
From Loc-Tody and Plougastel,
All come – till Monday – set up camp:
Three nights and three days there they dwell.

The salt marsh groans three nights, three days,
According to the ancient rite,
– Seraphic choir and drunken lays –
The *SPIRITUAL CANTICLES* recite:

* * *

Mère taillée à coups de hache,
Tout cœur de chêne dur et bon;
Sous l'or de ta robe se cache
L'âme en pièce d'un franc-Breton!

*

— Vieille verte à face usée
Comme la pierre du torrent,
Par des larmes d'amour creusée,
Séchée avec des pleurs de sang...

*

— Toi dont la mamelle tarie
S'est refait, pour avoir porté
La Virginité de Marie,
Une mâle virginité!

*

— Servante-maîtresse altière,
Très-haute devant le Très-Haut;
Au pauvre monde, pas fière,
Dame pleine de comme-il-faut!

*

— Bâton des aveugles! Béquille
Des vieilles! Bras des nouveau-nés!
Mère de Madame ta fille!
Parente des abandonnés!

*

— Ô Fleur de la pucelle neuve!
Fruit de l'épouse au sein grossi!
Reposoir de la femme veuve...
Et du veuf Dame-de-merci!

★ [★] ★

Mother, carved with hatchet strokes,
All heart of oak and hard and good,
Your golden dress beneath it cloaks
A free and Breton soul in the wood!

★

– Green crone with weathered face,
A stone out of the torrent's force,
Channelled where tears of love leave trace,
Dried with tears of blood that course…

★

– You whose dry and milkless breast,
By bearing the Virginity
Of Mary, recovered and was blest
With a male chastity!

★

– Lofty mistress and servitor,
Most high before the Highmost;
Not haughty to all those who're poor,
Of all that's proper Lady, Host!

★

– Stick for the blind! Crutch, supporter,
To old women! Arms for the newborn!
Mother of madam your daughter!
Kith and kin to lost and forlorn!

★

– O Flower of the fresh young lass!
Fruit of the wife with nursing breast!
For widows, altar and the mass…
For widowers, Lady-of-Mercy blest!

★

– Arche de Joachim! Aïeule!
Médaille de cuivre effacé?
Gui sacré! Trèfle-quatre-feuille!
Mont d'Horeb! Souche de Jessé!

★

– Ô toi qui recouvrais la cendre,
Qui filais comme on fait chez nous,
Quand le soir venait à descendre,
Tenant l'Enfant sur tes genoux;

★

Toi qui fus là, seule, pour faire
Son maillot neuf à Bethléem,
Et là, pour coudre son suaire
Douloureux, à Jérusalem!…

★

Des croix profondes sont tes rides,
Tes cheveux sont blancs comme fils…
– Préserve des regards arides
Le berceau de nos petits-fils!

★

Fais venir et conserve en joie
Ceux à naître et ceux qui sont nés.
Et verse, sans que Dieu te voie,
L'eau de tes yeux sur les damnés!

★

Reprends dans leur chemise blanche
Les petits qui sont en langueur…
Rappelle à l'éternel Dimanche
Les vieux qui traînent en longueur.

*

– Forebear! Arc of Joachim!
Four-leafed clover, holy mistletoe!
Copper medal worn and dim!
Stem of Jesse! Mount Horeb! – O,

*

You who covered the cinders first,
Then spun as locally they spin,
The CHILD *upon your knees you nursed*
As dusk of day was drawing in;

*

You who were there alone to make
His swaddling bands in Bethlehem
And also there to sew for his sake
The sad shroud in Jerusalem!...

*

Your wrinkled lines are crosses deep.
Your hair is white as any thread...
– From all the barren glances keep
Safe our grandsons' cradle-bed!

*

Ease their arrival; joyful keep
Those born and those whose birth is due.
Pour on the damned the drops you weep
Without God seeing what you do!

*

In their white gowns once more enfold
The little ones who are so ill...
To endless Sunday call the old
Who linger interminably still.

*

– Dragon-gardien de la Vierge,
Garde la crèche sous ton œil.
Que, près de toi, Joseph-concierge
Garde la propreté du seuil!

*

Prends pitié de la fille-mère,
Du petit au bord du chemin...
Si quelqu'un leur jette la pierre,
Que la pierre se change en pain!

*

– Dame bonne en mer et sur terre,
Montre-nous le ciel et le port,
Dans la tempête ou dans la guerre...
Ô Fanal de la bonne mort!

*

Humble: à tes pieds n'as point d'étoile,
Humble... et brave pour protéger!
Dans la nue apparaît ton voile,
Pâle auréole du danger.

*

– Aux perdus dont la vie est grise,
(– Sauf respect – perdus de boisson)
Montre le clocher de l'église
Et le chemin de la maison.

*

Prête ta douce et chaste flamme
Aux chrétiens qui sont ici...
Ton remède de bonne femme
Pour les bêtes-à-corne aussi!

*

— The Virgin's Guardian-Dragon, keep
The crib beneath your watchful scan.
May doorman Joseph, near you, sweep
The threshold always spick and span!

*

To unmarried mothers show compassion,
To the waif beside the road unfed ...
If someone casts a stone, then fashion
That stone into a bit of bread!

*

— O Lady, kind by earth and water,
Show us Heaven and the harbour-side,
Whether in storm or wartime slaughter ...
O Beacon of a good death, guide!

*

Humble: no star beneath your tread;
Humble ... courageous to defend!
Amid the clouds your veil is spread,
Pale halo of dangers that portend.

*

— To those whose life is hazed, lost people,
(— Saving your reverence — lost through booze)
Reveal to them the church and steeple
And the best way home to choose.

*

Lend your flame, gentle and pure,
To the Christians of this part ...
Lend your wise woman's cure
To the horned dumb beasts in the cart!

*

Montre à nos femmes et servantes
L'ouvrage et la fécondité...
– Le bonjour aux âmes parentes
Qui sont bien dans l'éternité!

*

Nous mettrons un cordon de cire,
De cire-vierge jaune, autour
De ta chapelle; et ferons dire
Ta messe basse au point du jour.

*

– Préserve notre cheminée
Des sorts et du monde-malin...
À Pâques te sera donnée
Une quenouille avec du lin.

*

Si nos corps sont puants sur terre,
Ta grâce est un bain de santé;
Répands sur nous, au cimetière,
Ta bonne odeur-de-sainteté.

*

– À l'an prochain! – Voici ton cierge:
(C'est deux livres qu'il a coûté)
... Respects à Madame la Vierge,
Sans oublier la Trinité.

* * *

... Et les fidèles, en chemise,
– Sainte Anne, ayez pitié de nous! –
Font trois fois le tour de l'église
En se traînant sur leurs genoux;

*

Show to our servants and our women
Employment and fertility...
– Give a 'Good day' to souls of kin in
Their comfortable eternity!

*

We'll put a yellow candle ring
Of virgin wax – and all the way –
Around your shrine; make sure to sing
Your low mass at the break of day.

*

– Preserve our paths from the wicked world,
From spells. And every Eastertide
We'll offer you a distaff furled
Around with a bit of wool beside.

*

If our bodies are putrid on earth,
A healthy bath your grace will be;
Sprinkle us in the churchyard turf
With your essence of sanctity.

*

– Here's to next year! – Your candle, here:
(For that it cost two francs as fee)
... Respects to madam the Virgin, dear,
Not forgetting the Trinity.

* * *

... In just their smocks the Faithful lurch,
– *Saint Anne, have pity on us, please!* –
Three times they go around the church,
Dragging themselves on hands and knees;

Et boivent l'eau miraculeuse
Où les Job teigneux ont lavé
Leur nudité contagieuse...
– *Allez: la Foi vous a sauvé!* –

C'est là que tiennent leurs cénacles
Les pauvres, frères de Jésus.
– Ce n'est pas la cour des miracles,
Les trous sont vrais: *Vide latus!*

Sont-ils pas divins sur leurs claies,
Qu'auréole un nimbe vermeil,
Ces propriétaires de plaies,
Rubis vivants sous le soleil!...

En aboyant, un rachitique
Secoue un moignon désossé,
Coudoyant un épileptique
Qui travaille dans un fossé.

Là, ce tronc d'homme où croît l'ulcère,
Contre un tronc d'arbre où croît le gui;
Ici, c'est la fille et la mère
Dansant la danse de Saint-Guy.

Cet autre pare le cautère
De son petit enfant malsain:
– L'enfant se doit à son vieux père...
– Et le chancre est un gagne-pain!

Là, c'est l'idiot de naissance,
Un *visité par Gabriel*,
Dans l'extase de l'innocence...
– L'innocent est près du ciel! –

And drink of the miraculous waters
Where scurvy Jobs wash head to sole
Their naked contagions and disorders...
– *Go: thy Faith hath made thee whole!* –

Joined, for the last supper, in this plot,
The poor brothers of Jesus, packed.
– Miracle gathering of beggars, it's not.
Vide latus! The holes are fact.

Divine, aren't they, displayed in stocks,
Crowned with a red halo, everyone,
Proprietors of wounds and pox,
These living rubies in the sun!...

Barking, a man with rickets shakes
A boneless stump about him – which
Elbows an epileptic who quakes
With the convulsions in a ditch.

A man's trunk grows an ulcer there,
Beside a trunk where mistletoe grows;
Here, a mother and daughter share
St Vitus' dance in dancing throes.

Another tends the running sore
Of his sickly little son.
– That he owes his old father for...
– The tumour's the breadwinning one!

There is a born-simple one,
Poor *visited-by-Gabriel* sod,
In an ecstasy of simple fun...
– The simple-minded's next to God! –

– Tiens, passant, regarde: tout passe…
L'œil de l'idiot est resté,
Car il est en état-de-grâce…
– Et la Grâce est l'Éternité! –

Parmi les autres, après vêpre,
Qui sont d'eau bénite arrosés,
Un cadavre, vivant de lèpre,
Fleurit – souvenir des croisés…

Puis tous ceux que les Rois de France
Guérissaient d'un toucher de doigts…
– Mais la France n'a plus de rois,
Et leur dieu suspend sa clémence.

– Charité dans leurs écuelles!…
Nos aïeux ensemble ont porté
Ces fleurs de lis en écrouelles
Dont ces *choisis* ont hérité.

– *Miserere* pour les ripailles
Des *Ankokrignets* et *Kakous!*…
Ces moignons-là sont des tenailles,
Ces béquilles donnent des coups.

Risquez-vous donc là, gens ingambes,
Mais gare pour votre toison:
Gare aux bras crochus! gare aux jambes
En *kyriè-éleison!*

… Et détourne-toi, jeune fille,
Qui viens là voir, et prendre l'air…
Peut-être, sous l'autre guenille,
Percerait la guenille en chair…

– Here, traveller, turn your eyes.
All passes... The idiot's eye is stayed,
For in a state of grace he lies...
– And Grace is Eternity purveyed! –

After vespers, in the rest to be
Sprinkled with holy water here,
A corpse, with living leprosy,
Flowers – a crusading souvenir!...

Next come those who once were healed
By a hand's turn of the Kings of France...
– No more French kings to give the chance,
And their God's mercy is repealed.

– Place charity on their plate!...
Our ancestors combined bequeathed
The fleur-de-lys of scrofula, state
These *chosen ones* as heirs received.

– *Miserere* for the merrymaking
Of the *Ankokrignets* and *Kakous!*...
Those crutches offer blows and aching;
Those stumps are torture tongs and screws.

Then risk it, nimble people there;
Beware your fleece, to keep it on:
Ware crooked hands! of legs beware
In *kyrie eleison!*

... And you, young lady, taking the air
To come and watch the show, withdraw...
Perhaps beneath the clouts they wear
Clout of the flesh may poke out raw...

C'est qu'ils chassent là sur leurs terres!
Leurs peaux sont leurs blasons béants:
– Le droit-du-seigneur à leurs serres!…
Le droit du Seigneur de céans! –

Tas d'*ex-voto* de carne impure,
Charnier d'élus pour les cieux,
Chez le Seigneur ils sont chez eux!
– Ne sont-ils pas sa créature…

Ils grouillent dans le cimetière
On dirait les morts déroutés
N'ayant tiré de sous la pierre
Que des membres mal reboutés.

– Nous, taisons-nous!… Ils sont sacrés.
C'est la faute d'Adam punie,
Le doigt d'En-haut les a marqués:
– La Droite d'En-haut soit bénie!

Du grand troupeau, boucs émissaires
Chargés des forfaits d'ici-bas,
Sur eux Dieu purge ses colères!…
– Le pasteur de Sainte-Anne est gras. –

. . . .

Mais une note pantelante,
Écho grelottant dans le vent
Vient battre la rumeur bêlante
De ce purgatoire ambulant.

Une forme humaine qui beugle
Contre le *calvaire* se tient;
C'est comme une moitié d'aveugle:
Elle est borgne, et n'a pas de chien…

They're hunting in their own chase!
Their coats of arms, the gaping skin:
– Their claws have *droit-de-seigneur* grace!...
And their Lord's right of way's within! –

Heaped *offerings* of rotten meat,
Charnel house of Heaven's elect,
Home in the Lord's House, the select!
– Aren't these his creatures, his élite...

They swarm the churchyard. You'd assume
The dead, quite lost amid the stones,
Had only dragged out of the tomb
The limbs with badly mended bones.

– Us, let us shut up!... They're holy.
Sentenced for Adam's fault they lie.
The Lord most High has touched them solely:
– Bless the right hand of the Most High!

They're scapegoats of the great flock
Loaded with crimes from here below.
God wreaks on them his furious shock!...
– Saint Anne's shepherd is fat and slow. –

.   .   .   .

But then these gasping sounds begin,
An echo, quaking on the breeze,
Comes battering the bleating din
Of this walking purgatory of disease.

It bellows, some sort of humankind,
Leaning against the *calvary's* side,
Like half – the better half – of a blind
Man: one-eyed; no dog to guide...

C'est une rapsode foraine
Qui donne aux gens pour un liard
L'*Istoyre de la Magdalayne*,
Du Juif-Errant ou d'*Abaylar*.

Elle hâle comme une plainte,
Comme une plainte de la faim,
Et, longue comme un jour sans pain,
Lamentablement, sa complainte…

– Ça chante comme ça respire,
Triste oiseau sans plume et sans nid
Vaguant où son instinct l'attire:
Autour des Bon-Dieu de granit…

Ça peut parler aussi, sans doute.
Ça peut penser comme ça voit:
Toujours devant soi la grand'route…
– Et, quand ç'a deux sous… ça les boit.

– Femme: on dirait hélas – sa nippe
Lui pend, ficelée en jupon;
Sa dent noire serre une pipe
Éteinte… – Oh, la vie a du bon! –

Son nom… ça se nomme Misère.
Ça s'est trouvé né par hasard.
Ça sera trouvé mort par terre…
La même chose – quelque part.

– Si tu la rencontres, Poète,
Avec son vieux sac de soldat:
C'est notre sœur… donne – c'est fête –
Pour sa pipe, un peu de tabac!…

A wandering minstrel it is, then,
Who for a farthing chants for you
The Historie of Mary Magdalen
Or *Abelard* or *The Wandering Jew.*

It wails in dirge-like unrestraint;
It's like a dirge of hunger-pangs,
Long as a day without bread hangs,
In lamentation, its complaint.

– And as it breathes so does it sing,
Sad bird, without a nest, unfledged,
Wandering wherever instinct bring:
Around these good Gods granite-edged ...

It can speak, too, without a doubt;
And as it sees, so it can think:
Ahead, the highway stretches out
Always ... – And, penny-won ... a drink.

– A woman: alas, you'd say – old rags
Hang from her; petticoat tied with string.
From her black tooth a pipe sags,
Gone out ... – Oh, life has the odd good thing! –

Her name ... her name is Want. And birth
She found came by an ill-chance;
She will be found dead on the earth ...
Somewhere – in the same circumstance.

– Poet, if you pass her on the way
With her old pack of soldier-type,
It's our sister ... Give her – it's holiday –
A bit of baccy for her pipe! ...

Tu verras dans sa face creuse
Se creuser, comme dans du bois,
Un sourire; et sa main galeuse
Te faire un vrai signe de croix.

Cris d'aveugle

(Sur l'air bas-breton Ann hini goz.*)*

L'œil tué n'est pas mort
Un coin le fend encor
Encloué je suis sans cercueil
On m'a planté le clou dans l'œil
L'œil cloué n'est pas mort
Et le coin entre encor

Deus misericors
Deus misericors
Le marteau bat ma tête en bois
Le marteau qui ferra la croix
Deus misericors
Deus misericors

Les oiseaux croque-morts
Ont donc peur à mon corps
Mon Golgotha n'est pas fini
Lamma lamma sabacthani
Colombes de la Mort
Soiffez après mon corps

And you'll see trenching her trenched face
A smile as if in wood; see, too,
Her scabbed and callused fingers trace
The true sign of the cross for you.

Blind Man's Cries

(To the Low Breton tune of 'Ann hini goz'.)

The slaughtered eye's not dead
By a beam still riveted
Without a coffin I am nailed
My eye upon the nail impaled
The nailed eye is not dead
By a beam still riveted

Deus misericors my head
Deus misericors my head
The hammer beats my head of wood
The hammer that iron-shod the rood
Deus misericors my head
Deus misericors my head

Do deathmute birds feel dread
At my body overhead
Unfinished is my Calvary
Lamma lamma sabacthani
The Doves of Death thirst red
For my body overhead

Rouge comme un sabord
La plaie est sur le bord
Comme la gencive bavant
D'une vieille qui rit sans dent
La plaie est sur le bord
Rouge comme un sabord

Je vois des cercles d'or
Le soleil blanc me mord
J'ai deux trous percés par un fer
Rougi dans la forge d'enfer
Je vois un cercle d'or
Le feu d'en haut me mord

Dans la moelle se tord
Une larme qui sort
Je vois dedans le paradis
Miserere, De profundis
Dans mon crâne se tord
Du soufre en pleur qui sort

Bienheureux le bon mort
Le mort sauvé qui dort
Heureux les martyrs, les élus
Avec la Vierge et son Jésus
Ô bienheureux le mort
Le mort jugé qui dort

Un Chevalier dehors
Repose sans remords
Dans le cimetière bénit
Dans sa sieste de granit
L'homme en pierre dehors
A deux yeux sans remords

Ringed as a porthole red
The wound in my side's bled
Like slavering gums and toothless laugh
Of some old crone upon her staff
Ringed as a porthole red
The wound in my side's bled

I notice gold rings spread
White sun bites my head
Two holes pierce me from a blade
Hell-forged and red-hot made
I notice gold rings spread
Heaven's fire bites my head

Out of my marrow fed
Twists a tear that's shed
I see Paradise in this
Miserere, De profundis
Wrung from my skull-bone thread
Tears of brimstone shed

Blessèd the good and dead
The dead safe in his bed
Blessèd each martyr, chosen one,
With the Virgin and her Son
O blessèd are the dead
Judged at rest in bed

A Knight sleeps like lead
No remorse in his head
In the hallowed burial ground
In his granite siesta sound
The stone man sleeps like lead
Remorseless eyes in his head

Ho je vous sens encor
Landes jaunes d'Armor
Je sens mon rosaire à mes doigts
Et le Christ en os sur le bois
À toi je baye encor
Ô ciel défunt d'Armor

Pardon de prier fort
Seigneur si c'est le sort
Mes yeux, deux bénitiers ardents
Le diable a mis ses doigts dedans
Pardon de crier fort
Seigneur contre le sort

J'entends le vent du nord
Qui bugle comme un cor
C'est l'hallali des trépassés
J'aboie après mon tour assez
J'entends le vent du nord
J'entends le glas du cor

Menez-Arrez.

Oh still felt in my head
Armor's yellow spread
I feel my rosary in my fingers
Christ in bone on wood lingers
I gape on you long-sped
O skies of Armor fled

Forgive the wild prayers said
Lord if it's fate ahead
My eyes are holy water bowls
Where the devil poked his finger-holes
Forgive the cries of dread
Lord against fate ahead

I hear the north wind spread
The horn call for the dead
It is the mort of those who're gone
In my turn I'm baying on
I hear the north wind head
Hear the horn knell spread

Menez-Arrez.

La Pastorale de Conlie

PAR UN MOBILISÉ DU MORBIHAN

> *Moral jeunes troupes excellent.*
>
> OFF.

Qui nous avait levés dans le *Mois-noir* – Novembre –
    Et parqués comme des troupeaux
Pour laisser dans la boue, au *Mois-plus-noir* – Décembre –
    Des peaux de mouton et nos peaux!

Qui nous a lâchés là: vides, sans espérance,
    Sans un levain de désespoir!
Nous entre-regardant, comme cherchant la France...
    Comiques, fesant peur à voir!

– Soldats tant qu'on voudra!... soldat est donc un être
    Fait pour perdre le goût du pain?...
Nous allions mendier; on nous envoyait paître:
    Et... nous paissions à la fin!

– S'il vous plaît: Quelque chose à mettre dans nos bouches?...
    – Héros et bêtes à moitié! –
... Ou quelque chose là: du cœur ou des cartouches:
    – On nous a laissé la pitié!

L'aumône: on nous la fit – Qu'elle leur soit rendue
    À ces bienheureux uhlans soûls!
Qui venaient nous jeter une balle perdue...
    Et pour rire!... comme des sous.

On eût dit un radeau de naufragés. – Misère –
    Nous crevions devant l'horizon.
Nos yeux troubles restaient tendus vers une terre...
    Un cri nous montait: Trahison!

The Pastoral of Conlie

BY A CONSCRIPT FROM MORBIHAN

Morale young troops excellent.

OFF.

Who had levied us in the *Black Month* – November –
Folded us in flocks up to the shins
To leave behind, in mud of the *Blacker Month* – December –
Sheepskins along with our own skins!

Who abandoned us there: empty, no hope, no chance,
Without a leaven of despair!
Gawping at one another as if we searched for France...
A comical fright to see us there!

– Just the soldiers you'd want!... so soldiers are poor bastards
Born to forget the taste for bread?...
We'd meant to beg; they sent us packing out to grass:
We grazed till the last shred!

– Please: Something just to put in our mouths tonight?...
– Partly heroes, partly beast! –
... Or something else here: heart or cartridges to bite:
We've been left pity, some feast!

Alms: we've been given some. – That let someone repay
Those blessèd Uhlans, full of booze!
Who came to toss the stray bullet or so our way...
And to laugh!... like handfuls of sous.

You'd have thought of a raft of shipwrecked sailors. – Misery –
Before the horizon, about to croak,
Our troubled eyes fixed, staring land out of the sea...
Then from us the cry 'Betrayal!' broke.

– Trahison!… c'est la guerre! On trouve à qui l'on crie!…
　　　　– Nous: pas besoin… – Pourquoi trahis?…
J'en ai vu parmi nous, sur la Terre-Patrie,
　　　　Se mourir du mal-du-pays.

– Oh, qu'elle s'en allait morne, la douce vie!…
　　　　Soupir qui sentait le remord
De ne pouvoir serrer sur sa lèvre une hostie,
　　　　Entre ses dents la mâle-mort!…

– Un grand enfant nous vint, aidé par deux gendarmes,
　　　　– Celui-là ne comprenait pas –
Tout barbouillé de vin, de sueur et de larmes,
　　　　Avec un *biniou* sous son bras.

Il s'assit dans la neige en disant: Ça m'amuse
　　　　De jouer mes airs; laissez-moi. –
Et, le surlendemain, avec sa cornemuse,
　　　　Nous l'avons enterré – Pourquoi!…

Pourquoi? dites-leur donc! Vous du Quatre-Septembre!
　　　　À ces vingt mille croupissants!…
Citoyens-décréteurs de victoires en chambre,
　　　　Tyrans forains impuissants!

– La parole est à vous – la parole est légère!…
　　　　La Honte est fille… elle passa –
Ceux dont les pieds verdis sortent à fleur-de-terre
　　　　Se taisent… – Trop vert pour vous, ça!

– Ha! Bordeaux, n'est-ce pas, c'est une riche ville…
　　　　Encore en France, n'est-ce pas?…
Elle avait chaud partout votre garde mobile,
　　　　Sous les balcons marquant le pas?

– Betrayal!... That's war! You learn the sort you're calling to!...
      – For us: no need... – Betrayed, why?...
There in the Homeland, I have seen more than a few
      So homesick of it that they die.

– How bitterly sweet life was giving us the slip!...
      Remorse in a sighing of its breath
Unable to accept the wafer on its lip
      With teeth gritted on violent death!...

– A big kid came to us. – Clueless he was, and lugged
      In by a pair of gendarme types –
All smeared and daubed with wine and sweat and tears, he hugged
      Beneath his arm his *Breton* pipes.

He sat down in the snow and said: 'It pleases me
      To play my songs; leave me.' – But by
The day after next to that, and with his bagpipes, we
      Saw to his burial. – But why!...

Why? You 4th-of-Septembrists! you tell why it is
      To twenty thousand bogged-in, speak!...
Citizen-decreers of chamber victories,
      Powerless, alien dictator clique!

– Come on! Your turn to speak. – Words are a glib pennyworth...
      Shame's a quick lay... Her heels are clean –
But those whose mildewed feet poke from the earth
      Die quiet... – For you, they're too green!

– Hah! Bordeaux, now there, that's a nice rich place...
      And still in France, I think it is?...
And your militia warm whatever way they face,
      Marking time under the balconies?

La résurrection de nos boutons de guêtres
　　　Est loin pour vous faire songer;
Et, vos noms, je les vois collés partout, ô Maîtres!...
　　　– La honte ne sait plus ronger. –

– Nos chefs... ils fesaient bien de se trouver malades!
　　　Armés en faux-turcs-espagnols
On en vit quelques-uns essayer des parades
　　　Avec la troupe des Guignols.

– *Le moral: excellent* – Ces rois avaient des reines,
　　　Parmi leurs sacs-de-nuit de cour...
À la botte vernie il faut robes à traînes;
　　　La vaillance est sœur de l'amour.

– Assez! – Plus n'en fallait de fanfare guerrière
　　　À nous, brutes garde-moutons,
Nous: ceux-là qui restaient simples, à leur manière,
　　　Soldats, catholiques, Bretons...

À ceux-là qui tombaient bayant à la bataille,
　　　Ramas de vermine sans nom,
Espérant le premier qui vînt crier: Canaille!
　　　Au canon, la chair à canon!...

– Allons donc: l'abattoir! – Bestiaux galeux qu'on rosse,
　　　On nous fournit aux Prussiens;
Et, nous voyant rouler-plat sous les coups de crosse,
　　　Des Français aboyaient – Bons chiens!

Hallali! ramenés! – Les perdus... Dieu les compte, –
　　　Abreuvés de banals dédains;
Poussés, traînant au pied la savate et la honte,
　　　Cracher sur nos foyers éteints!

The resurrection of our gaiter buttons here
        Is far enough off for you to ignore.
O Mastermen, stuck everywhere your names appear!…
        – Shame gnaws away at you no more. –

– Our leading men… were doing well to feel so ill!
        Dressed to kill like panto moodies;
And some were seen attempting to parade their fill
        With costume troops of Punch-and-Judys.

– *Morale: excellent* – Such kings had queans to reign
        Court in their sleeping bags each night…
And patent-leather boots require a gown and train;
        Valour's the handmaid of love on sight.

– Enough! – No need of fanfares to the war
        For us, sheep guard-dogs coarse and thick.
Us – ones who'd kept our simple ways from long before,
        Soldier, Breton, Catholic…

For those who, with their mouths gaped wide, in battle fell,
        Verminous mob of nameless ones,
Trusting the first of them who would approach to yell:
        'Cannon-fodder, to the guns!'…

– Right: to the shambles. – Scab-ridden, thrashable mutts
        Fed to the Prussians as we stood.
And, seeing us ground beneath the rifle-butts,
        Were Frenchmen baying – Good dogs, good!

The mort! survivors! – The lost… God counts them, every
                   name, –
        Drenched in common contempt our path,
Driven, dragging at heel our old boots and shame,
        Home, to spit on the cold hearth!

. . . .

– Va: toi qui n'es pas bue, ô fosse de Conlie!
     De nos jeunes sangs appauvris,
Qu'en voyant regermer tes blés gras, on oublie
     Nos os qui végétaient pourris,

La chair plaquée après nos blouses en guenilles
     – Fumier tout seul rassemblé…
– Ne mangez pas ce pain, mères et jeunes filles!
     L'*ergot* de mort est dans le blé.

                              1870

. . . .

– So: Conlie Ditch, you grave, not dead drunk yet!
   With our young, exhausted gore,
May people, seeing your rich grain sprout, forget
   Our vegetating, rotting bones; ignore

The flesh plastered to our blouses, shred to shred,
   – Dung heap self gathered, off meat...
– Mothers and young girls just do not eat this bread!
   The *ergot* of death is in the wheat.

1870

Gens de mer

Point n'ai fait un tas d'océans
Comme les Messieurs d'Orléans,
Ulysses à vapeur en quête...
Ni l'Archipel en capitan;
Ni le Transatlantique autant
Qu'une chanteuse d'opérette.

Mais il fut flottant, mon berceau,
Fait comme le nid de l'oiseau
Qui couve ses œufs sur la houle...
Mon lit d'amour fut un hamac;
Et, pour tantôt, j'espère un sac
Lesté d'un bon caillou qui coule.

– Marin, je sens mon matelot
Comme le bonhomme Callot
Sentait son illustre bonhomme...
– Va, bonhomme de mer mal fait!
Va, Muse à la voix de rogomme!
Va, Chef-d'œuvre de cabaret!

Not sailed, me, such heaps of seas
As these Gents of Orleans, these
Steam-boat Ulysses on a quest...
Not swaggered the Archipelago;
Nor Transatlantic high and low,
To match an opera-singer's breast!

It always floated, my cradle-bed.
Made like the nests of birds wave-bred
That hatch their eggs upon the sea...
A hammock was my bed for loving,
And, soon, I hope a sack for covering,
Ballast, a rolling stone will be.

– Seaman, I sense my sailor, though,
Just like that good fellow Callot
Sensed his illustrious good bloke...
– Cast off, good Jack, from my poor pen!
Cast off, Muse of gin-soaked croak!
Cast off, Masterpiece of the drinking den!

Matelots

Vos marins de quinquets à l'Opéra... comique,
Sous un frac en bleu-ciel jurent « Mille sabords! »
Et, sur les boulevards, le survivant chronique
Du *Vengeur* vend l'onguent à tuer les rats morts.
Le Jûn'homme infligé d'un bras – même en voyage –
Infortuné, chantant par suite de naufrage;
La femme en bain de mer qui tord ses bras au flot;
Et l'amiral ★★★ – Ce n'est pas matelot! –
– Matelots – quelle brusque et nerveuse saillie
Fait cette *Race à part* sur la race faillie!
Comme ils vous mettent tous, *terriens*, au même sac!
– Un curé dans ton lit, un' fill' dans mon hamac! –

. . . .

– On ne les connaît pas, ces gens à rudes nœuds.
Ils ont le mal de mer sur vos *planchers à bœufs*;
À terre – oiseaux palmés – ils sont gauches et veules.
Ils sont mal culottés comme leurs brûle-gueules.
Quand le roulis leur manque... il se sentent rouler:
– À terre, on a beau boire, on ne peut désoûler!

– On ne les connaît pas. – Eux: que leur fait la terre?...
Une relâche, avec l'hôpital militaire,
Des filles, la prison, des horions, du vin...
Le reste: Eh bien, après? – Est-ce que c'est marin?...

– Eux ils sont matelots. – À travers les tortures,
Les luttes, les dangers, les larges aventures,
Leur *face-à-coups-de-hache* a pris un tic nerveux
D'insouciant dédain pour ce qui n'est pas Eux...

Seamen

You sailors of the footlights of the Opera... comic,
Swearing 'Shiver me timbers!' in sky-blue frockcoats, spats.
Or, on the boulevards, that survivor – chronic –
Of 'The Avenger', selling stuff to kill dead rats;
The Young 'Un – who on a harbour trip – has lost an arm,
In hard*ship* singing out: 'Result of shipwreck, ma'am';
The woman sea-bather wringing her hands at seas;
And Admiral Spatter-dash. – None sailors! – None of these.
Sailors! – Real sailors – what abrupt, vigorous jumps
This *Race apart* takes on the race of brassless lumps!
How they lump you *lubbers* all together in one cart!
– A parson in your bed; in my hammock a tart. –

.   .   .   .

– You wouldn't know them, these men of crude ropes and ties.
They're seasick on your *terra farmer*, list, capsize.
On land – like web-foot birds – they're clumsy awkward types,
As ill-breeched as the stems of their throat-burning pipes.
When rollers desert them... they begin to roll all over:
– You might as well be sloshed on land; you can't get sober!

– You wouldn't know them. – What's the land do for them?...
Mere port of call: military hospital, pro tem,
Prison, punch-ups, wine, floozies, scars... The other stuff:
Well, what more 'd there be? – That's seaworthy enough?...

– They're sailors first and foremast. – From their ordeals, shit
        creeks,
Fights, far-flung escapades, dire straits, *narrowsqueaks*,
Their *adze-hewn* faces show a nervous tic of devil-
May-care contempt for all that's not for Them... sea-level.

C'est qu'ils se sentent bien, ces chiens! Ce sont des mâles!
– Eux: l'Océan! – et vous: les plates-bandes sales;
Vous êtes des *terriens*, en un mot, des *troupiers*:
– *De la terre de pipe et de la sueur de pieds!* –

– Eux sont les *vieux-de-cale* et *les frères-la-côte*,
Gens au cœur sur la main, et toujours la main haute;
Des natures en barre! – Et capables de tout...
– Faites-en donc autant!... Ils sont *de mauvais goût*...
– Peut-être... Ils ont chez vous des amours tolérées
Par un *grippe-Jésus*★ accueillant leurs entrées...
– Eh! faut-il pas du cœur au ventre quelque part,
Pour entrer en plein jour là – bagne-lupanar,
Qu'ils nomment le *Cap-Horn*, dans leur langue hâlée:
– Le cap Horn, noir séjour de tempête grêlée –
Et se coller en vrac, sans crampe d'estomac,
De la chair à chiquer – comme un nœud de tabac!

Jetant leur solde avec leur trop-plein de tendresse,
À tout vent; ils vont là comme ils vont à la messe...
Ces anges mal léchés, ces durs enfants perdus!
– Leur tête a du requin et du petit-Jésus.

Ils aiment à tout crin: Ils aiment plaie et bosse,
La Bonne-Vierge, avec le gendarme qu'on rosse;
Ils font des vœux à tout... mais leur vœu caressé
A toujours l'habit bleu d'un *Jésus-Christ*† rossé.

– Allez: ce franc cynique a sa grâce native...
Comme il vous toise un chef, à sa façon naïve!
Comme il connaît son maître: – *Un d'un seul bloc de bois!*
– *Un mauvais chien toujours qu'un bon enfant parfois!*

★ *Grippe-Jésus*: petit nom marin du gendarme.
† *Jésus-Christ*: du même au même.

They feel so self-sufficient, these rovers. They are men!
For Them, the Ocean! – yours, soiled garden plot and pen.
You're *landlubbers*; in a word, you're *saps*, old sweats:
– *Of pipe-clay claggy, foot-slog sweaty, drips and wets!* –

But them, they're *hold salts* and *messmates of the coast.*
Men with their hearts on their sleeves; and, most
Of all, high-handed; iron-souled! – Never outfaced…
– And can you claim as much as that!… They're *in bad taste*…
– Perhaps… They've birds among you that the *Jesus-nicker**
Turns a blind eye to, welcomes their entry quicker…
– Well, it must take some guts, or something near, to pay
A visit there – hard-labour brothel – in broad day!
Place they have nicknamed *Cape Horn* in their weathered tongue:
– The Cape Horn, dark home of the hailstorm far flung –
And stick themselves en masse without a belly-ache
To chew the flesh – just like a baccy quid they take!

Throwing their cash with surplus tenderness to spare
To the four winds. Like going to mass, they go there…
These ill-licked angels, these tough kids lost in the dark!
– Their features partly little Jesus, partly shark.

They love with fur flying: love dust-up and rough stuff;
The Holy Virgin; and the copper that they cuff.
They swear they'll fix the lot… but still their fondest urge
Is always for a battered *St Nick-alas†* in blue serge.

– And yet: this candid cynic has a native grace…
How well he sums a boss up in his artless ways!
And knows his master: – *Hacked from a solid block of wood!*
– *Always a dangerous dog; sometimes a child that's good!*

---

* *Jesus-nicker*: nickname of sailors for the police.
† *St Nick-alas*: another for the same.

. . . .

– Allez: à bord, chez eux, ils ont leur poésie!
Ces brutes ont des chants ivres d'âme saisie
Improvisés aux quarts sur le gaillard-d'avant...
– Ils ne s'en doutent pas, eux, poème vivant.

– Ils ont toujours, pour leur *bonne femme de mère*,
Une larme d'enfant, ces héros de misère;
Pour leur *Douce-Jolie*, une larme d'amour!...
Au pays – loin – ils ont, espérant leur retour,
Ces gens de cuivre rouge, une pâle fiancée
Que, pour la mer jolie, un jour ils ont laissée.
Elle attend vaguement... comme on attend là-bas.
Eux ils portent son nom tatoué sur leur bras.
Peut-être elle sera veuve avant d'être épouse...
– Car la mer est bien grande et la mer est jalouse. –
Mais elle sera fière, à travers un sanglot,
De pouvoir dire encore: – Il était matelot!...

– C'est plus qu'un homme aussi devant la mer géante,
Ce matelot entier!...
                    Piétinant sous la plante
De son pied marin le pont près de crouler:
Tiens bon! Ça le connaît, ça va le désoûler.
Il finit comme ça, simple en sa grande allure,
D'un bloc: – *Un trou dans l'eau, quoi!... pas de fioriture.* –

. . . .

On en voit revenir pourtant: bris de naufrage,
Ramassis de scorbut et hachis d'abordage...
Cassés, défigurés, dépaysés, perclus:
– Un œil en moins. – Et vous, en avez-vous en plus?

.   .   .   .

But then: they've their poetry among themselves aboard!
These brutes have drunken shanties heartily roared
Which they on watches in the foc'sle improvise...
– This, living poems themselves, they do not realize.

– At all times for that *good woman their mother* they find
A childlike tear; these heroes who have never whined;
And for their *Sweetheart* have a tear of love to spare her!...
In his own land – distant – every bronzed seafarer
Has a pale betrothed one waiting for his coming home
Whom he'd deserted one day for the lovely foam.
She's waiting waveringly... they're used to waiting there.
Meanwhile tattooed on their arm her name they bear.
Maybe, she'll be a widow long before a wife...
– For very wide the sea and jealous of all life. –
But through her tears and sobbing, very proud she'll be
To manage saying: – Sailor he was, and is to me!...

– He's more than a man, too, before the towering ocean,
This sailor through and through!...
                                        His sea-legs ride the motion,
The deck beneath him set to stave in: belay!
This'll sober his wits. He knows what's coming his way.
He meets his end like that, simple, with bearing, still
All of a piece: – *A hole in the water!... No flourish, frill.* –

.   .   .   .

Still some of them do get back, matchwood of wrecks,
A scurvy-ridden rabble, hash from boarding decks...
Broken, disfigured, uprooted, crippled, halt:
– 'One eye short!' – 'And you, got a spare one, in salt?'

– La fièvre jaune. – Eh bien, et vous, l'avez-vous rose?
– Une balafre. – Ah, c'est signé!… C'est quelque chose!
– Et le bras en pantenne. – Oui, c'est un biscaïen,
Le reste c'est le bel ouvrage au chirurgien.
– Et ce trou dans la joue? – Un ancien coup de pique.
– Cette bosse? – *À tribord?*… excusez: c'est ma chique.
– Ça? – Rien: une *foutaise*, un pruneau dans la main,
Ça sert de baromètre, et vous verrez demain:
Je ne vous dis que ça, sûr! quand je sens ma crampe…
Allez, on n'en fait plus de coques de ma trempe!
On m'a pendu deux fois… –

                  Et l'honnête forban
Creuse un bateau de bois pour un petit enfant.

– Ils durent comme ça, reniflant la tempête
Riches de gloire et de trois cents francs de retraite,
Vieux culots de gargousse, épaves de héros!…
– Héros? – ils riraient bien!… – Non merci: matelots!

– Matelots! – Ce n'est pas vous, jeunes *mateluches*,
Pour qui les femmes ont toujours des coqueluches…
Ah, les vieux avaient de plus fiers appétits!
En haussant leur épaule ils vous trouvent petits.
À treize ans ils mangeaient de l'Anglais, les corsaires!
Vous, vous n'êtes que des *pelletas* militaires…
Allez, on n'en fait plus de ces *purs, premier brin!*
Tout s'en va… tout! La mer… elle n'est plus *marin!*
De leur temps, elle était plus salée et sauvage.
Mais, à présent, rien n'a plus de pucelage…
La mer… La mer n'est plus qu'une fille à soldats!…

– Vous, matelots, rêvez, en faisant vos cent pas
Comme dans les grands quarts… Paisible rêverie
De carcasse qui geint, de mât craqué qui crie…

– 'Yellow fever?' – 'What about yours, then? In the pink?
– 'A scar?'– 'Ah, but it's signed. Something, you might think.'
– 'And the arm's skew-whiff!' – 'Yes, that was musket-fire.
The rest of it's a surgeon's handiwork, entire.'
– 'But that hole in your cheek?' – 'Old blow a pike did.'
– 'That lump? – *To starboard* then?... – 'Sorry: my baccy quid.'
– 'That, there?' – 'A *scratch*, nothing. Bullet in the palm.
Works like a barometer; you'll see, tomorrow: calm.
Can only tell you, when it twinges, though, this hand...
Well, they don't lay down keels these days of my brand!
They've hanged me twice...' –
                       And the honest rover
Hollows a wooden boat out for a kid in clover.

– They survive like that, sniffing the air for squall,
Rich with fame and three hundred francs pension in all,
Old spent cartridge ends, hero wrecks and bailers!...
– Heroes? – They'd horse-laugh!... – No thanks: sailors.

– Sailors! – You're not of their ilk, you *boater*-lads,
For whom the women have their soft spots, whims and fads...
Ah, the old sea-dogs had much prouder appetites!
They shrug their shoulders, find you petty little mites.
At thirteen they were eating Englishmen, these corsairs!
You, you're just army *fish-dock hands*, don't take on airs...
Give over. Not made now, these of the *first water*, prime.
Everything passes... The lot! The sea's no longer... maritime.
In their day it was a saltier and wider tract.
But now nothing's pure and virginal and intact...
The sea... the sea is nothing but a soldier's whore!...

– Dream on, you sea-dogs, in your pacing aft and fore,
As in the long watches... A peaceful daydream
Of carcass hulls that creak and rending masts that scream...

– Aux pompes!...
                    – Non: fini! – Les beaux jours sont passés:
– *Adieu mon beau navire aux trois mâts pavoisés!*

. . . .

Tel qu'une vieille coque, au sec et dégréée,
Où vient encor parfois clapoter la marée:
Âme-de-mer en peine est le vieux matelot
Attendant, échoué... – quoi: la mort?
                         – Non, le flot.

Île d'Ouessant. – Avril.

– Man the pumps!...
            – No: finished! – The good old days gone west:
Farewell, my splendid ship, your three masts fully dressed!

.   .   .   .

Like an old hulk, derigged, and high and dry,
Where sometimes the odd wave will ripple by,
The old salt is a sea-soul suffering inside,
Awaiting, aground... – what: death?
                              – No, high tide.

Isle of Ushant. – April.

Le bossu Bitor*

Un pauvre petit diable aussi vaillant qu'un autre,
Quatrième et dernier à bord d'un petit *cotre*...
Fier d'être matelot et de manger pour rien,
Il remplaçait le *coq*, le mousse et le chien;
Et comptait, comme ça, quarante ans de service,
Sur *le rôle* toujours inscrit comme – *novice!* –

... Un vrai bossu: cou tors et retors, très madré,
Dans sa coque il gardait sa petite influence;
Car chacun sait qu'en mer un bossu porte chance...
– Rien ne f...iche malheur comme femme ou curé!

Son nom: c'était Bitor – nom de mer et de guerre –
Il disait que c'était un tremblement de terre
Qui, jeune et fait au tour, l'avait tout démoli:
Lui, son navire et des cocotiers... au Chili.

. . . .

Le soleil est noyé. – C'est le soir – dans le port
Le navire bercé sur ses câbles, s'endort
Seul; et le clapotis bas de l'eau morte et lourde,
Chuchote un gros baiser sous sa carène sourde.
Parmi les yeux du brai flottant qui luit en plaque,
Le ciel miroité semble une immense flaque.

Le long des quais déserts où grouillait un chaos
S'étend le calme plat...
                      Quelques vagues échos...

------

* Le *bitors* est un gros fil à voile tordu en double et goudronné.

Arch Halyard, the Hunchback*

A poor little devil, he was, as good as any other,
Fourth, the last and least on board a tiny *cutter*...
Proud to be a sailor and to eat for free,
He did for cook, and dog, and cabin-boy, all three,
And had, in this way, four years of service borne,
Always recorded in the register: *greenhorn!* –

... A real hunchback, crook neck, twisted, devious, he;
He had a bit of influence in his cockleshell:
A hunchback brings good luck afloat, as all know well...
– Nothing buggers the luck like skirts or priests at sea!

His name: 'Arch' Halyard – sea-term twist and *nom de guerre* –
He'd tell about an earthquake once... in Chile where
It ruined him, young and finely honed, destroyed:
Himself, his boat, some coco-palms, all of it void.

. . . .

The sun was drowned. – It is evening – in harbour docked,
The boat sleeps alone, upon its cables rocked;
And the low ripples of the sluggish neap tide hiss,
Whisper under its deaf keel the grossest kiss.
Mid spills of floating tar like plate metal that gleams
The shimmered sky like some immense pool seems.

And on deserted quays that swarmed with chaos earlier
A dull calm spread...
                    The odd echo made a stir...

---

* Halyard is a thick sail rope twisted of two strands and tarred.

Quelque novice seul, resté mélancolique,
Se chante son pays avec une musique…
De loin en loin, répond le jappement hagard,
Intermittent, d'un chien de bord qui fait le quart,
Oublié sur le pont…
                              Tout le monde est à terre.
Les matelots farauds s'en sont allés – mystère! –
Faire, à grands coups de gueule et de botte… l'amour.
– Doux repos tant sué dans les labeurs du jour. –
Entendez-vous là-bas, dans les culs-de-sac louches,
Roucouler leur chanson ces tourtereaux farouches!…

– Chantez! La vie est courte et drôlement cordée!…
Hâle à toi, si tu peux, une bonne bordée
À jouer de la fille, à jouer du couteau…
Roucoulez mes Amours! Qui sait: demain!… tantôt…

… Tantôt, tantôt… la ronde en écrémant la ville,
Vous soulage en douceur quelque traînard tranquille
Pour le coller en vrac, léger échantillon,
Bleu saignant et vainqueur, au clou. – Tradition. –

.   .   .   .

Mais les soirs étaient doux aussi pour le Bitor,
Il était libre aussi, maître et gardien à bord…
Lové tout de son long sur un rond de cordage,
Se sentant somnoler comme un chat… comme un sage,
Se repassant l'oreille avec ses doigts poilus,
Voluptueux, pensif, et n'en pensant pas plus,
Laissant mollir son corps dénoué de paresse,
Son petit œil vairon noyé de morbidesse!…

– Un *loustic* en passant lui caressait les os:
Il riait de son mieux et faisait le gros dos.

.   .   .   .

Melancholy, left behind, crooning, some greenhorn
Noises abroad to himself the land where he was born...
Further and further off, come yelps of a dog aboard
That keeps the watch, upon the deck ignored,
Spasmodic, haggard...
                   Everybody's gone ashore.
Sailors gone off dandified – a mystery and more! –
To make, with great feats of gob and boot... love royal.
– Sweet relief so sweated for with daily toil. –
D'you hear, there, in the shady blind alley ways,
Those turtledoves coo-cooing all their lays!...

– Sing on! Life's short, the rigging weird and odd!...
Haul in, if you can, a good spree shore, shoot your wad
And play the girls, or play with knife, or spoon...
Bill and coo, my Loves! Who knows: tomorrow!... soon...

... Oh soon, yes, soon... the watch, in skimming off the town,
Avoiding trouble, takes some docile sluggard down
To stick him, all of a heap; an advance sample: one
Bruise-blue and bleeding champ, in jug. – Routinely done. –

. . . .

But these evenings were pleasant for Archie, too.
Free also, master and watch aboard, no crew...
His full length curling comfy on a coil of ropes,
Feeling himself doze... like sage or cat that slopes
Its furry fingers over its ear, luxurious,
Thoughtful, then without a thought, soft puss,
Letting the body slip, in indolence unwound;
His little odd-toned eye in nonchalance drowned!...

– Some passing *joker* then would stroke him dozing slack:
He'd laugh as best he could, and then he'd arch his back.

. . . .

Tout le monde a pourtant quelque bosse en la tête…
Bitor aussi – c'était de se payer la fête!

Et cela lui prenait, comme un commandement
De Dieu: vers la Noël, et juste une fois l'an.
Ce jour-là, sur la brune, il s'ensauvait à terre
Comme un rat dont on a cacheté le derrière…
– Tiens: Bitor disparu. – C'est son jour de sabbats.
Il en a pour deux nuits: réglé comme un compas.
– C'est un sorcier pour sûr… –
                                Aucun n'aurait pu dire,
Même on n'en riait plus; c'était fini de rire.

Au deuxième matin, le *bordailleur* rentrait
Sur ses jambes en pieds-de-banc-de-cabaret,
Louvoyant bord-sur-bord…
                                Morne, vers la cuisine
Il piquait droit, chantant ses vêpres ou matine,
Et jetait en pleurant ses savates au feu…
– Pourquoi – nul ne savait, et lui s'en doutait peu.
… J'y sens je ne sais quoi d'assez mélancolique,
Comme un vague fumet d'holocauste à l'antique…

C'était la fin; plus morne et plus tordu, le hère
Se reprenait hâler son bitor de misère…

. . . .

– C'est un soir, près Noël. – Le cotre est à bon port,
L'équipage au diable, et Bitor… toujours Bitor.
C'est le grand jour qu'il s'est donné pour prendre terre:
Il fait noir, il est gris. – L'or n'est qu'une chimère!
Il tient, dans un vieux bas de laine, un sac de sous…
Son pantalon à mettre et: – La terre est à nous! –

Now everybody has some quirk tucked in the brain...
Archie, as well – it was to have his fling again!

It always came to him like some command of God:
Near Christmas-tide and once a year the prod.
That day, at dusk, every-man-for-himself, he tore,
Just like a rat with stitched-up arse, ashore...
– Hang it, Archie's vanished. – Time for his revels, rumpus.
Two nights they took, fixed like points on the compass.
– He was a wizard, surely... –
        Where, no one ever could say.
No one laughed any more; laughter had had its day.

The second morning and the *spreeing-tackster*'s back,
On legs as bock-kneed as pub-table legs and tack-
Tacking half seas over...
       Made for the galley, fast,
Depressed, droning his vespers or matins, cast
His worn-out shoes, weeping, straight into the stove...
– Why – no one knew, and nor did he, poor cove.
... I have this sense of something there quite melancholy,
The vague smoke of a burnt offering in antiquity...

The end; and more depressed and twisted, the poor blighter
Set to and hauled his halyard of misery tauter, tighter...

. . . .

– An evening near Christmas. – The cutter in a good port; while
The crew has gone to the devil, Halyard's... still Halyard tortile.
It was the great day he'd picked to go ashore.
It's dark; he's a shade high. – Gold's a mirage by his score!
Inside an old wool sock he has a bag of sous...
On with the trousers and: – 'The earth is mine, that's whose!' –

... Un pantalon jadis *cuisse-de-nymphe-émue*,
Couleur tendre à mourir!... et trop tôt devenue
Merdoie... excepté dans les plis *rose-d'amour*,
Gardiens de la couleur, gardiens du pur contour...

Enfin il s'est lavé, gratté – rude toilette!
– Ah! c'est que ce n'est pas, non plus, tous les jours fête!...
Un cache-nez lilas lui cache les genoux,
   – Encore un coup-de-suif! et: La terre est à nous!
... La terre: un bouchon, quoi!... – Mais Bitor se sent riche:
D'argent, comme un bourgeois: d'amour, comme un caniche...
– Pourquoi pas le *Cap-Horn!**... Le sérail – Pourquoi pas!...
– Syrènes du *Cap-Horn*, vous lui tendez les bras!...

   · · · · · · · · · · · · · · · · · ·

Au fond de la venelle est la lanterne rouge,
Phare du matelot, *Stella maris* du bouge...
– Qui va là? – Ce n'est plus Bitor! c'est un héros,
Un Lauzun qui se frotte aux plus gros numéros!...
C'est Triboulet tordu comme un ver par sa haine!...
Ou c'est Alain Chartier, sous un baiser de reine!...
Lagardère en manteau qui va se redresser!...
– Non: C'est un bienheureux honteux – Laissez passer.
C'est une chair enfin que ce bout de rognure!
Un partageux qui veut son morceau de nature.
C'est une passion qui regarde en dessous
L'amour... pour le voler!... – L'amour à trente sous!

– Va donc Paillasse! Et le trousse-galant t'emporte!
Tiens: c'est là!... C'est un mur – Heurte encor!... C'est la porte:
As-tu peur! –
            Il écoute... Enfin: un bruit de clefs,

------

*   *Ce bagne-lupanar*
Qu'ils nomment le Cap-Horn, *dans leur langue hâlée.*
                   ('*Les Matelots*', p. 314)

... Trousers, once *thigh-pink-of-trembling-sylph* in shade,
And soft enough to die for!... too soon *goose-dung*areed were
    made...
Except where creases let some *rose-of-love* escape,
Guardians of the colour, guardians of the pure shape!...

At last, a cat-lick – washed and scraped away!
– Ah! since it isn't like all days are holiday!...
A lilac muffler muffled his knees from sight,
– A smarm of grease! then, and: the world is ours tonight!
... The world: a pub, more like! – But Archie he feels rich:
With cash like a bourgeois, with love like Fido's snitch...
– Why not *Cape Horn!**... The harem? – And why not! – Grim
Sirens of *Cape Horn*, spread and close your claws on him!...

. . . .

The far end of the alley are the red-light shores;
Light house for *seamen*, *Stella Maris* for the whores...
– Who goes there? – Not, surely, Archie's figure! A hero's,
Lauzun who rubbed shoulders with ones that headed zeros!...
It's Triboulet arching like a worm with hate!...
Or Alain Chartier kissed by one of queen's estate!...
Or else, cloaked Lagardère taking up his stance!...
– No: it's a shamefaced joymaker – Let him advance.
It's flesh and blood, well, at the least, a paring!
A partner wanting his part in some of nature's sharing.
That is a passion that always takes a furtive view,
Of love... To pinch a bit!... – Love at thirty sou!

– Go on, then, Clown! May miss cholera collar you!
You're there! Wall, that – knock on!... Door there. In a stew! –
Are you?
       He listens... At last: there comes the noise of keys,

---

* A visit there – hard-labour brothel – in broad day! / Place they have
nicknamed *Cape Horn* in their weathered tongue. ('Seamen', p. 315.)

Le judas darde un rais: – Hô, quoi que vous voulez?
– J'ai de l'argent. – Combien es-tu? Voyons ta tête...
Bon. Gare à n'entrer qu'un; la maison est honnête;
Fais voir ton sac un peu?... Tu feras travailler?... –
Et la serrure grince, on vient d'entrebâiller;
Bitor pique une tête entre l'huys et l'hôtesse,
Comme un chien dépendu qui se rue à la messe.
– Eh, là-bas! l'enragé, quoi que tu veux ici?
Qu'on te f...iche droit, quoi? pas dégoûté! Merci!...
Quoi qui te faut, bosco?... des nymphes, des pucelles
Hop! à qui le Mayeux? Eh là-bas, les donzelles!... –

Bitor lui prit le bras: – Tiens, voici pour toi, gouine:
Cache-moi quelque part... tiens: là... – C'est la cuisine.
– Bon. Tu m'en conduiras une... et propre! combien?...
– Tire ton sac. – Voilà. – Parole! il a du bien!...
Pour lors nous en avons du premier brin: *cossuses*;
Mais on ne t'en a pas fait exprès des *bossuses*...
Bah! la nuit tous les chats sont gris. Reste là voir,
Puisque c'est ton caprice; as pas peur, c'est tout noir. –

. . . .

Une porte s'ouvrit. C'est la salle allumée.
Silhouettes grouillant à travers la fumée:
Les amateurs beuglant, ronflant, trinquant, rendus;
– Des Anglais, jouissant comme de vrais pendus,
Se cuvent, pleins de tout et de béatitude;
– Des Yankees longs, et roide-soûls par habitude,
Assis en deux, et tour à tour tirant au mur
Leur jet de jus de chique, au but, et toujours sûr;
– Des Hollandais salés, lardés de couperose;
– De blonds Norvégiens hercules de chlorose;
– Des Espagnols avec leurs figures en os;
– Des baleiniers huileux comme des cachalots;
– D'honnêtes caboteurs bien carrés d'envergures,

The spy-hole shoots a ray: – Well, what d'you want? – Please,
I've got the cash. – How many are you? Show your face...
Good. Only one at a time. This house is a straight place;
Now can I see your stash?... You'll set it toiling, tar?... –
And the lock grinds. The door is set a bit ajar;
Between hostess and doorpost Archie dives his head,
Just as a cur spared hanging flies to mass instead.
– Hey, rabid, down, boy! What d'you want here, bow-shanks?
A lay, straight up? What? Not choosy are you? Thanks!...
What d'you want, humpy: nymphs, virgins? What's yours?...
Hey! Who's up for Punch? – Come on, stand to, you whores! –

Archie took her arm: – Look, doll, that's for you:
Hide me somewhere... here... – The kitchen. – This'll do.
– Good. Now fetch me one – and clean at that! How much?...
– Let's see your money. – See. – My word! So he's a touch
Well off!... In that case we've the finest: *well to do*;
But we don't have *hunchback* girls on purpose just for you...
Bah! at night all cats are grey. Wait, nosy-park,
Since that's your fad; and don't be scared, it's dark. –

. . . .

A door swung open, giving on the well-lit bar.
Silhouettes swarmed amid the fumes of fag, cigar:
The punters lowing, groaning, boozing, deadbeat;
– The English enjoying themselves stiff, like gallows meat.
Sleeping it off, gut-full, as blessed as an abbot;
– And lanky Yanks, dead drunk as is their usual habit,
Sitting in twos, and taking it in turns to hit
The wall, crack-shots, with baccy juice they spit;
– Then salty Dutchmen greasy with acne streaks and peaks;
– Blond Norwegians, hercules with chlorotic cheeks;
– And Spaniards with their features skeletal, gaunt;
– Whalers oily as the sperm-whales that they haunt;
– Blunt inshoremen, square-rigged, and broad of beam,

Calfatés de goudron sur toutes les coutures;
– Des Nègres blancs, avec des mulâtres lippus;
– Des Chinois, le chignon roulé sous un *gibus*,
Vêtus d'un frac flambant-neuf et d'un parapluie;
– Des chauffeurs venus là pour essuyer leur suie;
– Des Allemands chantant l'amour en orphéon,
Leur patrie et leur chope... avec accordéon;
– Un noble Italien, jouant avec un mousse
Qui roule deux gros yeux sous sa tignasse rousse;
– Des Grecs plats; des Bretons à tête biscornue;
– L'escouade d'un vaisseau russe, en grande tenue;
– Des Gascons adorés pour leur galant bagoût...
Et quelques renégats – écume du ragoût. –

Là, plus loin dans le fond sur les banquettes grasses,
Des novices légers s'*affalent* sur les Grâces
De corvée... Elles sont d'un gras encourageant;
Ça se paye au tonnage, on en veut pour l'argent...
Et, quand on *largue tout*, il faut que la viande
Tombe, comme un *hunier qui se déferle en bande*!

– On a des petits noms: *Chiourme, Jany-Gratis,*
Bout-dehors, Fond-de-Vase, Anspeck, Garcette-à-ris.
– C'est gréé comme il faut: satin rose et dentelle;
Ils ne trouvent jamais la mariée assez belle...
– Du velours pour frotter à cru leur cuir tanné!
Et du fard, pour torcher leur baiser boucané!...
À leurs ceintures d'or, faut ceinture dorée!
Allons! – *Ciel moutonné, comme femme fardée*
N'a pas longue durée à ces Pachas d'un jour...
– *N'en faut du vin! n'en faut du rouge!... et de l'amour!*

. . . .

Bitor regardait ça – comment on fait la joie –
Chauve-souris fixant les albatros en proie...
Son rêve fut secoué par une grosse voix:

Well caulked with tar on every scar and seam;
– Some white Negroes with mulattos blubber-lipped;
– Chinese with hair coiled underneath a *gibus,* equipped
With rolled umbrella, brand-new tails afoot;
– Stokers that have come to wipe away their soot;
– The Germans singing love, their country and their tankard,
In chorus to… accordion accompaniment anchored.
– A noble Italian plays with a cabin-boy whose big
Round eyes are rolling underneath his ginger wig;
– Bretons with lopsided heads; Greeks spiritless;
– A squad out of some Russian ship in full dress;
– Gascons adored for their flattering turn of phrase…
Scum of the spicy stews – the renegades and strays. –

And in the background on plump and cushioned benches
Fast greenhorns flopped upon the Graces, wenches
On fatigues… They were encouragingly plump ones.
You get the tonnage you require in paying lump sums.
And when you *cast off* then the meat slumps to it,
Like a *topsail broken out* when the crew jumps to it!

– They've all got nick-names: *Lou Screw, Jany Gratist,*
Endsa Way, Deep Shaft, Rifi Riggish, Handspike Artist.
– They're rigged up as required: rose-satin and lace.
Men never find the bride with such a pulling grace…
– To buff their naked leather tans, the velvet miss!
And here's the rouge to polish off their rawhide kiss!…
The golden waists *de rigueur* with gilded girdle's lure!
Huh! – *Fleecy skies like dolled-up women endure*
But short a session for these fleeting Pashas of decks…
– *We want more wine! And want the red!… and now sex!*

.   .   .   .

Archie observed – how pleasure's to be made – he was
A stray bat that eyed as prey the albatross…
His dream was broken into by a deep rough voice:

– Eh, dis donc, l'oiseau bleu, c'est-y fini ton choix?
– Oui: (Ses yeux verts vrillaient la nuit de la cuisine)
... La grosse dame en rose avec sa crinoline!...
– Ça: c'est *Mary-Saloppe*, elle a son plein et dort. –
Lui, dégainant le bas qui tenait son trésor:
– Je te dis que je veux la belle dame rose!...
– Ç'a-t'y du vice!... Ah-ça: t'es porté sur la chose?...
Pour avec elle, alors, tu feras dix cocus,
Dix tout frais de ce soir!... Vas-y pour tes écus
Et paye en double: On va t'*amatelotter*. Monte...
– Non ici... – Dans le noir?... allons faut pas de honte!
– Je veux ici! – Pas mèche, avec les règlements.
– Et moi je veux! – C'est bon... mais t'endors pas dedans...

Ohé là-bas! debout au quart, *Mary-Saloppe*!
– Eh, c'est pas moi *de quart*! – C'est pour prendre une chope,
C'est rien *la corvée*... accoste: il y a gras!
– De quoi donc? – Va, c'est un qu'a de l'or plein ses bas,
Un bossu dans un sac, qui veut pas qu'on l'évente...
– Bon: qu'y prenne son soûl, j'ai le mien! j'ai ma pente.
– Va, c'est dans la cuisine...

           – Eh! voyons-toi, Bichon...
T'es tortu, mais j'ai pas peur d'un tire-bouchon!
Viens... Si ça t'est égal: éclairons la chandelle?
– Non. – Je voudrais te voir, j'aime Polichinelle...
Ah je te tiens; on sait jouer Colin-Maillard!... –
La matrulle ferma la porte...
           – Ah tortillard!...

. . . .

– Charivari! – Pour qui? – Quelle ronde infernale,
Quel paquet crevé roule en hurlant dans la salle?...
– Ah, peau de cervelas! ah, tu veux du chahut!

– Well, tell me, bluebird, have you made your choice?
(His green eyes bored out through the kitchen's dark.) – Yes:
... The buxom one in pink, that wears the crinoline dress!...
– Her: *Dredger Mary*. She's had her fill and kips off duty. –
And he, drawing the trusty sock that held his booty,
– I say again I want the lovely one in pink!...
– You're wicked with it!... Well: so you're set on her chink?...
With her you'll make ten cuckolds if you still insist,
Ten fresh tonight!... Go on. You got the cash in your fist,
Pay double. You'll be *seamanned* off, *matlow*. Up then...
– No, here... – What, in the dark?... Get off! In this den
No need to be embarrassed! – In here. – Not on. Must keep
The house rules. – Here, I insist! – Well... not to sleep...

Hey, you there, stand to the watch, you, *Dredger Mary*!
– What now? It's not my *trick*! – It's just a drink, nothing hairy,
Not this *fatigue*... Come on, board him: a loaded hold,
He has! – What of? – Come on. His socks are full of gold,
Some hunchback in a poke that's not to take the air...
– Good: let him take his fill. I've had my share.
I've got my line. – Come on. The kitchen...

                              – Let's see you, Duck!
You're twisted but a corkscrew doesn't shake my pluck!
Right... if it's okay by you: light the candle, hunch?
– No. – But I'd like to see you. I like Mr Punch...
Ah, caught you; I know how to play this blindman's buff!...
The madam shut the door...

                    – Ah, you crooked scruff!...

. . . .

– Some racket! – What an infernal dance! – For whom?
What burst bag rolling howls across the room?...
– Ah, you sausage skin! Oh, so it's a romp, you carcass!

À poil! à poil! on va te *caréner* tout cru!
Ah, tu grognes, cochon! Attends, tu veux la goutte:
Tiens son ballon!... Allons, avale-moi ça... toute!
Gare au grappin, il croche! Ah! le cancre qui mord!
C'est le diable bouilli!... –

           C'était l'heureux Bitor.

– Carognes, criait-il, mollissez!... je régale...
– Carognes?... Ah, roussin! mauvais comme la gale!
Tu régales, Limonadier de la Passion?
On te régalera, va! double ration!
Pou crochard qui montais nous piquer nos *punaises*!
Cancre qui viens manger nos *peaux*!... Pas de foutaises,
Vous autres: Toi, *la mère*, apporte de là haut,
Un grand tapis de lit, en double et comme-y-faut!...
Voilà! –
      Dix bras tendus halent la couverture
– Le *tortillou* dessus!... On va la danser dure;
Saute, Paillasse! hop là!... –
             C'est que le matelot,
Bon enfant, est très dur quand il est *rigolot*.
Sa colère: c'est bon. – Sa joie: ah, pas de grâce!...
Ces dames rigolaient...
          – Attrape: pile ou face?
Ah, le malin! quel vice! il échoue en côté! –
... Sur sa bosse grêlaient, avec quelle gaîté!
Des bouts de corde en l'air sifflant comme couleuvres;
Les sifflets de gabier, rossignols de manœuvres,
Commandaient et rossignolaient à l'unisson...
– Tiens bon!... –
        Pelotonné, le pauvre hérisson
Volait, rebondissait, roulait. Enfin la plainte
Qu'il rendait comme un cri de poulie est éteinte...
– Tiens bon! il fait exprès... Il est dur, l'entêté!...

Strip off. Strip off. You'll be *careened* and starkers.
Ah, you're grunting, pig! Hang on. You want a tot.
Hold his gob-let steady!... Here, knock it back... the lot!
Watch for the grapnel, it hooks! Ah, the duffer bites!
He's the devil on the boil... –

It was Arch happiness. The heights!

– Bitches, he was yelling, ease off... It's me that's paying...
– Bitches?... Ah, cart-horse, evil as mange, quit neighing!
You're paying, are you, Squash-pusher at the Passion?
No, we'll be paying you, right! Double ration!
You crooked louse, mounting to nip our *bedbuggery*.
Crab-louse, come to eat us *hole-sale*. No more fuckery,
The rest of you: and, *madam*, fetch us from upstairs
A double bedcover just the job!... now, you corsairs,
Here goes! –
                 Ten arms stretch the cover out. Biff.
– Up with the *humpback!*... We're going to dance him stiff.
Leap, Pillockcase, hup, there!... –
                 With a sailor, good sort,
It's pretty rough stuff, his clowning and his *sport*.
His anger: ah, that's good. – His joy: ah, merciless!...
The ladies were *disporting*...
                 – Heads or tails! Yes?
Catch. The little devil! Wicked! gone beam end aground! –
... Rope's ends rained down on the hunchback with the sound
Of hissing snakes, the bo's'n's pipes, the nightingales
Of rigging, issued orders singing out, as one, their scales...
– Keep on!... –
                 Curled in a ball the poor hedgehog went
Flying, bouncing, rolling. And then the long lament
He let out like a squealing block had ceased...
– Keep on. He's faking. He's tough, the pighead beast!...

C'est un lapin! ça veut le jus plus pimenté:
Attends!... –
              Quelques couteaux pleuvent... *Mary-Saloppe*
D'un beau mouvement, hèle: – À moi sa place! – Tope
Amène tout en vrac! largue!... –
                   Le jouet mort
S'aplatit sur la planche et rebondit encor...

Comme après un doux rêve, il rouvrit son œil louche
Et trouble... Il essuya dans le coin de sa bouche,
Un peu d'écume avec sa chique en sang... – C'est bien;
C'est fini, matelot... Un coup de *sacré-chien*!
Ça vous remet le cœur; bois!... –
                  Il prit avec peine
Tout l'argent qui restait dans son bon bas de laine
Et regardant *Mary-Saloppe*: – C'est pour toi,
Pour boire... en souvenir. – Vrai? baise-moi donc, quoi!...
Vous autres, laissez-le, grands lâches! mateluches!
C'est mon amant de cœur... on a ses coqueluches!
... Toi: file à l'embellie, en double, l'asticot:
L'échouage est mauvais, mon pauvre saligot!... –

Son œil marécageux, larme de crocodile,
La regardait encore... – Allons, mon garçon, file! –

. . . .

C'est tout. Le lendemain, et jours suivants, à bord
Il manquait. – Le navire est parti sans Bitor. –

. . . .

Plus tard, l'eau soulevait une masse vaseuse
Dans le dock. On trouva des plaques de vareuse...
Un cadavre bossu, ballonné, démasqué
Par les crabes. Et ça fut jeté sur le quai,

He's got some spunk! He wants it hotting up, more vim:
Stand to!... –
     Several knives were raining down on him...
Then *Dredger Mary* with a noble impulse cried:
– Right now, let me stand to! – Agreed, they all replied!
Lower away wholesail. Cast off!... –
       The dead plaything fell flat
Upon the deck and went rebounding after that...

As if out of a pleasant dream he opened a lid,
His squint eye troubled... And with his bloody baccy quid
He wiped foam from the corner of his mouth... – Good.
It's over, sailor... Now, *hair of the dog!* That should
Put heart in you again; drink up!... –
       In pain, he took
The cash left in his trusty sock, and with a look
At *Dredger Mary* managed: – Yours, for you, the lot.
Drink it for me... a reminder. – Really? Well, shaft me! What!
... The rest of you, leave him alone, you cowards, swabs.
He's my true love... one has one's favourites, you yobs!
... Now, you; save yourself, quick, in the coming trough:
Go, at the double, plague, it's a bad grounding, rough,
My poor little sod!... –
     Crocodile tears, his oozy look
Still gazed at her... – Now come on, kid, sling your hook! –

. . . .

And that was it. The next and following days, he failed
To show. – And without Archie Halyard the cutter sailed. –

. . . .

Later, in the dock, the water raised and floated
A slimy mass. Shreds of a sailor's jersey noted...
A swollen hunchback corpse, faceless from crabs.
They threw it out upon the dockside slabs,

Tout comme l'autre soir, sur une couverture.
Restant de crabe, encore il servit de pâture
Au rire du public; et les gamins d'enfants
Jouant au bord de l'eau noire sous le beau temps,
Sur sa bosse tapaient comme sur un tambour
Crevé...
      – Le pauvre corps avait connu l'amour!

                Marseille. – La Joliette. – Mai.

Le Renégat

Ça c'est un renégat. Contumace partout:
      Pour ne rien faire, ça fait tout.
Écumé de partout et d'ailleurs; crâne et lâche,
Écumeur amphibie, à la course, à la tâche;
Esclave, flibustier, nègre, blanc, ou soldat,
Bravo: fait tout ce qui concerne tout état;
Singe, limier de femme... ou même, au besoin, femme;
Prophète *in partibus*, à tant par kilo d'âme;
Pendu, bourreau, poison, flûtiste, médecin,
Eunuque; ou mendiant, un coutelas en main...

La mort le connaît bien, mais n'en a plus envie...
Recraché par la mort, recraché par la vie,
Ça mange de l'humain, de l'or, de l'excrément,
Du plomb, de l'ambroisie... ou rien – Ce que ça sent. –

And, very like the other night, on blanketing.
The crabs' rejects, still it was provisioning
For public laughter; and the brats of kids that played
On sunny days beside the black water, laid
Into his swollen hump as if it were a drum
That split...

            – The corpse had known love, the poor bum!

Marseilles. – La Joliette. – May.

Renegade

Renegade, this one. Defaulter, wandering:
      Does anything not to do a thing.
Drifts nowhere and beyond; swashbuckler, yob,
Privateer, two-faced, on shipboard or shore job;
Lackey, freebooter, black, white, soldier – hired –
Hit-man, does anything and all required,
Ape, woman-hound; at need, a woman found;
Prophet *in partibus*, soul sold by the pound;
Hanged stiff, butcher, poison, soak, and quack;
Eunuch; beggar, cutlass handy to attack...

Death knows him well, won't give him house-room...
Spewed up by life and spewed out by the tomb,
He gorges on the human, gold, lead, shit,
Ambrosia... or nothing – the stench of it. –

– Son nom? – Il a changé de peau, comme chemise...
Dans toutes langues c'est: Ignace ou Cydalyse,
Todos los santos... Mais il ne porte plus ça;
Il a bien effacé son *T.F.* de forçat!...

– Qui l'a poussé... l'amour? – Il a jeté sa gourme!
Il a tout violé: potence et garde-chiourme.
– La haine? – Non. – Le vol? – Il a refusé mieux.
– Coup de barre du vice? – Il n'est pas vicieux;
Non... dans le ventre il a de la fille-de-joie,
C'est un tempérament... un artiste de proie.

.   .   .   .

– Au diable même il n'a pas fait miséricorde.
– Hale encore! – Il a tout pourri jusqu'à la corde,
Il a tué toute *bête*, éreinté tous les coups...

Pur, à force d'avoir purgé tous les dégoûts.

Baléares.

– His name? – He changes skins like shirts… but he's
Well known in every tongue: Ignatius, Cydalise,
Todos los Santos… Can't manage another one.
His *Hard Labour* label's well and truly run!…

– What drives him on… love? – He's had his fling!
He's dished the lot now: noose, and screw. – His thing
Is hate? – No. – Theft? – He's passed up better. – Jerk
Of vice's helm? – He's not a vicious berk;
No… inside he's like a good-time lay,
It's just a bent… he is an artist of prey.

. . . .

– He gives no quarter even to the devil.
– The heave ho still! – He's rotted, razed all level,
Bumped off what's dumb; fagged out all blows and busts…

Pure by way of purging all of his disgusts!

Balearic Isles.

Aurora

APPAREILLAGE D'UN BRICK CORSAIRE

> *Quand l'on fut toujours vertueux*
> *L'on aime à voir lever l'aurore…*

Cent vingt *corsairiens*, gens de corde et de sac,
À bord de la *Mary-Gratis*, ont mis leur sac.
– Il est temps, les enfants! on a roulé sa bosse…
Hisse! – C'est le grand-foc qui va payer la noce.
Étarque! – Leur argent les fasse tous cocus!…
La drisse du grand-foc leur rendra leurs écus…
– Hisse hoé!… *C'est pas tant le gendarm' qué jé r'grette!*
– Hisse hoà!… *C'est pas ça! Naviguons, ma brunette!*

Va donc *Mary-Gratis*, brick écumeur d'Anglais!
Vire à pic et dérape!… – Un coquin de vent frais
Largue, en vrai matelot, les voiles de l'aurore;
L'écho des cabarets de terre beugle encore…
Eux répondent en chœur, perchés dans les huniers,
Comme des colibris au haut des cocotiers:
> *« Jusqu'au revoir, la belle,*
> *« Bientôt nous reviendrons… »*

Ils ont bien passé là quatre nuits de liesse,
Moitié sous le comptoir et moitié sur l'hôtesse…
> *« … Tâchez d'être fidèle,*
> *« Nous serons bons garçons… »*

– Évente les huniers!… *C'est pas ça qué jé r'grette…*
– Brasse et borde partout!… *Naviguons, ma brunette!*
– *Adieu, séjour de guigne!…* Et roule, et cours bon bord…
Va, la *Mary-Gratis!* – au nord-est quart de nord. –

Aurora

CORSAIR BRIG PREPARING TO SAIL

> *When you are always virtuous*
> *You like to see the dawn rise...*

A hundred and twenty *corsairs*, gallows-cheats and crooks,
On board the *Mary-Gratis* slung their bags and hooks.
– It's time, you rascals; your rolling stone has run...
Haul away! – The jib-boom pays out for the fun.
Hoist sail! – Their cash may cuckold all of them...
The jib-boom's halyards will restore their funds pro tem....
– Haul, haul!... *It's not so much the copper I regret!*
– Haul, haul!... *It isn't that. Let's steer clear, my pet!*

Right, then, *Mary-Gratis*, you Brit-scouring brig!
Tack apeak and trip the anchor!... – A freshening pig
Of a wind like a true sailor shakes out sails of dawn;
The echo of cabarets ashore bellows, long drawn...
They answer in a chorus perched in topsail yards,
Like humming birds in coconut palms, these topsy bards:
>   *'Till next time, you lovely, you,*
>   *Soon we'll return, my fair...'*

They've spent to the full their four nights of excess;
Half under the counter, and half on the hostess...
>   *'... Try to be loyal and true,*
>   *We'll be good boys, we swear...'*

– Set the tops'ls!... *It's not that I regret...*
– Brace and tauten all sail!... *Let's steer clear, my pet.*
– *Unlucky port of call, goodbye!*... Stand off the shoal...
Tack, *Mary-Gratis* – to nor-nor-east. And roll. –

... Et la *Mary-Gratis*, en flibustant l'écume,
Bordant le lit du vent se gîte dans la brume.
Et le grand flot du large en sursaut réveillé
À terre va bâiller, s'étirant sur le roc:

>   *Roul' ta bosse, tout est payé*
>   *Hiss' le grand foc!*

. . . .

Ils cinglent déjà loin. Et, couvrant leur sillage,
La houle qui roulait leur chanson sur la plage
Murmure sourdement, revenant sur ses pas:
– Tout est payé, la belle!... ils ne reviendront pas.

... And *Mary-Gratis* freebooting the foam that hissed,
Skirting the eye of the wind, puts up in the mist.
The tide of the offing startled awake and made for
The shore, yawning in, to stretch on rocks its spume:
>*Go, rolling stone, all's paid for.*
>*Brace the jib-boom!*

.   .   .   .

They scud into the distance. Covering their wake, the swell
That rolled their shanty over to the beach, and fell,
Murmurs its muffled sound withdrawing in its track:
– All's paid, my lovely!... no, they won't be coming back.

Le novice en partance et sentimental

À LA DÉÇENTE DES MARINS C^{HES}
MARIJANE SERRE À BOIRE ET À
MANGER COUCHE À PIEDS ET À
CHEVAL.

DEBIT.

Le temps était si beau, la mer était si belle …
     Qu'on dirait qu'y en avait pas.
Je promenais, un coup encore, ma Donzelle,
     À terre, tous deux, sous mon bras.

C'était donc, pour du coup, la dernière journée.
     Comme-ça : ça m'était égal …
Ça n'en était pas moins la suprême tournée
     Et j'étais sensitif pas mal.

… Tous les ans, plus ou moins, je relâchais près d'elle
     – Un mois de mouillage à passer –
Et je la relâchais tout fraîchement fidèle …
     Et toujours à recommencer.

Donc, quand la barque était à l'ancre, sans malice
     J'accostais, novice vainqueur,
Pour mouiller un pied d'ancre, Espérance propice ! …
     Un pied d'ancre dans son cœur !

Elle donnait la main à manger mon décompte
     Et mes avances à manger.
Car, pour un *mathurin** faraud, c'est une honte :
     De ne pas rembarquer léger.

---

* *Mathurin : Dumanet* maritime.

The Greenhorn on the Point of Embarking and Sentimental

AT THE SAILORS' INN, MARI-
JANE PROVIDES FOOD & DRINK
BED & STABLING.

FREE HOUSE.

The weather was good, the sea so calm...
      You would have said that there was none.
I walked my girl once more upon my arm,
      The two of us, ashore, in sun.

It was this time for certain our final day.
      Just so. Yet all the same to me...
But none the less our best jaunt anyway;
      I showed some, what, sensitivity.

... Every year more or less I'd docked by her
      – A month to spend at anchorage. –
I'd leave her feeling freshly faithfuller...
      And ready to repeat the privilege.

So when the barque docked, without tricks
      I'd board her, a greenhorn's conquering art,
To find a mooring, propitious Hope!... to fix
      A mooring safely in her heart!

She gave her hand to splash my discounts round;
      Of my advances made a splash.
For swash-buccaneering Pistol* feels unbound
      Disgrace if back on board with cash.

---

* Pistol: maritime equivalent of braggart soldier.

J'emportais ses cheveux, pour en cas de naufrage,
Et ses adieux au long-cours.

Et je lui rapportais des objets de sauvage,
Que le douanier saisit toujours.

Je me l'imaginais pendant les traversées,
Moi-même et naturellement.

Je m'en imaginais d'autres aussi – censées
Elle – dans mon tempérament.

Mon nom mâle à son nom femelle se jumelle,
Bout-à-bout et par à peu-près:

Moi je suis Jean-Marie et c'est Mary-Jane elle...
Elle ni moi *n'ons* fait exprès.

... Notre chien de métier est chose assez jolie
Pour un leste et gueusard amant;

Toujours pour démarrer on trouve l'embellie:
– Un pleur... Et saille de l'avant!

Et hisse le grand foc! – la loi me le commande. –
Largue les *garcettes*,* sans gant!

Étarque à bloc! – L'homme est libre et la mer est grande –
La femme: un sillage!... Et bon vent! –

On a toujours, puisque c'est dans notre nature,
– Coulant en douceur, comme tout –

Filé son câble par le bout, sans *fignolure*...
Filé son câble par le bout!

– File!... La passion n'est jamais défrisée.
– Évente tout et pique au nord!

Borde la brigantine et porte à la risée!...
– On prend sa capote et s'endort...

---

* *Garcettes*. – Bouts de corde qui servent à serrer les voiles.

In case of wreck, I'd take from her a curl
       And her goodbyes to distant lands,
Would bring outlandish trinkets for my girl
       That finished up in excise hands.

And I'd imagine her on voyages, that's me,
       And natural enough, it is.
Imagined others too – made out to be
       Herself – in my intimacies.

My man's name twinned itself with hers,
       Back to back but nearly the same.
Jean-Marie; Mary-Jane our monickers…
       Neither chose *either* by the name.

… Our bitch of a business is a bit of a plum
       For a mettlesome footloose sex-pot.
For cutting loose a lull will always come:
       – Tears… and forging out like a shot!

Raise the jib-boom! – it's the law of the sea. –
       Up *hawse** and away! Gloves off, set sail!
Brace tight! – The sea is vast and man is free. –
       Woman: a wake!… Fair winds prevail! –

We've always, since it's in our nature, yes –
       As easy going as they come –
Run our cable right out, no *finesse*…
       Run out our cable and then some!

– Run out!… Passion's never let down at all.
       Set all sail; head north; for the deep!
Tauten the spanker and stand in to the squall!…
       – You wear your watch coat and you sleep…

------

* *Hawse*: an arrangement of anchors.

– Et file le parfait amour! à ma manière,
     – Ce n'est pas la bonne: tant mieux!
C'est encor la meilleure et dernière et première…
     As pas peur d'échouer, mon vieux!

Ah! la mer et l'amour! – On sait – c'est variable…
     Aujourd'hui: zéphyrs et houris!
Et demain… c'est un grain: Vente la peau du diable!
     Debout au quart! croche des ris!…

– Nous fesons le bonheur d'un tas de malheureuses,
     Gabiers volants de Cupidon!…
Et la lame de l'ouest nous rince les pleureuses…
     – Encore une! et lave le pont!

. . . .

Comme ça moi je suis. Elle, c'était la rose
     D'amour, et du débit d'ici…
Nous cherchions tous deux à nous dire quelque chose
     De triste. – C'est plus propre aussi. –

… Elle ne disait rien – Moi: pas plus. – Et sans doute,
     La chose aurait duré longtemps…
Quand elle dit, d'un coup, au milieu de la route:
     – Ah Jésus! comme il fait beau temps. –

J'y pensais justement, et peut-être avant elle…
     Comme avec un même cœur, quoi!
Donc, je dis à mon tour: – Oh! oui, mademoiselle,
     Oui… Les vents halent le *noroî*…

– Ah! pour où partez-vous? – Ah! pour notre voyage…
     – Des pays mauvais? – Pas meilleurs…
– Pourquoi? – Pour faire un tour, démoisir l'équipage…
     Pour quelque part, et pas ailleurs:

– And run off the perfect love! my way,
        – Might not be the right way but first rate!
It's still the best, the last and first, I'll lay…
        No fear of grounding, my old mate!

Ah! love and the sea! – You know – they're fickle, twin…
        Today: it's all light breeze and houri!
Tomorrow… squall: to flay the devil's skin!
        Stand to the night watch! Reef in! The fury!…

– We make a happy heap of luckless dears,
        Cupid's flying topmen, on spec!…
The western swell swills off the women's tears…
        – Here's another! and swills the deck!

. . . .

That's how I am. And she, the compass Rose
        Of Love, and of the pub, too…
Both seeking something sad to say, I suppose.
        – It was the proper thing to do. –

… She was saying nothing – Me: no more. – And I dare say
        The thing would have taken us forever…
When suddenly she said in the middle of the way:
        – Ah, Jesus, today what lovely weather. –

I'd just thought that, perhaps before she had…
        As if, guess what! we had one heart!
I said in turn: – Oh! yes, lass, yes, not bad…
        These winds, veering nor'west for a *start*…

– Ah! where you bound for? – Well! for our next trip…
        – For dreadful countries? – Not so good…
– Why? – To sail, limber up crew and ship…
        To somewhere, nowhere else, understood:

New-York... Saint-Malo... – Que partout Dieu vous garde!
  – Oh!... Le saint homme y peut s'asseoir;
Ça c'est notre métier à nous, ça nous regarde:
   Éveillatifs, l'œil au bossoir!

– Oh! ne blasphémez pas! Que la Vierge vous veille!
  – Oui: que je vous rapporte encor
Une bonne Vierge à la façon de Marseille:
   Pieds, mains, et tête et tout, en or?...

– Votre navire est-il bon pour la mer lointaine?
  Ah! pour ça, je ne sais pas trop,
Mademoiselle; c'est l'affaire au capitaine,
   Pas à vous, ni moi matelot.

– Mais le navire a-t-il un beau nom de baptême?
  – C'est un *brick*... pour son petit nom:
Un espèce de nom de dieu... toujours le même,
   Ou de sa moitié: *Junon*...

– Je tremblerai pour vous, quand la mer se tourmente...
  – Tiens bon, va! la coque a deux bords...
On sait patiner ça! comme on fait d'une amante...
   – Mais les mauvais maux?... – Oh! des sorts!

– Je tremble aussi que vous n'oubliez mes tendresses
   Parmi vos reines de là-bas...
– Beaux cadavres de femme: oui! mais noirs et singesses...
   Et puis: voyez, là, sur mon bras:

C'est l'*Hôtel de l'Hymen, dont deux cœurs en gargousse*
   Tatoués à perpétuité!
Et *la petite bonne-femme en frac de mousse*:
   C'est vous, en portrait... pas flatté.

New York... St Malo... – God watch you anywhere!
      – Oh!... That saintly man may sit back now:
That's our own special job, how we take care:
      Look-sharpers, eye upon the bow!

– Oh! don't blaspheme! The Virgin watch the while!
      – So, and for you shall I get hold
Of a fine Virgin in the Marseilles style:
      Feet, hands, the head, and rest, of gold?...

– Is your ship in good shape for the high seas?
      – Ah! that I wouldn't really know,
Girl; that's the captain's business, if you please,
      Not yours, nor mine, plain matelot.

– But surely it has a good baptismal name?
      – *Brig*, you call it... for its first name, though:
A sort of god's name... it's always done the same,
      Or his other half: *Juno*, d'you know...

– I'll be anxious over you when the seas swirl...
      – Stay calm, a hull's got two sides...
You know how to coax it as you do a girl...
      – And if the worst comes?... – Oh, fate decides!

– I'm anxious, too, that you'll forget my touch...
      Among your queens, far off, abroad...
– Fine carcasses of women: blacks, apes and such...
      But look: here, on my arm well moored:

The Hymen Hotel, cartouche, with two hearts
      Tattooed in perpetuity!
And this *trim girl in cabin-boy gear* imparts:
      The image of you... no flannel, see!

– Pour lors, c'est donc demain que vous quittez?... – Peut-être.
       – Déjà!... – Peut-être après-demain.
– Regardez en appareillant, vers ma fenêtre:
       On fera bonjour de la main.

– C'est bon. Jusqu'au retour de n'importe où, m'amie...
       Du Tropique ou Noukahiva.
Tâchez d'être fidèle, et moi: sans avarie...
       Une autre fois mieux!... Adieu-vat!

                         Brest-Recouvrance.

– Well, then, tomorrow's when you leave?... – Could be.
    – So soon?... – Could be the next day or two.
– While getting shipshape then, glance up to see
    My window: I'll wave good luck to you.

– Good. Till I'm back from who knows where on the map,
    From Noukahiva or some Tropic clime,
Try to be faithful; me, too: without mishap...
    'Bye!... Helm aweather! Better next time!

Brest-Recouvrance.

La Goutte

Sous un seul hunier – le dernier – à la cape,
Le navire était soûl; l'eau sur nous faisait nappe.
– Aux pompes, faillis chiens! – L'équipage fit – non. –

– Le hunier! le hunier!...
                C'est un coup de canon,
Un grand froufrou de soie à travers la tourmente.

– Le hunier emporté! – C'est la fin. Quelqu'un chante. –
– Tais-toi, Lascar! – Tantôt. – Le hunier emporté!...
– Pare le foc, quelqu'un de bonne volonté!...
– Moi. – Toi, lascar? – Je chantais ça, moi, capitaine.
– Va. – Non: la goutte avant? – Non, après. – Pas la peine:
La grande tasse est là pour un coup... –
                            Pour braver,
Quoi! mourir pour mourir et ne rien sauver...
– Fais comme tu pourras: Coupe. Et gare à la drisse.
– Merci –
        D'un bond de singe il saute, de la lisse,
Sur le beaupré noyé, dans les agrès pendants.
– Bravo! –
          Nous regardions, la mort entre les dents.

– Garçons, tous à la drisse! à nous! pare l'écoute!...
(Le coup de grâce enfin...) – Hisse! barre au vent toute!
Hurrah! nous abattons!... –
                Et le foc déferlé
Redresse en un clin d'œil le navire acculé.
C'est le salut à nous qui bat dans cette loque
Fuyant devant le temps! Encor paré la coque!
– Hurrah pour le lascar! – Le lascar?...
                        – À la mer.
– Disparu? – Disparu – Bon, ce n'est pas trop cher.

The Tot

Under a single tops'l – the last – at the cape,
Sheets of water on us; ship a drunken ape.
– 'Man the pumps, you curs!'– Crew yelled – no – back.

– 'The tops'l! Tops'l, quick!'...
                 – Then comes a cannon crack.
Through the gale a great swish of ripped silk gone winging.

– 'Tops'l's gone! – We're done for.' Some idiot was singing. –
– 'Belt up, Lascar.' – 'Finished now.' – 'Tops'l's torn clear!'...
– 'Hoist the stays'l! Anyone game, some volunteer!'...
– 'I'll do it.' – 'You, Lascar?' – 'I sang out so, cap'n.'
– 'All right.' – 'No, first a tot?' – 'After.' – ''appen:
No problem. Davy Jones's Liquor's down there for a shot... –
Risk that! Dying for nothing, not even for a tiny tot.'...
– 'Do what you can first: cut it loose. Ware the halyard lash.'
– 'Thanks' –
         From the rail, with monkey spring he bounded, rash,
To the drowned bowsprit where the tackle dragged and
      weighed.
– 'Bravo!' –
         Death's taste in the mouth, we watched, dismayed.

– 'All hands to the ropes! Here. Prepare the lower rig!'...
(The mercy blow at last...) – 'Haul. Weather the helm!' A big:
'Hurrah! She's paying off!...' –
            The stays'l, unfurled, swelled,
Righting in a flash the stern-down ship, and held.
It was our safety flapping in that rag in our flight
Before the weather. The hull still seemed all right!
– 'Hurrah for the Lascar!' – 'Where's the Lascar?... – 'Lost?''
'Overboard?'– 'Overboard.'– 'Well, not too great a cost.'

. . . .

– Ouf! c'est fait – Toi, Lascar! – Moi, Lascar, capitaine,
La lame m'a rincé de dessus la poulaine,
Le même coup de mer m'a ramené gratis…
Allons, mes poux n'auront pas besoin d'onguent-gris.

– Accoste, tout le monde! Et toi, Lascar, écoute:
Nous te devons la vie… – Après? – Pour ça?… – La goutte!
Mais c'était pas pour ça, n'allez pas croire, au moins…
– Viens m'embrasser! – Attrape à torcher les grouins.
J'suis pas beau, capitain', mais, soit dit en famille,
Je vous ai fait plaisir plus qu'une belle fille?…

. . . .

Le capitaine mit, ce jour, sur son rapport:
– *Gros temps. Laissé porter. Rien de neuf à bord.* –

À bord.

. . . .

'Phew! Done it!' – 'Lascar still with us?' – 'Yes, skipper, me,
Washed from the bowsprit by a breaking sea,
The same that washed me back again on deck...
Well, my fleas won't need much treatment. Heck!'

– 'Assemble all hands! And, Lascar, listen, know what?
We owe our lives to you.'... – 'So?' – 'For that?'– 'A tot!
Don't ever think I did it just for that, a guzzle.'...
– 'Let me embrace you!' – 'Hug and rub dry, muzzle to
     muzzle.
Not handsome, skipper, but, among ourselves, we'd say:
I've given you more pleasure than a good-time lay?'...

. . . .

The captain in his log had only to record:
– *'Foul weather. Ran on before. Nothing new aboard.'* –

                                        Aboard.

Bambine

Tu dors sous les panais, capitaine Bambine
Du remorqueur havrais *l'Aimable Proserpine*,
Qui, vingt-huit ans, fis voir au Parisien béant,
Pour vingt sous: *L'OCÉAN! L'OCÉAN!! L'OCÉAN!!!*

Train de plaisir au large. – On double la jetée –
En rade: *y a-z-un peu d'gomme*... – Une mer démontée –
Et *la cargaison* râle: – Ah! commandant! assez!
Assez, pour notre argent, de tempête! cessez! –

Bambine ne dit mot. Un bon coup de mer passe
Sur les infortunés: – Ah, capitaine! grâce!...
– C'est bon... si ces messieurs et dam's ont leur content?...
C'est pas pour mon plaisir, moi, v's'êtes mon chargement:
Pare à virer... –

         Malheur! le coquin de navire
Donne en grand sur un banc... – Stoppe! – Fini de rire...
Et talonne à tout rompre, et roule bord sur bord
Balayé par la lame: – À la fin, c'est trop fort!... –

Et *la cargaison* rend des cris... rend tout! rend l'âme.
Bambine fait les cent pas.
             Un ange, une femme
Le prend: – C'est ennuyeux ça, conducteur! cessez!
Faites-moi mettre à terre, à la fin! c'est assez! –

Bambine l'élongeant d'un long regard austère:
– À terre! q'vous avez dit?... vous avez dit: à terre...
À terre! pas dégoûtaî!... Moi-z'aussi, foi d'mat'lot,
J'voudrais ben!... attendu q'si t'-ta-l'heure l'prim'flot

Bambine

You're pushing up the daisies, Captain Bambine,
Ex- the le-Havran tug *The Sweet Proserpine*, keen
For twenty-eight years to offer gaping Paris a notion
For sous of: *THE OCEAN! THE OCEAN!! THE OCEAN!!!*

Excursion train at sea. – It smoothly rounds the pier –
In the roadstead: *a bit upper crust* ... – Seas rear. –
The *cargo*'s at its death rattle: – 'Ah, captain, enough!
Enough; we've had our money's worth of this rough stuff.' –

Bambine says nothing. On the luckless ones a sea breaks: –
'Ah, captain! have mercy, have mercy for our sakes!' ...
– 'Fair-dos ... if these ladies and gents have had their share? ...
It's no pleasure of mine. You're my shipment. Prepare
To go about!' ... –

                        Bad luck! The rogue of a boat planks
Itself down slap on a shoal ... – 'Stop now! No more pranks ...'
She bottoms enough to break up and rolls gunwale down,
Swept by the waves: – 'Give over; too much of this, clown! ...'

The cargo hawks up screams ... hawks everything! and spirit next.
Bambine paces to and fro.
                        An angel, a woman, vexed,
Collars him: – 'All this is irritating, driver! Drop it!
Have me put ashore. That's enough now! Stop it!' –

Bambine lay alongside her with a long hard stare:
– 'Ashore! You said? ... You said "Ashore"! Ashore ... Spare
Me, you don't want much! ... On my word as sailor, me too.
I'd like it a lot! ... since if the first breaker don't slew

Ne soulag' pas la coque: vous et moi, mes princesses,
J'bêrons ben, sauf respect, la lavure éd'nos fesses! –

Il reprit ses cent pas, tout à fait mal bordé:
– À terre!... j'crâis f...tre ben! Les femm's!... pas dégoûté!

Havre-de-Grâce. La Hève. – Août.

Cap'taine Ledoux

À LA BONNE RELÂCHE DES CABOTEURS
VEUVE-CAP'TAINE GALMICHE
CHAUDIÈRE POUR LES MARINS – COOK-HOUSE
BRANDY – LIQŒUR
– POULIAGE –

Tiens, c'est l'cap'tain' Ledoux!... et quel bon vent vous pousse?
– Un *bon frais*, m'am' Galmiche, à fair'plier mon pouce:
R'lâchés en avarie, en rade, avec mon *lougre*...
– Auguss'! on se hiss' pas comm' ça desur les g'noux
Des cap'tain's!... – Eh, laissez, l'chérubin! c'est à vous?
– Mon portrait craché hein?... – Ah...

Ah! l'vilain p'tit bougre.

Saint-Mâlo-de-l'Isle.

Her off, then you and me, princesses, will get,
Most likely, no disrespect, our arses swilling wet!' –

Absolutely sprung, he went on pacing to and fro:
– 'Ashore!… Bugger me! Women!… they don't want much.
Oh no!'

Havre-de-Grâce. La Hève. – August.

Cap'n Gentle

THE GOOD HAVEN FOR COASTERS
CAPT. GALMICHE'S WIDOW
WASH-HOUSE FOR SAILORS — COOK-HOUSE
BRANDY — LICQUER
— TACKLE —

Well, skipper Gentle!… And what fair wind blows you in?
– A *freshener*, Mrs Galmiche, that bends the thumbs like skin:
Put in through damage in the roads with my *lugger*…
– Gus! you don't clamber up on the knees of a cap'n
Like that!… – Oh, he's all right, the cherub! Yours, happen,
Isn't he? – My spitting image, eh?… – Ah…

Ah! the hideous little bugger.

St Mâlo-de-l'Isle.

Lettre du Mexique

La Vera-Cruz, 10 février.

« Vous m'avez confié le petit. – Il est mort.
Et plus d'un camarade avec, pauvre cher être.
L'équipage… y en a plus. Il reviendra peut-être
       Quelques-uns de nous. – C'est le sort –

« Rien n'est beau comme ça – Matelot – pour un homme;
Tout le monde en voudrait à terre – C'est bien sûr.
Sans le désagrément. Rien que ça: Voyez comme
       Déjà l'apprentissage est dur.

« Je pleure en marquant ça, moi, vieux *Frère-la-côte*.
J'aurais donné ma peau joliment sans façon
Pour vous le renvoyer… Moi, ce n'est pas ma faute:
       Ce mal-là n'a pas de raison.

« La fièvre est ici comme Mars en carême.
Au cimetière on va toucher sa ration.
Le zouave a nommé ça – Parisien quand-même –
       Le jardin d'acclimatation.

« Consolez-vous. Le monde y crève comme mouches.
… J'ai trouvé dans son sac des souvenirs de cœur:
Un portrait de fille, et deux petites babouches,
       Et: marqué – *Cadeau pour ma sœur.* –

« Il fait dire à *maman*: qu'il a fait sa prière.
Au père: qu'il serait mieux mort dans un combat.
Deux anges étaient là sur son heure dernière:
       Un matelot. Un vieux soldat. »

Toulon, 24 mai.

Letter from Mexico

Vera Cruz, February 10th.

'You entrusted the kid to me. – He's dead.
And more than one with him, poor little sprat.
The crew... exists no more. It may be that
        Some will get back. – Fate has its head. –

'Nothing as good as that – Sailoring – for a man;
Everyone ashore wants to sail – That's sure enough.
But for the hardship. Nothing but that: you can
        See: even apprenticeship is tough.

'Saying this, me, an old sea-dog, I weep salt.
I'd cheerfully have risked my neck to send
Him back to you, no messing... It's not my fault:
        This outbreak makes no sense, old friend.

'As regular as clockwork the fever's back here.
You get your square ration in the burial ground.
The Zouave has called it – a Parisian, that's clear –
        The zoo's *settling-in* pound.

'Console yourself. They die off here like flies.
... I came across these souvenirs in his bag:
A girl's picture; Turkish slippers, tiny size,
        With: "For my sister" – on a tag. –

'He said to tell his *mum* he'd said his prayers.
To father: he'd rather died in action, older.
Two angels with him at the last, confreres:
        A sailor. And an old soldier.'

Toulon, 24th May.

Le Mousse

Mousse: il est donc marin, ton père?...
– Pêcheur. Perdu depuis longtemps.
En découchant d'avec ma mère,
Il a couché dans les brisants...

Maman lui garde au cimetière
Une tombe – et rien dedans. –
C'est moi son mari sur la terre,
Pour gagner du pain aux enfants.

Deux petits. – Alors, sur la plage,
Rien n'est revenu du naufrage?...
– Son garde-pipe et son sabot...

La mère pleure, le dimanche,
Pour repos... Moi: j'ai ma revanche
Quand je serai grand – matelot! –

Baie des Trépassés.

Cabin Boy

Well, kid, dad a seaman, you say?...
– Fisherman. Lost a long time ago.
Got up from mother's bed one day
And went to sleep with the waves below...

Mum keeps a grave by, anyway,
In the churchyard – nothing in it, though. –
Her husband's me on earth; my pay
Provides the littl'uns with the dough.

Two toddlers. – Nothing washed ashore
Out of the wreckage? – Nothing more
Than his pipe-pouch, clog, thrown up...

Sundays mum weeps for rest... Me:
I'll have revenge upon the sea,
– Sailor, me! – when I'm grown up. –

Deadmen's Bay.

Au vieux Roscoff

BERCEUSE EN NORD-OUEST MINEUR

Trou de flibustiers, vieux nid
À corsaires! – dans la tourmente,
Dors ton bon somme de granit
Sur tes caves que le flot hante…

Ronfle à la mer, ronfle à la brise;
Ta corne dans la brume grise,
Ton pied marin dans les brisans…
– Dors: tu peux fermer ton œil borgne
Ouvert sur le large, et qui lorgne
Les Anglais, depuis trois cents ans.

– Dors, vieille coque bien ancrée;
Les margats et les cormorans
Tes grands poètes d'ouragans
Viendront chanter à la marée…

– Dors, vieille fille-à-matelots;
Plus ne te soûleront ces flots
Qui te faisaient une ceinture
Dorée, aux nuits rouges de vin,
De sang, de feu! – Dors… Sur ton sein
L'or ne fondra plus en friture.

– Où sont les noms de tes amants…
– La mer et la gloire étaient folles! –
Noms de lascars! noms de géants!
Crachés des gueules d'espingoles!…

Où battaient-ils, ces pavillons,
Écharpant ton ciel en haillons!…
– Dors au ciel de plomb sur tes dunes…

To Old Roscoff

LULLABY IN NORTH-WEST MINOR

Bolt-hole for freebooters, old nest
Of pirates! – sleep throughout the storm
Your heavy granite slumber; rest
On your cellars haunted by tides that swarm...

Snore like the breeze; like the sea, snore;
Your horn in the grey fog roar;
Your sea-legs in the breaking combers...
– Sleep: you can shut your shifty eye
Open on the sea and used to spy
Three hundred years on English roamers.

– Sleep, old hull; well anchored, ride;
The cormorant and ember-goose
Your great poets of hurricanes let loose
Will come and sing above the tide...

– Sleep now, seamen's ancient whore;
These waves will get you drunk no more
Though once they gave you a golden belt
On nights turned red with wine, with gore,
With fire! – Sleep... On your breast no more
In sizzling fry will such gold melt.

– Where now your lovers' names, old flames?...
– Mad was the sea, glory a craze! –
The names of lascars, giants' names!
Spewed in the blunderbusses' sprays...

Where have they flapped to, your old flags
That used to tear your sky to rags!...
– Sleep under lead skies, on your dunes recline...

Dors: plus ne viendront ricocher
Les boulets morts, sur ton clocher
Criblé – comme un prunier – de prunes…

– Dors: sous les noires cheminées,
Écoute rêver tes enfants,
Mousses de quatre-vingt-dix ans,
Épaves des belles années…

. . . .

Il dort ton bon canon de fer,
À plat-ventre aussi dans sa souille,
Grêlé par les lunes d'hyver…
Il dort son lourd sommeil de rouille.

– Va: ronfle au vent, vieux ronfleur,
Tiens toujours ta gueule enragée
Braquée à l'Anglais!… et chargée
De maigre jonc-marin en fleur.

Roscoff. – Décembre.

Sleep: no more will cannonballs shower
Down dead, bounced off your belfry-tower
Riddled with grapeshot – like a vine...

– Sleep: under black chimneys, hark,
Hear your children dreaming away,
Cabin-boys, ninety if a day,
Wrecks of the golden times, the ark!...

.   .   .   .

Your fine old iron cannon's asleep,
Belly-flopped, also, in the dust,
Hailed on by wintry moons... how deep
And sound its sleep, heavy with rust.

– Come: snore in the wind, old snorer, boom.
Keep your angry muzzle poking
Towards the English!... charged and smoking
With weedy furze in fullest bloom.

Roscoff. – December.

Le Douanier

ÉLÉGIE DE CORPS-DE-GARDE
À LA MÉMOIRE DES DOUANIERS
GARDES-CÔTES MIS À LA RETRAITE
LE 30 NOVEMBRE 1869

Quoi, l'on te fend l'oreille! est-il vrai qu'on te rogne,
Douanier?... Tu vas mourir et pourrir sans façon,
Gablou?... – Non! car je vais t'empailler – Qui qu'en grogne! –
Mais, sans te déflorer: avec une chanson;
Et te coller ici, boucané de mes rimes,
Comme les varechs secs des herbiers maritimes.

    – Ange gardien culotté par les brises,
      Pénate des falaises grises,
      Vieux oiseau salé du bon Dieu
      Qui flânes dans la tempête,
      Sans auréole à la tête,
      Sans aile à ton habit bleu!...

      Je t'aime, modeste amphibie
      Et ta bonne trogne d'amour,
      Anémone de mer fourbie
      Épanouie à mon *bonjour!*...
      Et j'aime ton *bonjour*, brave homme,
      Roucoulé dans ton estomac,
      Tout gargarisé de rogomme
      Et tanné de jus de tabac!
      J'aime ton petit corps de garde
      Haut perché comme un goéland
            Qui regarde
      Dans les quatre aires-de-vent.

      Là, rat de mer solitaire,
      Bien loin du contrebandier

The Customsman

GUARDHOUSE ELEGY
TO THE MEMORY OF COASTGUARD
CUSTOMSMEN PENSIONED OFF
30 NOVEMBER 1869

What, you, too, cashiered! But tell me, is it true,
Excise man, you've also been excised?... You'll die and rot
Without ceremony, *bag-nab*?... – No! you won't, not you.
I'm going to stuff you. – No matter who complains! – But not
Deflower you: with a song; and hang you up here,
Smoked in my rhymes like seaweed, dried and sere.

    – Guardian-angel, breeched with wind-whiffs,
      Penates of the lone grey cliffs,
      Salty old bird of almighty God,
      Kicking your heels in storm and squall,
      No halo round your head at all,
      Wingless, you blue-coated clod!...

      Bashful amphibian, I like you, see?
      Your good and ruddy mug, I love;
      Polished sea-anemone,
      To my *good-day* blooming, guv...
      I like your *good-day*, fine bloke,
      Out of your belly rumbled loose,
      All gargled through a boozy croak
      And weathered in tobacco juice!
      I like your little look-out post,
      Perched high like a gull, eyes skinned,
            Watching the coast
      To the four quarters of the wind.

      There, solitary, water rat,
      Far off the scent of contraband,

Tu rumines ta chimère:
– Les galons de brigadier! –

Puis un petit coup-de-blague
Doux comme un demi-sommeil...
Et puis: bâiller à la vague,
Philosopher au soleil...

La nuit, quand fait la rafale
La chair-de-poule au flot pâle,
Hululant dans le roc noir...
Se promène une ombre errante;
Soudain: une pipe ardente
Rutile... – Ah! douanier, bonsoir.

· · · · · · · · · · · · · · · · ·

– Tout se trouvait en toi, bonne femme cynique.
Brantôme, Anacréon, Barême et le Portique;
Homère-troubadour, vieille Muse qui chique!
Poète trop senti pour être poétique!...
– Tout: sorcier, sage-femme et briquet phosphorique,
Rose-des-vents, sacré gui, lierre bacchique,
Thermomètre à l'alcool, coucou droit à musique,
Oracle, écho, docteur, almanach, empirique,
Curé voltairien, huître politique...
– Sphinx d'assiette d'un sou, ton douanier souvenir
Lisait le bordereau même de l'avenir!

– Tu connaissais Phœbé, Phœbus, et les marées...
Les amarres d'amour sur les grèves ancrées
Sous le vent des rochers; et tout amant fraudeur
Sous ta coupe passait le colis de son cœur...
– Tu reniflais le temps, quinze jours à l'avance,
Et les noces: neuf mois... et l'état de la France;
Tu savais tous les noms, les cancans d'alentour,
Et de terre et de mer, et de nuit et de jour!...

You ruminate daydreams: that
You'll get – officer stripes, so grand! –

Then, a little bit of a smoke,
Sweet as a cat-nap… That done:
A yawning fit the waves provoke,
Philosophize in the sun…

Night, when the rising squall brings
Gooseflesh to pallid billowings
Howling like wolves in black rocks…
A wandering shadow on its toes;
Suddenly: a lit pipe glows…
– Ah, officer, good evening. – Old fox.

.   .   .   .

– Everything's found in you, goodwife cynic, you're:
Brantôme, Anacreon, Ready Reckoner, Stoic, the hoar
Old Muse, chewing a quid; Homer the Troubadour;
Poet too heartfelt to be poet any more!…
– The lot: midwife and phosphor flint-stone, war-
Lock, compass card, the sacred mistletoe, oracle-lore,
Alcohol thermometer, musical cuckoo clock; you're
Bacchanal ivy, echo, doctor, back-number bore,
Empiricist, voltairean priest, political numbskull… for,
– Sphinx-taxer of our hard tacks – your excise memory
Would check the docket even of futurity!

– You knew Phoebe, Phoebus, and the tides, all and each…
The ropes of love that anchor up and down the beach,
Under the lee of the rocks; each cheating lover come
To smuggle the parcel of his heart under your thumb…
– You'd nose the weather out a fortnight in advance,
And weddings: nine months… and the state of France;
You knew the names and all the scandals close to hand,
Of the day and of the night, of sea and of the land!…

Je te disais ce que je savais écrire…
Et nous nous comprenions – tu ne savais pas lire –
Mais ta philosophie était un puits profond
Où j'aimais à cracher, rêveur… pour faire un rond.

. . . .

Un jour – ce fut ton jour! – Je te vis redoutable:
 Sous ton bras fiévreux cahotait la table
 Où nageait, épars, du papier timbré;
 La plume crachait dans tes mains alertes
 Et sur ton front noir, tes lunettes vertes
 Sillonnaient d'éclairs ton nez cabré…

 – Contre deux rasoirs d'Albion perfide,
 Nous verbalisions! tu verbalisais!
 « *Plus les deux susdits… dont un baril vide…* »
 J'avais composé, tu repolissais…

. . . .

– Comme un songe passé, douanier, ces jours de fête!
Fais valoir maintenant tes droits à la retraite…
– Brigadier, brigadier, vous n'aurez plus raison!…
– Plus de longue journée à gratter l'horizon,
Plus de sieste au soleil, plus de pipe à la lune,
Plus de nuit à l'affût des lapins sur la dune…
Plus rien, quoi!… que *la goutte* et le ressouvenir…
– Ah! pourtant: tout cela c'est bien vieux pour finir!

– Va, lézard démodé! Faut passer, mon vieux type;
Il faut te voir t'éteindre et s'éteindre ta pipe…
Passer, ta pipe et toi, parmi les vieux culots:
L'administration meurt, faute de ballots!…

Telle que, sans rosée, une sombre pervenche
Se replie, en closant sa corolle qui penche…

I'd tell you what I knew I'd be writing... We'd
A good understanding between us – you couldn't read –
But your philosophy was a well, oh, so profound,
In which I loved to spit, dreamer... to make a round.

. . . .

One day – it was your day! – I saw your doughty side:
    Under your fevered arms the table shied;
    Where crazy headed sheets, scattered, splashed;
    In your alerted hands the pen spat flecks.
    And on your black features your greenish specs,
    Wrinkling your bucking nose, their lightning flashed...

    – Against two dry sticks of perfidious Albion,
    We summoned the verbals; a summons you verbalized!
    'Plus *the two aforesaid... one keg empty*' – and on.
    I had composed, you polished and revised...

. . . .

– Like a forgotten dream, officer, your heydays!
Assert you rights now to the pension phase...
– Officer, officer, you won't be in the right!...
– No more raking horizons through the hours of light;
No more siestas in the sun, nor pipes in the moon;
No more eyes skinned for bucks from dune to dune...
Nothing more, what!... but little *tots* down memory lane...
– Ah! well: all that's old hat enough to end, in the main!

– Get on, you're out of the Ark! You must pass, old bloke;
Must see yourself put out and put out your pipe smoke...
Shelved, your pipe and you, among old briars, old smut:
The administration's dying for lack of case – and butt!...

As without the dew, a sombre periwinkle settles
Into itself, closing its flower, drooping its petals...

Telle, sans contrebande, on voit se replier
La capote gris-bleu, corolle du douanier!...
Quel sera désormais le terme du problème:
– L'ennui contemplatif divisé par lui-même? –
Quel balancier rêveur fera donc les cent pas,
Poète, sans savoir qu'il ne s'en doute pas...
Qui? sinon le douanier. – Hélas, qu'on me le rende!
Dussé-je pour cela faire la contrebande...

. . . .

– Non: fini!... réformé! Va, l'oreille fendue,
Rendre au gouvernement ta pauvre âme rendue...
Rends ton gabion, rends tes *Procès-verbaux divers*;
Rends ton bancal, rends tout, rends ta chique!...

Et mes vers.

Roscoff. – Novembre.

So, without contraband, you see the greatcoat, grey-
Blue flower of the excise, fold itself away!...
What will end this predicament now he's on the shelf:
– Ruminating tedium at loggerheads with itself? –
What dreamer pendulum pace to and fro a bit,
Poet without knowing he's written out of it...
Who now, if no excise man? – Heigh-ho, may I have him back!
To get him should I give smuggling a little crack?...

.   .   .   .

– No: finished!... dismissed! Come on, cash-eared poll,
Hand the government back your overtaxed poor soul...
Hand back your gabion; your *official reports*, long, terse;
Hand back your clay more, your all, last quid!...

> And my verse.

Roscoff – November.

Le Naufrageur

Si ce n'était pas vrai – Que je crève!

. . . .

J'ai vu dans mes yeux, dans mon rêve,
La Notre-Dame des brisans
Qui jetait à ses pauvres gens
Un gros navire sur leur grève...
Sur la grève des Kerlouans
Aussi goélands que les goélands.

Le sort est dans l'eau: le cormoran nage,
Le vent bat en côte, et c'est le *Mois Noir*...
Oh! moi je sens bien de loin le naufrage!
Moi j'entends là-haut chasser le nuage!
Moi je vois profond dans la nuit, sans voir!

Moi je siffle quand la mer gronde,
Oiseau de malheur à poil roux!...
J'ai promis aux douaniers de ronde,
Leur part, pour rester dans leurs trous...
Que je sois seul! – oiseau d'épave
Sur les brisans que la mer lave...

. . . .

Oiseau de malheur à poil roux!

– Et qu'il vente la peau du diable!
Je sens ça déjà sous ma peau.
La mer moutonne!... Ho, mon troupeau!
– C'est moi le berger, sur le sable...

L'enfer fait l'amour. – Je ris comme un mort –
Sautez sous le *Hû!*... le *Hû* des rafales,

The Wrecker

If it weren't true – fix my demise!

.   .   .   .

I've seen in dream, and in my eyes,
Our LADY OF THE BREAKERS throw
Up for her poor on the strand below
A vessel of a massive size ...
On the Kerlouan strand, you know,
As seagull as the seagulls go.

Fate is in the waves; the cormorant's afloat.
The gale beats inshore; the *Black Month* it would be ...
Oh! me, I sense the wreck though far remote!
Me, I can hear clouds race above, and note!
Me, deep into night without the eyes I see!

Me, oh I whistle when sea roars,
Bird of ill-omen with feathers red ...
I've promised the excise of these shores
Their cut to keep holed up instead ...
Wreck-haunter bird – steer clear of me! –
On reefs washed over by the sea ...

.   .   .   .

Bird of ill-omen with feathers red!

– May it flay the devil with its roar!
And in my bones I sense it near.
The sea's white fleeces! ... My flock, here!
– It's me, the shepherd of the shore ...

All hell's in rampant orgy. – I laugh like a corpse –
Leap under the *Hup*pity! ... *Hup* of the gales,

Sur les *noirs taureaux sourds, blanches cavales!*
Votre écume à moi, *cavales d'Armor!*
Et vos crins au vent!... – Je ris comme un mort –

    Mon père était un vieux *saltin,**
    Ma mère une vieille *morgate*...†
    Une nuit, sonna le tocsin:
    – Vite à la côte: une frégate! –
    ... Et dans la nuit, jusqu'au matin,
    Ils ont tout rincé la frégate...

    – Mais il dort mort le vieux *saltin,*
    Et morte la vieille *morgate*...
    Là-haut, dans le paradis saint,
    Ils n'ont plus besoin de frégate.

            Banc de Kerlouan. – Novembre.

---

* *Saltin*: pilleur d'épaves.
† *Morgate*: pieuvre.

On the *dull black bulls, white horses,* manes and tails!
Your lather's mine, you *swift Armorican horse!*
Your tousled mains the wind's!... – I laugh like a corpse. –

My father was a *wreck*-er, too.
Mother, an old *vampire,* she...
One night the warning hullabaloo:
– Quick, to the shore. Frigate alee! –
... During the night till dawn broke through,
They rinsed it cleaner than the sea...

– The old *wrecker*'s dead asleep.
Dead the old *vampire* as well...
In blessèd paradise they keep
No watch for frigates in the swell.

The Kerlouan Bank. – November.

À mon cotre le Négrier

VENDU SUR L'AIR DE
« ADIEU, MON BEAU NAVIRE! » ...

Allons file, mon cotre!
Adieu mon Négrier.
Va, file aux mains d'un autre
Qui pourra te noyer...

Nous n'irons plus sur la vague lascive
Nous gîter en fringuant!
Plus nous n'irons à la molle dérive
Nous rouler en rêvant...

– Adieu, rouleur de cotre,
Roule mon Négrier,
Sous les pieds plats de l'autre
Que tu pourras noyer.

Va! nous n'irons plus rouler notre bosse...
Tu cascadais fourbu;
Les coups de mer arrosaient notre noce,
Dis: en avons-nous bu!...

– Et va, noceur de cotre!
Noce, mon Négrier!
Que sur ton pont se vautre
Un noceur perruquier.

... Et, tous les crins au vent, nos chaloupeuses!
Ces vierges à sabords!
Te patinant dans nos courses mousseuses!...
Ah! c'étaient les bons bords!...

To My Cutter 'The Slaver'

VENDORED TO THE TUNE OF
'GOODBYE, MY SPLENDID BOAT!'

Well, off you go, old cutter!
Adieu, adieu; my 'Slaver'.
Sail, skippered by some strutter
Who'll sink you for the favour...

We'll go no more on the lusty swell,
  Nor heel ourselves with flair!
Nor go for a gently drifting spell
  To roll in dreams somewhere...

  – Fare well, my rolling cutter,
  Roll and pitch, my 'Slaver',
  Into that flat-foot nutter.
  You could sink the shaver.

So! we'll no longer swan off cruising...
  As once, old raver, zonked out;
The pound of waves watered our boozing,
  Haven't we've soaked in it, plonked out!...

  – Go it, old rake, my cutter!
  Half seas over, my 'Slaver'!
  Get wallowing in your gutter
  A toupé'd, old-fart raver.

– Think, hair all tousled, all our combers!
  Those port-hold virgins! would
Stroke you along our course of foamers!...
  Ah, those ship-bawds, they were good!...

         – Va, pourfendeur de lames,
         Pourfendre, ô Négrier!
         L'estomac à des dames
         Qui *paîront leur loyer.*

… Et sur le dos rapide de la houle,
         Sur le roc au dos dur,
À toc de toile allait ta coque soûle…
         – Mais toujours d'un œil sûr! –

         – Va te soûler, mon cotre:
         À crever! Négrier.
         Et montre bien à l'autre
         Qu'on savait louvoyer.

… Il faisait beau quand nous mettions en panne,
         Vent-dedans, vent-dessus;
Comme on pêchait!… Va: je suis dans la panne
         Où l'on ne pêche plus.

         – La mer jolie est belle
         Et les brisans sont blancs…
         Penché, trempe ton aile
         Avec les goëlands!…

Et cingle encor de ton fin mât-de-flèche,
         Le ciel qui court au loin.
Va! qu'en glissant, l'algue profonde lèche
         Ton ventre de marsouin!

         – Va, sans moi, sans ton âme;
         Et saille de l'avant!…
         Plus ne battras ma flamme
         Qui chicanait le vent.

– Go, wave-cleaver, skimming;
Cleave in two, my 'Slaver',
The bellies of those women
Who'll *cough up* without haver.

... And on the swift back of the swell,
At the hard-ridged rock would fly
With a rag of a rig your sloshed cockleshell ...
– But with a well-spliced eye! –

– Get sloshed, my cutter, high:
Dead pissed! Show, my 'Slaver',
That guy with your glad aye-aye
You put about with savour.

... In fine weather we would heave to off shore,
Wind filling, wind aback;
And what we fished! ... Now: I'll fish no more;
Shelled out; no tick, no tack.

– The sea is jolly fine,
The breakers foaming white ...
Dip your wing, incline
With the seagulls' flight! ...

Beat with your handsome mast the sky
That scuds away. Go! glide
On so the deep weed lips your spry
Porpoise bellying side!

– Go without me, your soul,
And thrust your prow into the seas! ...
No more to fly my banderole
That flirted with the breeze.

Que la risée enfle encor ta *Fortune**
     En bandant tes agrès!
– Moi: plus d'agrès, de lest, ni de fortune…
     Ni de risée après!

     … Va-t'en, humant la brume
     Sans moi, prendre le frais,
     Sur la vague de plume…
     Va – Moi j'ai trop de frais. –

Légère encor est pour toi la rafale
     Qui frisotte la mer!
Va… – Pour moi seul, rafalé, la rafale
     Soulève une flot amer!…

     – Dans ton âme de cotre,
     Pense à ton matelot
     Quand, d'un bord ou de l'autre,
     Remontera le flot…

– Tu peux encor échouer ta carène
     Sur l'humide varech;
Mais moi j'échoue aux côtes de la gêne,
     Faute de fond – à sec –

               Roscoff. – Août.

---

* Large voile de beau temps.

Derisory squalls still swell your *Fore–tune**
       In tautened rig and tackle.
– Me: no more rigging, mast-ery, fortune ...
       Afterwards, no cackle!

       ... Go away; snuff up the haze
       Without me, take the air,
       On the waves' feathery sprays ...
       Go – I'm a nillion-aire. –

Still light for you the flaws that frizz
       The main! Sail off ... – For me
– All washed up, floored, alone, it is
       A bitter rising sea! ...

       – In your cutter soul just try,
       Think of your shipmate now,
       When waves are breaking high
       On port or starboard bow ...

– You can still run your keel aground,
       In reeking seaweed chocks;
But, grounded me, in Skint Cove Sound;
       High and dry – on the rocks –

            Roscoff. – August.

---

* Fortune: in French, a big sail for fair weather.

Le Phare

Phœbus, de mauvais poil, se couche.
   Droit sur l'écueil:
S'allume le grand borgne louche,
   Clignant de l'œil.

Debout, Priape d'ouragan,
   En vain le lèche
La lame de rut écumant…
   – Il tient sa mèche.

Il se mate et rit de sa rage,
   Bandant à bloc;
Fier bout de chandelle sauvage
   Plantée au roc!

– En vain, sur sa tête chenue,
   D'amont, d'aval,
Caracole et s'abat la nue,
   Comme un cheval…

– Il tient le lampion au naufrage,
   Tout en rêvant,
Casse la mer, crève l'orage,
   Siffle le vent,

Ronfle et vibre comme une trompe,
   – Diapason
D'Éole – Il se peut bien qu'il rompe,
   Mais plier – non. –

The Lighthouse

Phoebus, blood up, settles for the night.
      Erect on the reef,
The tall and shifty one-eyed light
      Winks at the chief.

Erect, Priapus of hurricane,
      Rutting waves eddy
And lap at him, foaming in vain...
      – His shaft stays steady.

Raises his mast, laughs at his passion,
      Tensing up tight;
His proud, wild candle, flashing,
      Rock-firm, night-light!

– In vain upon his hoary head,
      Upstream, down-course,
Clouds wheel and swoop, well-sped,
      Just like a horse!...

– He aims his lamp against wreck,
      All the while dreaming,
The sea breaks, the storms trek,
      The wind is screaming,

Blares and quavers like a horn –
      Tuning fork
Of Aeolus – He might break, overborne,
      – Not bend – his stalk.

Sait-il son Musset: À la brune
      Il est jauni
Et pose juste pour la lune
      Comme un grand I.

… Là, gît debout une vestale
      – C'est l'allumoir –
Vierge et martyre (sexe mâle)
      – C'est l'éteignoir. –

Comme un lézard à l'eau-de-vie
      Dans un bocal,
Il tirebouchonne sa vie
      Dans ce fanal.

Est-il philosophe ou poète?…
      – Il n'en sait rien –
Lunatique ou simplement bête?…
      – Ça se vaut bien –

Demandez-lui donc s'il chérit
      Sa solitude?
– S'il parle, il répondra qu'il vit…
      Par habitude.

. . . .

– Oh! que je voudrais là, Madame,
      Tous deux!… – veux-tu? –
Vivre, dent pour œil, corps pour âme!…
      – Rêve pointu. –

Vous percheriez dans la lanterne:
      Je monterais…
– Et moi: ci-gît, dans la citerne…
      – Tu descendrais –

Does he know his Musset? At twilight
    He's yellow, high
Placed nicely for the moon's highlight,
    Like a big I.

... An upright vestal lodges there –
    The light, that's her. –
Virgin and martyr (male of the pair)
    – He's the extinguisher. –

Like a lizard in eau-de-vie
    In a fish-bowl,
He corkscrews his life to be
    The lampion's soul.

Is he poet or philosopher?...
    – Not that he knows. –
Lunatic or simply stupider?...
    – Much the same, those –

Ask the value that he gives
    His isolation?
– If he speaks, he'll say he lives...
    By habituation.

. . . .

– Oh, how I'd like to live up there,
    – Paired!... – Madam, would you? –
Tooth for eye, body for soul share!...
    – A pointed dream-do. –

You'd perch yourself up in the lamp:
    I'd mount to the crown...
– Me: here lies in the tank (damp)...
    – You'd slip right down. –

Dans le boyau de l'édifice
   Nous promenant,
Et, dans *le feu* – sans artifice –
   Nous rencontrant.

Joli ramonage… et bizarre,
   Du haut en bas!
– Entre nous… l'érection du phare
   N'y tiendrait pas…

         Les Triagots. – Mai.

In the column of the light,
       Walking, we two;
And, in the *shaft* – no trick or sleight –
       We'd rendezvous.

Nice chimney-sweeping... but dottily,
       From top to bottom!
– That erection... between you and me
       Wouldn't last... shotten.

Les Triagots. – May.

La fin

> *Oh! combien de marins, combien de capitaines*
> *Qui sont partis joyeux pour des courses lointaines*
> *Dans ce morne horizon se sont évanouis!...*
> . . . .
> *Combien de patrons morts avec leurs équipages!*
> *L'Océan, de leur vie a pris toutes les pages,*
> *Et, d'un souffle, il a tout dispersé sur les flots.*
> *Nul ne saura leur fin dans l'abîme plongée...*
> . . . .
> *Nul ne saura leurs noms, pas même l'humble pierre,*
> *Dans l'étroit cimetière où l'écho nous répond,*
> *Pas même un saule vert qui s'effeuille à l'automne,*
> *Pas même la chanson plaintive et monotone*
> *D'un aveugle qui chante à l'angle d'un vieux pont.*
>
> v. HUGO, *Oceano nox.*

Eh bien, tous ces marins – matelots, capitaines,
Dans leur grand Océan à jamais engloutis...
Partis insoucieux pour leurs courses lointaines
Sont morts – absolument comme ils étaient partis.

Allons! c'est leur métier; ils sont morts dans leurs bottes!
Leur *boujaron** au cœur, tout vifs dans leurs capotes...
– *Morts*... Merci: la *Camarde* a pas le pied marin;
Qu'elle couche avec vous: c'est votre bonne femme...
– Eux, allons donc: Entiers! enlevés par la lame!
       Ou perdus dans un grain...

Un grain... est-ce la mort ça? la basse voilure
Battant à travers l'eau! – Ça se dit *encombrer*...
Un coup de mer plombé, puis la haute mâture
Fouettant les flots ras – et ça se dit *sombrer*.

———
* *Boujaron*: ration d'eau-de-vie.

The End

How many seamen, captains and their ships,
Who set out happily on distant trips
Have vanished under this horizon's gloom!...

. . . .

How many masters dead with all their crews;
Sea takes their every page of life and news,
And with a breath disperses them on tides
And none shall know their end plunged in the deep...

. . . .

None know their names, not even the mean stone
In the strait graveyard where echoes answer us;
Not the green willow shedding autumn leaves;
Not even the dirge that a blind man heaves,
Huddled by a bridge, plaintive, monotonous.

V. HUGO, *Oceano nox.*

Well, then, all those seamen – captain, crew, corsair,
Forever swallowed up in their vast High Seas...
Embarked on distant voyages without a care –
All dead – as they were before they left the quays.

So what! it's their job; with their boots on, dead!
Alert, in their duffels, *tots** in heart and head...
– *Dead* men... No, thanks: *Lady Death* – no sea-legs at all.
She's your good woman: in your bed let her sleep...
– As for these, come off it: this lot lay with the deep!
          Or lost in a squall...

A squall... is that death, then? The reefed sail
Beating through the waves! – That's called *floundering...*
A heavy sea like lead breaks over. The topmasts flail
Whipping the tops of waves – and that's called *foundering.*

———

* *Tot*: ration of brandy.

– Sombrer – Sondez ce mot. Votre *mort* est bien pâle
Et pas grand'chose à bord, sous la lourde rafale…
Pas grand'chose devant le grand sourire amer
Du matelot qui lutte. – Allons donc, de la place! –
Vieux fantôme éventé, la Mort change de face:
           La Mer!…

Noyés? – Eh allons donc! Les *noyés* sont d'eau douce.
– Coulés! corps et biens! Et, jusqu'au petit mousse,
Le défi dans les yeux, dans les dents le juron!
À l'écume crachant une chique râlée,
Buvant sans hauts-de-cœur *la grand'tasse salée*…
      – Comme ils ont bu leur boujaron. –

. . . .

– Pas de fond de six pieds, ni rats de cimetière:
Eux ils vont aux requins! L'âme d'un matelot
Au lieu de suinter dans vos pommes de terre,
        Respire à chaque flot.

– Voyez à l'horizon se soulever la houle;
        On dirait le ventre amoureux
D'une fille de joie en rut, à moitié soûle…
        Ils sont là! – La houle a du creux. –

– Écoutez, écoutez la tourmente qui beugle!…
C'est leur anniversaire – Il revient bien souvent –
Ô poète, gardez pour vous vos chants d'aveugle;
– Eux: le *De profundis* que leur corne le vent.

… Qu'ils roulent infinis dans les espaces vierges!…
        Qu'ils roulent verts et nus,
Sans clous et sans sapin, sans couvercle, sans cierges…
– Laissez-les donc rouler, *terriens* parvenus!

                À bord. – 11 février.

– Foundering – Weigh the word. Your *death's* all pale
And nothing much, on board, against a heavy gale...
Not much beside the sea-salt's bitter jeer as he's
Battling away. – Come off it. Give him sea-room, space –
Your stale old Phantom, Death, changes her face:
The Sea's!...

Drowned? – Give over! It's freshwater sailors that *drown*.
– Foundered! all hands and gear! Right to cabin-boy down,
Defiance in their eyes, air blue through their teeth, they roar!
Spitting at the spray their death-rasp baccy plug,
Drinking without spewing *Davy Jones's Liquor* mug...
– Like tots they'd slugged before. –

. . . .

– No six-foot hole for them; no graveyard rats to scratch:
All of them gone to the sharks! A sailor's soul and pride
Instead of seeping out into the potato patch
Breathes in each tide.

– Look to the horizon; a heavy sea is running.
It moves like the randy belly behaves
Of a good-time girl who's half-seas-overcoming...
That's where they are! – Lapse in the waves. –

– Hark! Hark, how the tempest's bellowing prolongs!...
It's their birthday. – It comes round often and more –
O poet, keep for yourself your blind man's songs.
– For these, the *De Profundis* that the storm-winds roar.

... And may they roll in virgin expanses boundlessly...
Green and naked may they roll a bit,
No nails, no coffins, no lid, no candles, groundlessly...
Upstart landlubbers, you let them roll in it!

On board. – 11th February.

Sonnet posthume

Dors: ce lit est le tien… Tu n'iras plus au nôtre.
– Qui dort dîne. – À tes dents viendra tout seul le foin.
Dors: on t'aimera bien – L'aimé c'est toujours l'Autre…
Rêve: La plus aimée est toujours la plus loin…

Dors: on t'appellera beau décrocheur d'étoiles!
Chevaucheur de rayons!… quand il fera bien noir;
Et l'ange du plafond, maigre araignée, au soir,
– Espoir – sur ton front vide ira filer ses toiles.

Museleur de voilette! un baiser sous le voile
T'attend… on ne sait où: ferme les yeux pour voir.
Ris: Les premiers honneurs t'attendent sous le poêle.

On cassera ton nez d'un bon coup d'encensoir,
Doux fumet!… pour la trogne en fleur, pleine de moelle
D'un sacristain très-bien, avec son éteignoir.

Posthumous Sonnet

Sleep: this is your bed... To ours no more you'll come.
– Sleep's a good dinner. – Your teeth will hit the unserved hay.
Sleep: you'll be well loved now –The loved one's always some
Other... Dream: The most loved she's always far away...

Sleep: they will call you nifty star-demounter now.
Beam-spurrer!... when it's dark enough; shepherd's delight,
– Hope – ceiling angel, starveling spider, in the night,
Will spin its gossamers across your vacant brow.

Veil-muzzler! a kiss beneath the clothes is all
For you... no one knows where: shut your eyes to see.
Laugh: The host of high honours waits under the pall.

Someone'll lay it on thick to your face, a right puffer,
Scent-sational, game smell!... a budding mug of mettle free
From a worthy sexton ready with his snuffer.

Rondel

Il fait noir, enfant, voleur d'étincelles!
Il n'est plus de nuits, il n'est plus de jours;
Dors... en attendant venir toutes celles
Qui disaient: Jamais! Qui disaient: Toujours!

Entends-tu leurs pas?... Ils ne sont pas lourds:
Oh! les pieds légers! – l'Amour a des ailes...
Il fait noir, enfant, voleur d'étincelles!

Entends-tu leurs voix?... Les caveaux sont sourds.
Dors: il pèse peu, ton faix d'immortelles;
Ils ne viendront pas, tes amis les ours,
Jeter leur pavé sur tes demoiselles...
Il fait noir, enfant, voleur d'étincelles!

Rondel

Child, stealer of gleams, isn't it dark?
There are no more days and no more night;
Sleep ... waiting for those girls that gave a stark:
'Never!' All those that gave an 'Always might!'

D'you hear their steps? ... Their tread is very light:
Oh, how clean the heels are! – Love's a lark ...
Child, stealer of gleams, isn't it dark?

D'you hear their voice? ... The vaults are deaf. Sleep tight:
No weight, your immortelles won't leave a mark;
Your friends the bears won't come now, little sprite,
To cast their flags on your painted ladies ... Hark,
Child, stealer of gleams, isn't it dark?

Do, l'enfant, do…

Buona vespre! *Dors: Ton bout de cierge…*
On l'a posé là, puis on est parti.
Tu n'auras pas peur seul, pauvre petit?…
C'est le chandelier de ton lit d'auberge.

Du fesse-cahier ne crains plus la verge,
Va!… De t'éveiller point n'est si hardi.
Buona sera! *Dors: Ton bout de cierge…*

Est mort. – Il n'est plus, ici, de concierge:
Seuls, le vent du nord, le vent du midi
Viendront balancer un fil-de-la-Vierge.
Chut! Pour les pieds-plats, ton sol est maudit.
– Buona notte! *Dors: Ton bout de cierge…*

Hushaby, Baby

Buona vespre! *Sleep: Your bit of candle-end...*
They've put in place for you and left you quite.
But you're not frightened, are you, little mite?...
It's the night-light of your inn-bed for friend.

No fear that rod or bum-book will offend...
None with the neck to wake you up tonight.
Buona sera! *Sleep: Your bit of candle-end...*

Is out! – No caretakers hereabouts attend:
Only the north and south winds in their flight
Will let a dancing gossamer descend.
Hush! To flatfoots your ground's accursed. – Good night.
Buona notte! *Sleep: Your bit of candle-end...*

Mirliton

Dors d'amour, méchant ferreur de cigales!
Dans le chiendent qui te couvrira
La cigale aussi pour toi chantera,
Joyeuse, avec ses petites cymbales.

La rosée aura des pleurs matinales;
Et le muguet blanc fait un joli drap...
Dors d'amour, méchant ferreur de cigales.

Pleureuses en troupeau passeront les rafales...

La Muse camarde ici posera,
Sur ta bouche noire encore elle aura
Ces rimes qui vont aux moelles des pâles...
Dors d'amour, méchant ferreur de cigales.

Tin Whistle

With love, you naughty cicada-shoer, sleep!
And there, in the couchgrass your covering,
For you the cicada will also sing
Joyfully, with his tiny cymbals' cheep.

Fresh tears each morning the dew shall weep;
Lily-of-the-valley's pretty sheet will cling...
With love, you naughty cicada-shoer, sleep.

The squalls like weeping women will flock past like sheep...

Here will the deathly Muse sit lingering.
On your black lips she yet again will spring
Rhymes that will cut the pale ones marrow-deep...
With love, you naughty cicada-shoer, sleep.

Petit mort pour rire

Va vite, léger peigneur de comètes!
Les herbes au vent seront tes cheveux;
De ton œil béant jailliront les feux
Follets, prisonniers dans les pauvres têtes ...

Les fleurs de tombeau qu'on nomme Amourettes
Foisonneront plein ton rire terreux ...
Et les myosotis, ces fleurs d'oubliettes ...

Ne fais pas le lourd: cercueils de poètes
Pour les croque-morts sont de simples jeux,
Boîtes à violon qui sonnent le creux ...
Ils te croiront mort – Les bourgeois sont bêtes –
Va vite, léger peigneur de comètes!

Little Corpse Good for a Laugh

Light groomer of comet-tails, go, quick!
Grass blown in the wind shall be your hair;
And from your eyes, wide open, flare
Will o' the wisps, lags of the poor heads' nick …

Grave flowers, Love-in-the-Missed, spread thick
Your earthy laugh … forget-me-nots stare,
Of oubliettes the flower and pick …

Don't come over heavy: a simple trick
For death-mutes, poets' coffins, they're
Violin cases sounding a hollow air …
They'll think you're dead – The bourgeois are thick –
Light groomer of comet-tails, go, quick!

Male-fleurette

Ici reviendra la fleurette blême
Dont les renouveaux sont toujours passés...
Dans les cœurs ouverts, sur les os tassés,
Une folle brise, un beau jour, la sème...

On crache dessus; on l'imite même,
Pour en effrayer les gens très-sensés...
Ici reviendra la fleurette blême.

– Oh! ne craignez pas son humble anathème
Pour vos ventres mûrs, Cucurbitacés!
Elle connaît bien tous ses trépassés!
Et, quand elle tue, elle sait qu'on l'aime...
– C'est la male-fleur, la fleur de bohème. –

Ici reviendra la fleurette blême.

Baneflower

Pale, she'll return, sweet-nothing's flower
Whose spring is always over and blown...
In open hearts, on heaps of bone,
Sown by a mad breeze, some fine hour...

She's spat on; even faked, to cower
And scare the most-sensible... Unsown,
Pale, she'll return, sweet-nothing's flower.

– Don't scare at her curse's lowly power,
Cucurbits, on your ripe bellies thrown!
Full well to her her dead are known!
Killing, she knows she's loved... – She's our
Baneflower, the bohemian flower. –

Pale, she'll return, sweet-nothing's flower.

À Marcelle

LA CIGALE ET LE POÈTE

Le poète ayant chanté,
      Déchanté,
Vit sa Muse, presque bue,
Rouler en bas de sa nue
De carton, sur des lambeaux
De papiers et d'oripeaux.
Il alla coller sa mine
Aux carreaux de sa voisine,
Pour lui peindre ses regrets
D'avoir fait – Oh: pas exprès! –
Son honteux monstre de livre!…
– « Mais: vous étiez donc bien ivre?
– Ivre de vous!… Est-ce mal?
– Écrivain public banal!
Qui pouvait si bien le dire…
Et, si bien ne pas l'écrire!
– J'y pensais, en revenant…
On n'est pas parfait, Marcelle…
– Oh! c'est tout comme, dit-elle,
Si vous chantiez, maintenant! »

To Marcelle

THE CICADA AND THE POET

The poet, having sung out, soon
         Changed his tune,
Seeing his Muse, half cut to starboard,
Roll to the base of her cloud of cardboard
Down on to scraps of manuscript,
And tinsel finery all ripped.
He went and glued his nose to pore
On the windows of the girl next door
To picture for her his remorse
For making – Not on purpose, of course! –
His shameful monstrous book of verse!…
– So: were you drunk and much the worse?
– Drunk on you!… And is that wrong?
– Scrivener of hackneyed song!
Who might have said it well enough…
And, just as well, not written the stuff!
– I was thinking, going over it…
That nobody is perfect, Marcelle…
– Oh! come, she said, it sounds full well
That now you're crowing over it!

Sous un portrait de Corbière

EN COULEURS FAIT PAR LUI
ET DATÉ DE 1868

Jeune philosophe en dérive
Revenu sans avoir été,
Cœur de poète mal planté:
Pourquoi voulez-vous que je vive?

L'amour!... je l'ai rêvé, mon cœur au grand ouvert
Bat comme un volet en pantenne
Habité par la froide haleine
Des plus bizarres courants d'air;
Qui voudrait s'y jeter?... pas moi si j'étais ELLE!...
Va te coucher, mon cœur, et ne bats plus de l'aile.

J'aurais voulu souffrir et mourir d'une femme,
M'ouvrir du haut en bas et lui donner en flamme,
Comme un punch, ce cœur-là, chaud sous le chaud soleil...

Alors je chanterais (faux, comme de coutume)
Et j'irais me coucher seul dans la trouble brume
Éternité, néant, mort, sommeil, ou réveil.

Ah si j'étais un peu compris! Si par pitié
Une femme pouvait me sourire à moitié,
Je lui dirais: oh viens, ange qui me consoles!...

Under a Portrait of Corbière

IN COLOUR MADE BY HIMSELF
AND DATED 1868

> Young philosopher drifting back
> Before he'd even been for a start,
> With weedy stunted poet heart:
> Why want me to live – weird jack.

Love!... I dreamed it, heart wide open flung,
Flapping like shutters hung half mast,
Abiding in the icy blast
Of the weirdest draughts that swung;
Who'd want to throw themselves there?... not me, if HER!...
Heart, go to bed, don't flap your wings any further.

I would've wished to suffered and die of a woman – martyr,
Open myself from top to toe, give her, in ardour
Like a punch, this here heart, mulled in the sun's baking...

And then I'd sing (off-key as usually with me)
And go to bed alone in the thick mist Eternity,
Nothingness, stone-dead, sleeping or waking.

Ah, if only understood a bit! If out of pity, some if,
A woman could half-smile at me, I'd tell her in a jiff:
Oh, come to me, consoling angel, come and smile some!...

. . . .
… Et je la conduirais à l'hospice des folles.

On m'a manqué ma vie!… une vie à peu près;
Savez-vous ce que c'est: regardez cette tête.
Dépareillé partout, très bon, plus mauvais, très
Fou, ne me souffrant… Encor si j'étais bête!

La mort… ah oui, je sais: cette femme est bien froide,
Coquette dans la vie; après, sans passion.
Pour coucher avec elle il faut être trop roide…
Et puis, la mort n'est pas, c'est la négation.

Je voudrais être un point épousseté des masses,
Un point mort balayé dans la nuit des espaces,
            … Et je ne le suis point!

Je voudrais être alors chien de fille publique,
Lécher un peu d'amour qui ne soit pas payé;
Ou déesse à tous crins sur la côte d'Afrique,
Ou fou, mais réussi; fou, mais pas à moitié.

.   .   .   .
... And I would lead her to the lunatic asylum.

My life's been missed to me!... almost a life, in fact;
Do you know what it is: take a look at this head.
All lopsided, very good, that worse, most cracked,
Not bearing me... Yet if I were dumb beast instead!

Death... ah yes, I know: that woman's very frigid,
A cock-teaser in life; afterwards, no passion to give.
To sleep with her you need to be much too rigid...
And then, she isn't there, it's absolutely negative.

I want to be a point dusted from the masses, no traces,
A dead point swept away into the night of spaces,
                ... And I am not the point!

I want to be, then, lap dog to a common whore,
Lick a bit of love which wouldn't have to be bought;
Or goddess with flying mane on an African shore,
Or mad, successfully: mad but not by halves distraught.

Une mort trop travaillée

C'était à peu près un artiste,
C'était un poète à peu près
S'amusant à prendre le frais
En dehors de l'humaine piste.

Puis, écœuré de toute envie
En équilibre sur la vie
Et, ne sachant trop de quel bord...
Il se joua, lui contre *un mort*.

Au *bac*... – Au bac à qui perd gagne
Il perdit, ou, comme on voudra
Donc, dans trois mois, il se tûra!
Pour aller vivre à la campagne

... Trois mois... Ce n'est pas qu'il se pleure...
C'est un avenir à vingt ans,
Trois mois pour dorer de bon temps
La pilule du grand quart d'heure...

Vingt-quatre heures, c'est l'ordinaire,
Mais lui faisait tout en flânant
Et voulait prendre de l'élan
Puisqu'il n'avait qu'un saut à faire –

Tant en prit (jusqu'à sa pantoufle,
Avant soi voulant tout laver)
Qu'enfin il lui restait de souffle,
Juste assez pour se le souffler.

Or, jusqu'au bout dans ses toilettes
Suivant ses instincts élégants,

A Death too Worked at

He was a sort of artist hack,
He was a poet almost, amusing
Himself in the fresh air, cruising
Miles off the well-beaten track.

Then, sick of all desire, in knife-
Edge equilibrium with life,
Not knowing which game to play ...
He played himself *a dead man*; they

Played *bac* ... – At bac where loser wins
He lost, or, as one will, therefore,
He'll kill himself in three months more!
Going to live in the sticks, wither shins

... Three months ... He doesn't wail his lot ...
A future, that, at twenty-one,
Three months for gilding in good sun
The pill for fifteen grand minutes' slot ...

Twenty-four hours it'd commonly take,
But him, he loafed at it a while,
Wishing to do it with some style
Since he had just one leap to make –

So much he took (slippers and stuff,
Wanting to wash out all before him)
Till at the last only a puff
Or so was left to breathe and floor him.

Then, following his elegant instincts,
He finished with his grooming, drew

Lâchant la vie avec ses gants
Prit la mort avec des pincettes.

Il fit donc faire en Angleterre
Deux fins pistolets de *Menton*,
L'un, pour s'appuyer au menton
Et l'autre pour faire la paire.

Le pistolet, c'est un peu bête –
Outil presque médicinal –
Mais, pour lui, ça n'allait pas mal
Qui manquait de plomb dans la tête.

Et, ma foi, pour se fondre l'âme,
C'est aussi neuf que le poison,
C'est aussi chaud que le charbon
Ou que le creuset d'une femme!

C'est une affaire de calibre,
De goût, de dégoût ou d'argent –
Laissons-le donc trois mois chargeant
Ses pistolets. – Il est bien libre. –

Et puis, quels bijoux que ces armes
En acier mat, un peu trop sec.
Ça donnait un froid non sans charmes,
Frisson chaud à coucher avec!

Il les avait fait faire exprès,
Voulant dans son suprême excès
Que ce fût une bouche vierge
Qui lui mouchât son dernier cierge.

Il avait fait graver son nom
En spirale sur le canon,

Life off with his gloves, one, two,
And next he picked up death with pincers.

Two handsome pistols he had made
By *Mental-Bohne*, England, one for chin
To lean upon and then its twin
To make the pair since he had paid.

Bit of a beast, your pistol – med.,
Almost a medical instrument –
Not bad for him in the event
As he'd a lack of cranial lead.

My word, for soul-dissolving, shot
Is just as fresh as a poison dose
And just as hot as coals or close
To any woman's melting-pot!

A question of calibre, that,
Of taste, distaste, or cash the case –
Let us allow him three months' grace
To load his guns. – Off his own bat. –

And then, what jewels as these arms
In matt steel, a little too stiff.
That gives a chill not without charms,
A warm thrill for sleeping with!

He'd had them made to order, yes,
Wishing that in his last excess
It ought to be a virgin mouth
That snuffed his final candle out.

His name he had engraved around
The barrel, spiral, and as found

Et comme autour d'un mirliton
Cet aphorisme simple et sage
En vers que je vous transcris tels:
« Ici, ce qui manque aux mortels
Pour savoir mourir, c'est l'usage.

Ces pistolets sont une pose.
Eh bien posez comme il posa.
Allez, bourgeois, c'est quelque chose
De poser encor devant *ça!* – »

Il écrivit à sa maîtresse,
Comme on le fait en pareil cas …
– Et même quand on n'en a pas
Alors, c'est « Amanda » l'adresse –

Lui pour que sans pleurer ni rire, elle chantât
Il lui mit ça sur l'air de « J'ai du bon tabac »
                    Mon rat,

« Lis-moi jusqu'au bout, lis ça comme un conte.
Je me suis tué pour tuer le temps.
Je te lègue tout: comme fin de compte
Je laisse après moi : vingt ans, dont 20 francs.

« Puis ces pistolets : l'un dans ta ruelle
Avec mon amour, au mur accroché,
Comme objet d'art et, que lui soit fidèle
À ce dernier feu que j'aurai lâché.

« L'autre encor chargé, mets-le dans ma boîte,
Réveille-matin réglé pour ma nuit,
Dans cette couchette un peu trop étroite
Pour mettre au pied ma descente de lit.

On tin whistles, he had wound
This wise, plain aphorism reading
In verses I transcribe as going:
'Here, what mortals lack, for knowing
The way to die, it is the breeding.

'Pistols like these, they are a pose,
Well, pose then just as he has posed.
Come on, bourgeois, for against *those*
It's something to pose, hard-nosed! –'

He wrote, then, to his mistress expressly,
As in similar cases is done…
– And even when you haven't one
Then, 'Amanda' his addressee –

She, not to have to laugh or weep, she sang a stint.
He set it to the tune 'I've good tobacco'
                My skin-flint,

'Read me right through, read it like a tale.
To kill the time I've killed myself, one round.
I leave you everything: the sum-total, wholesale,
I leave behind is: twenty years at twenty pound.

'Also these pistols: the one that's there beside your bed
With all my love, hanging close by on the wall
Just like a work of art and, may it be faithful through all
To you down to this last shot I'll discharge, true lead.

'The other, loaded still, deposit in my box,
Alarm-clock set to go off for my night,
In that bunk a bit too cramped to let my socks
Manoeuvre my descent out of the bed at light.

« Si tu m'as aimé, ne ris pas ma Belle,
Je ne me fais pas, va, d'illusions.
Mais j'étais très mâle et toi très femelle
Et tu m'as aimé… par convulsions.

« Si tu m'as aimé, qu'allais-je donc dire,
Te donner peut-être des rendez-vous?
Tiens, je ris par chic, je veux, je veux rire!…
Eh bien! viens pendant qu'on mettra les clous. »

    Il se demanda si son âme
    Allait crever comme un abcès
    Ou s'éteindre comme une flamme,
    Puis il se dit: Eh bien! après?

Le moment venu (faiblesse physique)
Il s'ingurgita (c'est assez petit)
Un cruchon de rhum, toni-viatique,
Pour se mettre enfin plus en appétit –

Il se mit devant son armoire à glace
(Chez le photographe il n'eût pas fait mieux)
Pour se voir un peu tomber avec grâce,
Se jetant encor de la poudre aux yeux.

    Froid et brûlant baiser, il colla sur sa bouche
    La bouche où son dernier soupir est arrêté!…
    Il tombe, le coup part, suivi d'un éclair louche
    Et la charge…
                Excellente; il s'est juste raté!

MORALE

Drôle de balle et drôle pistolet!
Il en porte aujourd'hui les marques:
Il est marchand de contremarques
À la porte du Châtelet.

'If you have loved me, do not laugh, my Beauty,
I never harboured, come now, any illusions yet,
But I was very male, all female, you, to-at-T,
And you have loved me ... by convulsions, pet.

'If you have loved me what would I have to say?
Give you perhaps some assignations? Hold on,
I laugh for show, I want, I want to laugh away!...
Oh well, come before they nail me down and gone.'

    He wondered if his soul
    Would burst like a boil or not
    Or douse itself like coal,
    Then mused: 'Oh well, so what?'

The moment came (in body weak)
He golloped down a jug of rum
(A small one) tonic last-rite freak
To make the final hunger come –

He placed himself before a mirrored cupboard
(Photographer opined he couldn't have done better)
To see him fall a bit with grace, well scuppered,
Still throwing powder in his eyes like pepper.

    Cold and burning kiss, he stuck to her lips
    The mouth in which his final sigh is stopped!...
    He fell, the shot fired, a dodgy flash rips
    And the blast...

            Splendid; just missed, not dropped!

MORAL

Pistol, a weirdo bore, odd ball!
He bears the marks still to this day:
And at the gate of the Châtelet
He's merchant of countermarks and all.

Deux dédicaces des « Amours jaunes »

I   SUR L'EXEMPLAIRE DE M. LE VACHER

Exemplaire de mon genare.

Mon blazon pas bégueule
Est comme moi faquin
Nous bandons à la gueule
Fond troué d'arlequin.

II   SUR L'EXEMPLAIRE DE M. LE GAD

Nous sommes tous les deux deux fiers empoisonneurs.
À vous les estomacs, Le Gad, à moi les cœurs!

Un distique

Mon cher, on m'a volé... – Que je plains ton malheur!
– Oui, mon cher, un album. – Que je plains le voleur!

Two Dedications of *Les Amours jaunes*

I   IN M. LE VACHER'S COPY

Copy for my son-in-law.

My coat of arms not strait-laced
Is just my scoundrel twin
Bend to the gob gag-faced
Ground pierced with Harlequin.

II   IN M. LE GAD'S COPY

We're both of us proud poisoners, I of hearts
And you, Le Gad, of stomach and other parts!

A Couplet

My dear fellow, I've been robbed. – Such bad luck, good grief!
Yes, an album's gone. – What bad luck on the thief!

Paris diurne

Vois aux cieux le grand rond de cuivre rouge luire,
Immense casserole où le Bon Dieu fait cuire
La manne, l'arlequin, l'éternel plat du jour.
C'est trempé de sueur et c'est poivré d'amour.

Les Laridons en cercle attendent près du four,
On entend vaguement la chair rance bruire,
Et les soiffards aussi sont là, tendant leur buire;
Le marmiteux grelotte en attendant son tour.

Tu crois que le soleil frit donc pour tout le monde
Ces gras graillons grouillants qu'un torrent d'or inonde?
Non, le bouillon de chien tombe sur nous du ciel.

Eux sont sous le rayon et nous sous la gouttière
À nous le pot-au-noir qui froidit sans lumière…
Notre substance à nous, c'est notre poche à fiel.

Ma foi j'aime autant ça que d'être dans le miel.

Paris by Day

In the skies the big red round of copper's dawning, look:
Huge casserole where the Good God puts manna to cook,
Leftovers, the everlasting chef's choice of the day.
It's soused in sweat and over-spiced with love-game play.

The Mutt-skullions ring the cookhouse in the way.
Vague rustles of the past-its-sell-by-date chick-chook.
Holding their flagon out are soaks with booze to hook.
One down-and-out shakes waiting his turn long-stay.

So, do you think the sun fries up, for all, this nosh
Of greasy gobbets in torrential gold awash?
No, it's the dog's remainders slop on us from the sky.

Them, they're beneath the beams; we're under the gutter's
    spite,
For us, the luckless, beefs stone-cold without the light…
Subsistence for us our pocket full of bitter wry.

My word, I like that as much as in clover to lie.

Paris nocturne

Ce n'est pas une ville, c'est un monde.

– C'est la mer: – calme plat – et la grande marée,
Avec un grondement lointain, s'est retirée.
Le flot va revenir, se roulant dans son bruit –
– Entendez-vous gratter les crabes de la nuit...

– C'est le Styx asséché: Le chiffonnier Diogène,
Sa lanterne à la main, s'en vient errer sans gêne.
Le long du ruisseau noir, les poëtes pervers
Pêchent; leur crâne creux leur sert de boîte à vers.

– C'est le champ: Pour glaner les impures charpies
S'abat le vol tournant des hideuses harpies.
Le lapin de gouttière, à l'affût des rongeurs,
Fuit les fils de Bondy, nocturnes vendangeurs.

– C'est la mort: La police gît – En haut, l'amour
Fait la sieste en têtant la viande d'un bras lourd,
Où le baiser éteint laisse sa plaque rouge...
L'heure est seule – Écoutez:... pas un rêve ne bouge

– C'est la vie: Écoutez: la source vive chante
L'éternelle chanson, sur le tête gluante
D'un dieu marin tirant ses membres nus et verts
Sur le lit de la morgue... Et les yeux grand'ouverts!

Paris by Night

It's not a city, it's a world.

– It is the sea: – dead calm – and the spring tide,
Giving a snarl a long way off, has gone outside.
The tide will come in again, wallowing in its roar –
– D'you hear the nocturnal crabs scuttering on the shore...

– It's the dried-up Styx: and rag-and-bone man Diogenes,
His lantern in his hand, is wandering at his ease.
Along the black gutters, cussed poets fish for read-
Herrings, each baiting his lines from his hollow head.

– It's the Fields: and hideous harpies wheel and flap
To glean the leper-lint in every filthy scrap.
*Smart-alley*cats on the alert for rats take flight
From Bondy's sons, the harvesters of night.

– It's death: and the police are lying low. – And love,
Sucking the joint of a heavy hand naps up above
Where the extinguished kiss leaves a red smudge...
The hour is solitary – Listen:... no dreams budge

– It's life: Listen: the spring water sings
The eternal song over the slimy head that brings
The sea-god dragging out his limbs, all green and naked,
On to the mortuary bed... And his eyes are wide-awake!

Petit coucher

(RISETTE)

Le plaisir te fut dur, mais le mal est facile.
    Laisse-le venir à son jour.
À la Muse camarde on ne fait plus d'idylle;
    On s'en va sans l'Ange – à son tour –

Ton drap connaît ta plaie, et ton mouchoir ta bile;
    Chante, mais ne fais pas le four
D'aller sur le trottoir quêter dans ta sébile,
    Un sou de dégoût ou d'amour.

Tu vas dormir: voici le somme qui délie;
La Mort patiente joue avec ton agonie,
    Comme un chat maigre et la souris;

Sa patte de velours te pelotte et te lance.
Le paroxysme encor est une jouissance:
    Tords ta bouche, écume… et souris.

Minor Bedtime

(FETCHING LITTLE LAUGH)

Pleasure was hard on you but pain's easy enough.
    Let it come in its own time of day.
With the grave-faced Muse, one cuts the idyll stuff;
    Without the Angel, goes – in turn – away.

Your bed-sheets know your hurt, your hankie knows your huff;
    Sing but don't go in for that flop and stray
About the streets with your wooden bowl, a begging scruff,
    For a penn'orth of love or disgust to drop your way.

You're going to sleep: here comes the nap to set you free;
And patient Death plays with your final agony;
    Like a skinny cat with the mouse meanwhile;

Her velvet paw, it tucks you in and tosses you.
And then the paroxysm's a pleasuring do:
    Twist your mouth, foam at it … and smile.

[Moi ton amour?]

Moi ton amour? – Jamais! – Je fesais du théâtre
Et pris sous le *manteau d'Arlequin*, par hasard
Le sourire écaillé qui lézardait ton plâtre
La goutte de sueur que buvait ton bon fard.

Ma langue s'empâtait à cette bouillie âcre
En riant nous avons partagé le charbon
Qui donnait à tes yeux leur faux reflet de nacre,
À tes cils d'albinos le piquant du chardon.

Comme ton havanais, sur ta lèvre vermeille
J'ai léché bêtement la pommade groseille
Mais ta bouche qui rit n'a pas saigné ... jamais.

L'amende est de cent sous pour un baiser en scène ...
Refais ton tatouage, ô Jézabel hautaine,
Je te le dis sans fard, c'est le fard que j'aimais.

[Me, your lover?]

Me, your lover? – Never! – Theatricals, an act.
I took by chance, in the *guise of Harlequin,*
The descaling smile with which your plaster cracked
The bead of sweat your powder soaked from skin.

My tongue was whitened with that sour caker.
In laughter we had shared the charcoal stick
Which gave your eyes the bogus look of nacre,
And your albino lashes the thistle-like prick.

And from your ruby lips I licked, dumb mutt,
Your lap-dog, the red-*current* make-up, but
Your mouth that laughed didn't bleed... Ever. – Poor tyke.

The fine was fifty pence for a stage kiss...
Re-do your tattooage, proud Jezebel, this
I tell you, no varnish, it's the paint I like.

Pierrot pendu

I

La femme est une pilule
Que tu ne sais plus dorer
Ta lyre, outil ridicule
[......................]

II

C'est fini la comédie,
À la Morgue les Amours!
Arrêtons sur la my-die
La patraque de nos jours.

III

À la maîtresse chérie
De ton chanvre laisse un bout.
Elle fut la galerie
Qui l'admira malgré tout.

IV

Va, ça lui portera veine
– Ce dernier nœud de licol
Pour toucher dans la quinzaine
Un vrai monsieur en faux-col.

V

Qu'elle corne, la corneuse:
C'est aussi pur mais le soir [?]
Qu'elle râle, la râleuse
Et qu'elle trotte au trottoir.

Clown Hanged

I

Woman is a pill
You can't tell how to gild
Your lyre ridiculous skill
[Swallow or not, you're killed.]

II

The comedy's over, ay,
To the Morgue with Love plays!
Let's stop at the mid-die
The turnip of our days.

III

Leave the dear mistress her haul,
End of your noose, since she
Has been, despite it all,
The admiring gallery.

IV

That'll bring her a break
– The last knot in the rope,
Within the fortnight to make
A right mister, stiff-collar dope.

V

Let her blow her horn, miss horner:
By evening it's pure but but
Let her gasp, miss stamp-and-stormer,
And walk the streets, tut, tut.

Footnotes marked in the text of the poems by asterisks are by Corbière himself.

WRY-BLUE LOVES

The title of Corbière's collection is a nightmare to translate. The word *jaune* has many connotations which cannot be suggested by one word in English; its basic meaning is yellow, and as such associates the loves with autumn; the word is also used to suggest pornography and, used with words like *souris*, suggests a forced or wry smile. There is also the suggestion of 'yellow' fever. The smile and illness might be hinted at in English by 'Jaundiced Loves' but this omits the pornographic suggestion. Pol Konig records this as uppermost in Corbière's mind and Walzer records that the original book, printed by a house that specialized in erotic works, appeared under their colophon which would have identified it as a book of erotic and licentious poems. With this in mind, and seeking the terseness of the original, I have had to settle on 'Wry-Blue Loves', which may suggest some of these things.

To Marcelle: The Poet and the Cicada (p. 29)

This, and the last poem in the collection, is a parody of La Fontaine's fable 'The Cicada and the Ant'. Marcelle was the name Corbière used in publication for the actress he had fallen in love with and followed to Paris although she was already committed to a Count Rodolphe de Battine. Her real name was Armida-Josefina Cuchiani. She was a buxom blonde with more pretensions to the stage than to intellect, considered somewhat vulgar according to Le Gad, the proprietor of the café that Corbière frequented in Roscoff. According to others she was dark-haired.

THAT

Wry-Blue Loves is divided into sub-titled sections. There is, however, a confusion, largely caused by Corbière's probable oversight, as to whether 'That' should be the first section title as well as a poem title, since unlike in later sections poem titles provide the running head in this part in the first edition. It is probably a printing error. Walzer presumed that Corbière intended it to be a section title. It certainly makes a fittingly offhand label for a section which may be seen as an overture establishing motifs woven through the rest of the collection: the desperate love affair; his attitudes to poetry, and his attitude to his own thwarted life. It also establishes some key phrases and ideas.

That? (p. 31)

The word *Ça* ('That') has many contexts and idiomatic uses in French that cannot be represented by this direct translation. But Corbière's attitude is clearly shown by his inconsequential 'quotation' from Shakespeare.

Huron: the Indian name, language, cited by many early theorists of the idea of 'the noble savage'.
Paulin Gagne (1808–1876) was a lawyer and incorrigible pen-pusher who, among other eccentric endeavours, invented an international language he called 'Gagnemonopanglotte'.
Musset, the well-known romantic French poet whom Corbière pokes fun at in 'Grand Opera', 'Doors and Windows' and 'The Lighthouse'.

Corbière's line rendered here as 'Art doesn't recognize me. I know no art...' has been used to link him to Verlaine as a precursor of his sentiment: 'Take literature and wring its neck.'

Paris (p. 35)

This sequence of sonnets records Corbière's first responses to Paris where he went in spring 1872 in pursuit of 'Marcelle'.

In line 3 of the third sonnet, Corbière invents a neologism *dégoûteux* which suggests a person whose habitual temperament is a natural feeling of disgust for most things. Corbière returns to the idea of disgust on several occasions: in 'Epitaph' he writes, as translated here:

> And in distaste his taste was fine ...

In 'Poet by Default', he writes:

> In my distastes above all, my taste is exquisite ...

The reference to the manchineel tree is a dig at Hugo whom Corbière frequently attacks, most obviously in 'A Youngster on the Way Out' (p. 97). To sleep under this tree was thought to run the risk of sudden death.

The lines in italic are from a very popular folk song widely published in France.

Epitaph (p. 45)

The edition of *Les Amours jaunes*, Vanier (1891), contained the shorter version of this 'Epitaph' which follows on pp. 50–51.

WRY-BLUE LOVES

To Eternity Madam (p. 53)

This poem is a burlesque translation of a poem on the same theme in the second part of *Faust* by Goethe.

The penultimate line contains four rhymes to match *femme* that Corbière takes from Hugo to knock his rhetoric. (And that of many other French romantics, as the rhymes are not uncommonly collocated in love poems.) A neat English equivalence is not easy to find.

Modish Bohemia (p. 57)

There is a theory that this poem is a veiled attack on Villiers de l'Isle-Adam, the first verse referring to his candidature to the Greek throne and the 'three tails' referring to his triplet of a name. The spoof armorial bearings are nothing like his, however, and were used by Corbière beneath one of his self-caricaturing cartoons.

Chic: the word here translated 'modish' has many nuances in French but has a general sense of up-to-date stylishness. According to Pierre-Olivier Walzer, Corbière uses it in a sense current among artists of his time to suggest a kind of routine artiness, a sort of Royal Academy modishness. It is used more usually in the poem 'To My Dog Pope'.

It is doubtful whether Corbière was ever in Jerusalem. This writing location has been used by Florian Le Roy, as Walzer cites, to strengthen the de l'Isle-Adam connection. It is sometimes the case that such writing-locations are used by Corbière thematically and ironically rather than literally.

Fair Lady (p. 63)

This is an ironic version of the courtly love tradition perhaps as it relates to Corbière's pursuit of Marcelle. The tradition is referred to again in *Serenade of Serenades* and obliquely in 'Poet by Default'.

1 Sonnet (p. 67)

Though contemptuous of the strict sonnet-form here, Corbière did write several in various styles and line-lengths, including a reverse sonnet 'The Toad'. Despite his scorn, he is not as iconoclastic of form as he pretends since his poems retain rhyme and metre though he often ignores the precise classical rules for their use. It was the mellifluousness of French verse and its diction, regulation caesuras that he seems most impatient of.

He may have written this sonnet after an excursion in the Pyrenees while convalescing in Luchon. The name of the peak as the location of the piece is spurious, ironic.

Sonnet to Sir Bob (p. 69)

Corbière liked to spatchcock languages together in his poems and gives the location of the writing of this poem as 'The Britisch Channel' (*sic*).

Steam-Boat (p. 71)

In the last verse the word *fortune*, translated almost literally as 'fore-tune', also means a type of sail used in fine winds and weather. This pun also occurs in 'To My Cutter "The Slaver"'.

Pudenty-Anne (p. 75)

Corbière's title, 'Pudentiane', appears to derive from St Pudentiana, an Italian saint, but the word also suggests from the Latin an over-developed sense of sexual modesty.

This is, in fact, a very free sonnet. The italics, except the last, make free with the Ten Commandments and the injunctions of the Church.

After the Rain (p. 77)

A satirical encounter with a supposed or actual street girl, this poem may be compared with 'Good Fortune and a Fortune' (p. 91).

The Marchioness of Amaëgui: this is a knock at Musset who sang of an Andalusian with tanned breast, 'pale as a fine Autumn evening! She is my mistress, my lioness, the marchioness of Amaëgui!'
Sabine: The name is a knock at Hugo:

> Gastibelza, the man with the carbine
>> Sang like this:
> "Has anyone known my donna Sabine?...
>
> Has any of you known Sabine,
>> My señora?"

Carbine: a joke name referring to the extract above.
Batignol: used as a name for a Parisian accent of a *quartier* popular with artists at the time.

To a Rose (p. 85)

Here again, Corbière attacks traditional romantic notions through the time-tried imagery of the rose of love. 'D'Aÿ' is a *première classe* champagne from the region of its name.

To the Memory of Zulma (p. 89)

This poem is composed on only two rhymes in the original. There is a play on 'holes in the moon'. 'To make a hole in the moon' is an idiom for disappearing without making payment.

Good Fortune and a Fortune (p. 91)

A gloss on a poem by Baudelaire, 'A Une Passante' (To a Passing Woman).

To Just a Woman Friend (p. 93)

A line important to the understanding of Corbière occurs in this poem: 'Mon amour, à moi, n'aime pas qu'on l'aime' ('My love of myself does not love / like itself to be loved').

In this poem also occurs the neologism *mal-aimée* (ill-beloved), picked up by Apollinaire and others.

A Youngster on the Way Out (p. 97)

This poem is difficult for English readers fully to appreciate, being written on contemporary French literary issues. Some background information may help.

'Sick youngster with gait slow' is a reference to famous verses by Charles-Hubert Millevoye (1782–1816): 'La Chute des feuilles' (The Falling of the Leaves).

Lamartine: a daughter of Lamartine's, Julia, died at the age of ten in Beirut during an eastern tour on December 7th 1832. Lamartine recorded his grief at this in a poem 'Gethsemane, or the Death of Julia', eighty verses long. Corbière could not stand its flowing harmony, its public display of private feeling. He returns to the attack later in 'The Son of Lamartine and Graziella'. The next verse alludes to Lamartine's book *Harmonies Poetic and Religious* which contains a poem 'A Tear or Consolation'. The subscribers were those to a monthly magazine, *A Plain Course in Literature*, which appeared from 1856 to 1859.

Hégésippe Moreau (1810–1838): the tubercular, romantic bard of the Voulzie was treated several times in the Charity Hospital where he eventually died. One of his poems mentions the agonies of Gilbert who appears later in this piece:

> Poor Gilbert, what must you have suffered!

Escousse, Victor: the pen-name of Victor de Lasserre (1813–1832), a clerk and romantic poet. He had two fairly successful plays performed but could not sustain the failure of a third written in collaboration with a friend Auguste Lebras. They decided on a suicide pact and gassed themselves in Lasserre's room. Corbière clearly knew of the affair through several poems written on the tragedy – one, *Rolla*, by Alfred de Musset.

Gilbert, Nicolas (1751–1780): author of a famous poem on a farewell to life, published in nearly every anthology of eighteenth-century poetry and known by heart to thousands of French people, a plangent but fairly mindless piece.

Lacenaire: a notorious assassin, executed in 1836, whose writings including poems were published and became a sensation. Corbière probably heard of him through a poem of Moreau's which satirized the whole affair.

Sanson was in fact the executioner, more particularly of Chénier, mentioned later in the poem and below.

Hugo: in this further attack on Hugo – which has a cryptic critical accuracy on some aspects of his work – Corbière is making fun of the title of chapter two of the fifth book of *Notre Dame de Paris* (Our Lady of Paris), which is 'Ceci tuera Cela' (This will kill That). This was Hugo's terse expression of the idea that the press would kill off the church; that printing would polish off architecture. The last line of this verse is a mocking echo of a famous line of Hugo's at the close of 'Ultima Verba' in *Les Châtiments*, VII, xiv in defiance of the Emperor: 'And if there remain but one, I shall be that one.'

Chénier, André (1762–1794): French poet of classical leanings who was executed during the Revolution.

I've read them to death! ...: this half-line alludes to another of Hugo's:

> Alas, I have seen young girls die of it.

In French, it is a direct echo of 'en ai vu mourir' in Hugo, but 'en ai lus mourir', in Corbière, is a piece of odd French, difficult to give the flavour of.

Pipe to the Poet (p. 109)

A variation on Baudelaire's poem 'La Pipe' (The Pipe).

The Toad (p. 111)

This is a sonnet in reverse.

René Martineau records that in Corbière's flat in Paris a bell, activated by the door, attracted one's attention to the horrible sight over the chimney of a dried-out, flattened toad nailed to the wall.

Woman (p. 113)

The correction has been used which Corbière made in a copy of the first edition of *Les Amours jaunes*, where he changed the word *jour* in the last line to *drap*, typical self-mockery. *Jour* is the usual version printed.

Poor Kid (p. 121)

The epigraph links this sonnet with 'Woman'; the theme and approach suggest a practice run for the major poem 'Poet by Default'. See also 'Under a Portrait of Corbière' (p. 417).

Downer (p. 123)

The mood and tone of this poem is developed in 'Poet by Default'.

Poet by Default (p. 127)

The footnote giving 'Penmarc'h' as the place of writing is symbolic; it is the cliff, in Breton mythology, where Tristan was brought to die while awaiting Iseult. The poem was probably written at Christmas 1871, his first alone at Morlaix after the Marcelle affair.

SERENADE OF SERENADES

This, with *Rondels for After*, the final section of the book, is probably the only true sequence in *Les Amours jaunes* in which poems directly pick up and reflect each other in theme and image.

Night Sonnet (p. 139)

The linking image of all these poems is that of the serenading troubadour beneath the window of his impervious love.

One-String Guitar (p. 141)

The dislike of the light here reflects on Corbière's disgust with his own appearance which elsewhere drives him to identify himself with the toad.

Roof (p. 145)

The terse opening refers to the last line of the previous poem.

Litany (p. 147)

The poem makes ironic use of the Magnificat.

Rosary (p. 149)

The Spanish here is not accurate.

Elizir d'Amor (p. 151)

Corbière's 'Elizir' is neither Spanish nor Italian in its spelling.

Venery (p. 155)

Multiple puns in this poem make connexions between Venus and venery, deer and dears. It helps, perhaps, to know that the word 'beams' here can also refer to parts of antlers as well as door-frames and so forth.

Hours (p. 159)

This poem, somewhat surprisingly, is regarded in France as a most effective piece of word music and has been set to music – not a frequent occurrence with Corbière.

If-Key Song (p. 161)

The French verb in the last line of verse 2 is a Corbièrean neologism; unfortunately, English already has a standard equivalent.

The last line is a variation on lines in the poem 'Madrid' by Musset: 'Open your window only to me.'

Doors and Windows (p. 165)

The last verse is a parody of the poem 'Andalouse' by Musset:

> I want this evening serenades
>> Enough to damn the alcaids
>> From Tolosa to Guadaletta.

Grand Opera (p. 167)

The penultimate stanza, again, is mocking the poem cited immediately above.

Room with Lattice Windows (p. 173)

'To murder the language like a Spanish cow' is a traditional expression to refer to those who speak French badly. Possibly here a joke at the expense of his own Spanish and Italian.

FLUKES

The title word *Raccrocs* has many overtones and usages; it can mean a 'fluke' in billiards, a 'stroke of luck', or a 'prostitute's trick'.

Letting Slip (p. 177)

Many critics have felt the influence Villon must have had on Corbière. This poem provides the clearest direct evidence as he gives his version of the legacy ploy made famous by Villon in his *Testament*. Curiously, Corbière does not use Villon's ballade stanza but rather the metre of the song mentioned in the epigraph. As with Villon, the poem is full of puns and word-play difficult to recreate succinctly. *Isaac Laquedem*: the Flemish name for The Wandering Jew.

To my Mousy-Mare (p. 183)

This poem is paired and contrasted in theme and form with the next poem.

To the Docile Girl Friend (p. 185)

See note immediately above.

To my Dog Pope (p. 187)

The epigraph, again, shows Corbière's shakiness with the English he had picked up.

To a Young Lady (p. 191)

The name Érard refers to a maker of pianos. Érard also developed the pedal harp.

The poem has been taken, with '1 Sonnet', as an attack on the formalist approach to poetry: notation and metrics without real feeling. (The theme of young ladies and their piano pieces becomes an obsessive theme in the work of Laforgue.)

Uncouraged (p. 193)

The title is an invention to match one of Corbière's, an ironic glance at 'encouraged'.

Rhapsody of the Deaf Man (p. 197)

It is thought that Corbière, by no means a healthy person, suffered a period of deafness which gave rise to this poem. In the last verse there is a pun impossible to hint at: a 'dark lantern' in French may be thought of as a 'deaf' lantern.

Mixed Twins (p. 201)

This is one of the few poems where Corbière admits that his ironic, sardonic habituation of feeling is a protection to more compassionate emotion. The last line is, perhaps, the most powerful in its expression of this until the Rondels for After.

The Litany of Sleep (p. 205)

This proto-surrealist piece which chases the association of ideas and manic rhyme compulsion is full of puns and quibbles many of which are impossible to suggest. For example, the phrase 'blue devils' was colloquial for the regiment of the Chasseurs Alpins. The nearest English would be 'red devils' – a hopeless anachronism.

Romance Gone Flat (p. 217)

The opening section has many punning slangy French references to birds. Hence, rather desperate measures like the extra 'f' in 'half-finching'. Other puns like 'demi John' and 'brandy-legged' must serve to indicate the exuberance of the master of the 'supernumerary pun'.

Galimard, Ducornet: well-known painters in the Second Empire. Galimard (1813–1880) was a Salon favourite who painted both religious and secular works, including the designs of stained glass windows. Ducornet was born in Lille, unfortunately without arms, and painted with his feet.

The Cortège of the Poor Bloke (p. 225)

The dates for the writing of this poem could well be true since Corbière was in Paris at this time. The epigraph street name was associated with prostitution. The whole poem is an ironic elaboration on a painter's being rejected from the Salon.

bill hook: in Val Warner's version of this poem (*The Centenary Corbière*, Carcanet, 1975) she solves the problem of Corbière's pun on Courbet brilliantly with her deflating splitting of 'billhook'. Christopher Pilling (*These Jaundiced Loves*, Peterloo, 1995) followed suit. Sometimes the solution is found by a translator.

Al Frisko (p. 229)

The French title to this piece may suggest 'fleeting shades' but also, literally, 'breakfast or picnic in the sun'. The same phrase occurs earlier in 'After the Rain', the last line of verse 4, where a different translation has been adopted.

The poem is set in the Bois de Boulogne. The opening place names, here given as '*Birds' Eyes*' and '*Wild Thyme*', are of areas associated with prostitution.

Veder Napoli poi mori (p. 233)

The title is a dialectical form of the famous Italian saying translated as 'See Naples and Die'.

In the last line of the French text, the word *bon* is ungrammatical but it is what Corbière wrote.

The writing locations are given and dated in Italian by Corbière for this and the next two poems.

Mesoniello: perhaps refers to a musical drama *Masaniello or the Neapolitan Fisherman* by Moreau and Lafortelle, to music by Carafa. Mesoniello was a fisherman in the seventeenth century who led a popular uprising in Naples against the Spanish.

ruolz: an early process of electroplating with silver or gold.

Soneto a Napoli (p. 239)

The title and epigraph are oddly spelt Italian, perhaps an attempt to convey local habits of speech.

The Son of Lamartine and Graziella (p. 243)

As well as a bit of a soft spot for him, Corbière had a healthy contempt for many aspects of Lamartine's work and personality. This is the second attack on him for emotional posturing in harmonious verse. See also 'A Youngster on the Way Out' (p. 97). Corbière was not given to 'sincere' and flowing emotional outbursts and generally had a dislike of over-euphonious verses. All his revisions seem to move in the direction of abruptness and apparent dislocation of metric.

The Bard of St Point is a heavy irony. Lamartine was buried at St Point. The word translated *bard* (cygne) is commonly associated with Vergil in French, just as its direct English translation is associated chiefly with the 'swan' of Avon. Possibly, Corbière's italic is nudging us to think of a play on 'Point' to mean 'Not at all' as well.
raffle, verse 4: a rare nautical usage that means ropes, tackle, spars, left in a rubbishy heap.
Jocelyn, verse 7, refers to a narrative poem by Lamartine in which a priest hero takes refuge from war in a cave where he lives with another boy who turns out to be a girl in disguise. Despite his love for her, he leaves her to keep his priestly vocation.

The location and month are given in Italian. Corbière was in Italy at this time.

Libertà (p. 249)

It is possible but not likely that Corbière was once in this jail.

Hidalgo! (p. 257)

The location is given in Spanish.

Pariah (p. 259)

The closing poem of this section is reminiscent of some of Villon's methods and attitudes. Like the first poem in this section, it has a more genuine 'feel' to it than the more literary poems in between.

The human Self's detestable: the quotation is from Pascal.

ARMORICA

In this section, we return to what might be called the heartland of Corbière, the coastal areas of Brittany.

A Rich Man in Brittany (p. 269)

The abbot Jacques Delille (1738–1813) was an acclaimed translator of Vergil into French verse. The apparent quotation from him is not, however, accurate or close.

Saint Ivor Orr of Eitherore (p. 273)

The titular and other saints in this piece seem lost in obscurity if indeed they existed at all, though Breton tradition is full of minor localized saints that cure headaches and so forth.

Cunégonde: the wife of the emperor Henry II. Accused of marital infidelity she proved her innocence before God by walking unharmed on red-hot ploughshares.

The Wandering Minstrel and the Pardon of St Anne (p. 279)

Often regarded, with 'Poet by Default' and 'The Pastoral of Conlie', as the best of Corbière's work in this general area, the poem divides into three sections: a hymn of celebration which manages to combine a genuine sense of the people's devotion with the distancing puns and wordplay of Corbière's own feeling. The second is a passionately sympathetic sequence for the sufferings of humanity, followed by the climactic appearance of the wandering minstrel. It is in this poem where he combines real compassion with an ironic technique and bewilderingly rapid change of mood and tone that Corbière is closest to the best passages in Villon.

Ankokrignets: a collocation of two Breton words by Corbière which would seem to signify 'Gnawed Death', suggesting, perhaps, the skeleton.

Kakous: Breton, signifying lepers.

Blind Man's Cries (p. 297)

Unusually for Corbière, this piece was not punctuated. He also made the rhyme-scheme with a plangent running rhyme in *-or*. The rhyme in 'dead' was chosen to give a similar strength of sound – and because there was not much alternative.

The Pastoral of Conlie (p. 303)

The poem is based on accounts that Corbière had received from his brother-in-law Aimé Vacher, a volunteer who deserted, temporarily, to see his new-born daughter. Rodolphe de Battine may also have supplied some of the detail. By the order of Gambetta, and commanded by Count Émile de Keratry, fifty thousand troops were stupidly immobilized in the mire of the camp at Conlie, near le Mans, for fear of a royalist uprising.

The references to the black and blacker months in the opening verse are references to the Breton names for November and December.

SEAFARERS

The opening poem, printed in italic by Corbière, serves as an introduction to the section, attacking the romantic sentimentalization of sailors as seen in theatre and opera. One sympathizes with his attitude but his attempt to redress the balance hereafter has a tendency to sentimentalization in the other direction.

Seamen (p. 313)

This poem has many verbal and thematic echoes of the work of Corbière's father.

Lines 15–16: the word translated 'throat-burning pipes' is a colloquial word directly reminiscent of Baudelaire's use of it in 'The Albatross', as are these lines as a whole.

Arch Halyard, the Hunchback (p. 323)

The punning French title, 'Le bossu Bitor', represents a nickname for the hunchback presented in the poem but it cannot be succinctly conveyed in English as it has several layers. As Corbière's note reveals, a *bitors* is a twisted tarred rope or yarn used by sailors. The English equivalent is 'spun yarn' which hardly makes a usable name and suggests an active rogue rather than a victim. In addition, the words *bitte et bosse* are a maritime command given to tie up the ship on docking and signified to sailors the coming of the excitement and relief of shore-leave. The title chosen here suggests a British name that could equally be used to torment a person with a curved spine. The naval echo has to go to the surname.

La Joliette: the name of one of the docks in Marseilles.

Aurora (p. 345)

The italics are snippets of sea songs popular in Corbière's time.

The Greenhorn on the Point of Embarking and Sentimental (p. 349)

Pistol: Corbière's note is on pseudo-proper names; there is no Shakespearean reference.

Hawse: Corbière's note actually refers to the French for reef-points. He may have been punning; this is the nearest I could match. The French term in archaic use could apply to girls of easy virtue.

Adieu-vat!: the last words in the French poem, a play on the phrase *va-t-à Dieu*, are difficult to render. When a ship was coming too close inshore this nautical expression was used – literally, 'turn to God', indicating the danger of the situation requiring immediate manoeuvre. But Corbière reverses the phrase here, making it ambivalent: even while wishing someone goodbye and to the mercy of God, the greenhorn's thoughts are still on the sea – the shore is the danger.

Bambine (p. 363)

The captain is apparently based on a real person. He is recorded as the skipper of 'The Normandy' in 1837, and is mentioned by Stendhal in *Memoirs of a Tourist*.

Cap'n Gentle (p. 365)

A tavern sign, as used in this epigraph, also occurs in 'The Greenhorn on the Point of Embarking and Sentimental'.

Letter from Mexico (p. 367)

The French for a zoo is, literally, 'a garden of acclimatization' – a play on words that is difficult to convey in this poem.

Zouave: a soldier, usually an Algerian infantryman.

The Wrecker (p. 383)

The last line of the first verse is obscure in the French. Literally, 'As seagulls as the seagulls' which might refer to several aspects of gulls.

Corbière includes a footnote on lines 29–30, to explain two sailors' slang words here translated 'wrecker' and 'vampire'. Suitable equivalents were not forthcoming so this has rendered his footnote useless. The one rendered 'vampire' has also a literal suggestion of 'octopus' and a figurative use as 'sponger'.

To my Cutter 'The Slaver' (p. 387)

Corbière sold his cutter to acquire a better one to impress Marcelle. The earlier poem 'Steam-Boat' seems to concern one of their few voyages together.

In verse 14, Corbière puns on a French sail name, *fortune*: hence the desperate measure here.

The Lighthouse (p. 393)

Like a big I, in verse 7, is another joking reference to an image used by Musset of a moon above a steeple as a dotted *i*.

The End (p. 399)

A final attack on what Corbière considered the sentimentalization of seamen by Hugo (whom he slightly misquotes). It has been thought by some that these sea poems celebrating storm and wreck were an over-compensation by the author for the invalid life which rendered him unlikely to emulate his sea-captain father. Others record that he had a perverse pleasure in taking people for trips into storms. It is also recorded that he stayed on an island one night and left his mother worrying in fear for his survival.

RONDELS FOR AFTER

This is the second section of the book which may be regarded as a true sequence. Some critics have taken the series of wonderfully delicate and touching poems as a response to the death of a young child. Others have found them to decorate with a gossamer-like irony the theme of the *poète maudit*. Corbière embellished his own copy with funerary images.

Needless to say, Corbière does not use the rondel or rondeau form exactly.

Hushaby, Baby (p. 407)

Corbière printed *nocte*, a slip for *notte*.

Little Corpse Good for a Laugh (p. 411)

The title also occurs as a line in 'Romance Gone Flat'.

Baneflower (p. 413)

There is a dispute as to whether Corbière intended *Mâle-Fleurette* (Male-flower) or *Male-Fleurette* (Evil flower). He probably meant the latter; he was notoriously shaky on circumflex accents. Most early printings are without the accent. Besides, he would not object to a pun here. *Fleurette* can mean floweret, posy or 'sweet-nothing' in the lovers' sense. The title also glances at *Les Fleurs du mal* (The Flowers of Evil) by Baudelaire.

To Marcelle: The Cicada and the Poet (p. 415)

Corbière signs off as he began with a swipe at Marcelle and La Fontaine.

OTHER POEMS

Under a Portrait of Corbière (p. 417)

This poem is interesting in that it anticipates several images and lines that later appear in 'Poet by Default'. It seems almost a trial run for the ideas developed in that poem.

A Death too Worked at (p. 421)

This more or less completed poem was found among a few papers of Corbière that had been preserved. Unpolished, the punctuation is a bit odder than his usual style but the poem is interesting in how it intimates, in individual lines and ideas, poems to come: 'To the Memory of Zulma', 'Poet by Default', and, fleetingly, one or two others.

bac: baccarat, a card game where you play against the banker. Corbière's abbreviation has been kept, although not a current English contraction.

Two Dedications of Les Amours jaunes (p. 429)

IN M. LE VACHER'S COPY (p. 429)

Oddly Corbière's epigraph refers to him as son-in-law whereas they were brothers-in-law. Perhaps, some think, a sign of Corbière's thwarted wish to emulate his father.

IN M. LE GAD'S COPY (p. 429)

The dedicatee was a friend and the proprietor of the café in Roscoff where Corbière liked to hang out.

A Couplet (p. 429)

Recovered by Charles Le Goffic who also observed its similarity to a famous epigram of d'Écouchard-Lebrun. Laforgue also makes fun of the fashion for albums but would not have seen this poem.

Paris by Day (p. 431)

Corbière was in the habit of adding new poems to his copy of *Les Amours jaunes*. Clearly the lack of response to the book had not made him stop writing; revisions were also written into the text. Some of these new poems are difficult to assemble from this way of working but several were complete enough to be reconstructed by scholars. This one has various drafts written into Corbière's copy, some with a heavy hand.

Paris by Night (p. 433)

This was also written with corrections in Corbière's copy.

Minor Bedtime (p. 435)

Without alterations, if not extempore, this sonnet-like poem seems to have been written as a fair copy in Corbière's *Les Amours jaunes*.

Clown Hanged (p. 439)

This poem was written in pencil in Corbière's copy. The text is very faint, and there are variants. The version translated here was originally recovered and published by Yves-Gérard Le Dantec and included by Pierre-Olivier Walzer in the *Œuvres complètes*. There are some doubtful readings as the square bracket indicates and the last line of the first verse was never found. The line in square brackets is my plaster of Paris. The seventh line is also something of a mystery to French people as well as to translators. A tentative theory might be that it is a bit of Corbière's odd English to mean 'my death' – a desperate near visual pun on the French for midday.

The poem is interesting because it seems, almost in a time-warp, to anticipate the Pierrot theme in Laforgue and much of his tone and attitude. There is no way Laforgue might have seen it, however, so far as can be judged.

Index of French First Lines

Index of English First Lines

Index of English Titles

Translations by Peter Dale from Anvil

Dante: The Divine Comedy

The Divine Comedy is a foundation stone of European poetry. Simultaneously a journey through life and a spiritual biography, a portrait of the internecine Italy of Dante's time and a pilgrim's progress through the tripartite afterworld of Catholic mythology, it is also, paradoxically, a devotional work and one of the strangest love poems ever written.

More than 10 years in the making, this *terza rima* version is clear, accurate and compelling. Peter Dale includes a perceptive introduction on the poem's history and its influence on English poetry.

Poems of Jules Laforgue

'He is an exquisite poet, a deliverer of nations . . . a father of light", said Ezra Pound in 1918. Part symbolist and part impressionist, Laforgue was not only one of the most innovative and individual of French poets but also among the most entertaining. He died in Paris in 1887 aged just 27. Peter Dale captures the resourceful energy and panache of his poetry in translations which are by turns as playful, wild, clear, obscure and impossible as the French poems.

'[Dale] conveys much of the letter of the original as well as the spirit . . . The collection is hard to over-praise'

– D. J. ENRIGHT, *The Observer*

Poems of François Villon

Villon was born in Paris in 1431. History records a life of destitution and ill health, robbery and murder, torture and exile. While what became of Villon after his 32nd year is unknown, the poems he produced in just six years capture in witty, intelligent and candid verse the low and high life of Paris. Together they stand as a body of work with few rivals in the literature of his own or of any other country.

'The modernity of François Villon as well as the permanency of his genius have found in Peter Dale their best interpreter'

– LOUIS BONNEROT

'One despaired of ever finding anyone to "capture" [Villon] in English. But it's been done. Here it is. Hats off'

– LAWRENCE DURRELL

More French Poetry in Bilingual Editions from Anvil

Guillaume Apollinaire: Selected Poems
Translated and introduced by Oliver Bernard

A cross-section of the most dynamic modernist French poet's work. 'Oliver Bernard's translations . . . are immediately engaging in their vividness and humour.' – CHRISTOPHER RICKS, *New Statesman*

Charles Baudelaire
Translated and introduced by Francis Scarfe
Volume I: The Complete Verse   Volume II: The Poems in Prose

Francis Scarfe's prose versions are both scrupulous and inventive. 'No one must underestimate the value of the present enterprise to even the most advanced student of French literature.' – MICHAEL GLOVER, *British Book News*

Gérard de Nerval: The Chimeras
Translated by Peter Jay, with an essay by Richard Holmes

'The rendering of Gérard de Nerval's justly celebrated and mysteriously allusive sonnet sequence in English is a formidably difficult enterprise, and translator and publisher are to be congratulated.' – MICHAEL GLOVER, *Books and Bookmen*

Arthur Rimbaud: A Season in Hell and Other Poems
Translated by Norman Cameron

Robert Graves thought Norman Cameron unsurpassed as a translator of Rimbaud. *Une Saison en enfer* is here accompanied by thirty-three other poems and introduced by Michael Hamburger.

Paul Verlaine: Femmes / Hombres: Women / Men
Translated by Alistair Elliot

' . . . in Verlaine's clandestine collections of erotic verse, Mr Elliot succeeds marvellously . . . astonishing, beautiful poems, astonishingly and beautifully rendered.' – D.M. THOMAS